Other Books by Bill Holm

Boxelder Bug Variations
The Dead Get By with Everything
The Music of Failure (paper)
published as *Prairie Days (cloth)*

An Alphabet of China Essays

COMING HOME CRAZY

BILL HOLM

Introduction by
Harrison E. Salisbury

MILKWEED EDITIONS

COMING HOME CRAZY

© 1990, text by Bill Holm
© 1990, design by R.W. Scholes

All rights reserved
Printed in the United States of America
Published in 1990 by *Milkweed Editions*
430 First Avenue North, Suite 400
Minneapolis, Minnesota 55401
Books may be ordered from the above address

96 95 94 93   10 9 8 7
ISBN: 0-915943-42-5

Publication of *Coming Home Crazy* is made possible in part by grant support from the Elmer and Eleanor Andersen Foundation; the Eugene C. Sit and Gail V. Sit Foundation; the Literature Program of the National Endowment for the Arts; the Arts Development Fund of United Arts; the Dayton Hudson Foundation for Dayton's and Target stores; First Bank System Foundation; the General Mills Foundation; Jerome Foundation; the Minnesota State Arts Board through an appropriation by the Minnesota State Legislature, with additional funds to support this activity from the National Endowment for the Arts; a McKnight Foundation Award administered by the Minnesota State Arts Board; the Northwest Area Foundation; Star Tribune/Cowles Media Company; and by generous individuals.

The author wishes to acknowledge the publication of several of the essays in this book in the following publications: "D.H. Lawrence in China," the *New York Times Book Review*; "Book Smuggling," *Minnesota Libraries*; "Banking," "Kindergarten," and "Pastorale," *Stora* (published in Sweden); part IV of "Xmas," *Minnesota Monthly*; part II of "Xmas," and "Papers, Please," *Minnesota Times*. The author thanks Louis Simpson for permission to quote "The Inner Part" from his *Selected Poems*.

Library of Congress Cataloging-in-Publication Data

Holm, Bill, 1943–
    Coming home crazy : China essays / by Bill Holm.
        p.   cm.
    ISBN 0-915943-42-5   ∞
    1. China—Description and travel—1976-   2. Holm, Bill, 1943-
—Journeys—China. I. Title.
DS712.H65   1989   89-36394
915.104'58—dc20   CIP

The paper used in this publication meets the minimum requirements of American National Standard for Information Sciences—Permanence of Paper for Printed Library Materials, ANSI Z39.48-1984.

This book is dedicated with love to:
Marcy Brekken, whom I went to China to meet without knowing
she was there. She is the greatest gift of my craziness.

The memory of Oscar Tonn and to his wife Helen, St. Agathe,
Manitoba, my neighbors in China, and friends who tried to fix
everything with humor and patience and skill.

My Chinese students and friends. I meant to name you all,
and now I cannot. If this book finds you in a saner time,
remember that you have my gratitude for everything, and, my heart.

INTRODUCTION

China is the oldest society in the world—reckon it as 5,000 or 6,000 years—a long, long time, many, many dynasties, many, many people, possibly one billion 200 million citizens at present count, all black-haired, maybe 162,500,000,000,000 hairs, give or take a few beards and baldies, a lot of hair follicles.

In the centuries since the Han people emerged along the Yellow River they have experienced every event human beings can imagine—war, famine, drought, genocide, torture, slavery, pinnacles of art, poetry, technology (including gunpowder and paper-making), triumph, despair, conquest and oppression.

Through the eons China has come to see herself as the Middle Kingdom located high above ordinary mortals and just under heaven, surrounded by Barbarians, that is, people not born with jet eyes, olive skin, jet hair, repoussé noses (so they believe). The Chinese did not see themselves as God's chosen people; they saw themselves as *the* people. All others belonged to some lesser species.

I told a wise Chinese once that Boston thought of itself as the Hub of the Universe. Ah, yes, he laughed, but you know, of course, that China is the universe.

China is the universe. Into this world of worlds there entered a couple of years ago a giant from the soil of Minnesota, a Minneota man, blood of the blood of Minnesota, a Lutheran by birth, a hymn singer, a lover of Bach, a poet, a scholar steeped in the culture of the world, of Europe, of Greece and Rome and even South Dakota, a man of powerful frame, flowing beard no longer red, now streaked with gray, head of reddish hair, a man six-feet-five-inches tall, weight well over 240 pounds (he lost a good many in a few Chinese months), a man who drank Hamm's beer or *Tsingtao*, aquavit or *mao tai* with equal aplomb, an explorer walking the China land, seeing it for the first time, sensing China's eternal vitality, a people worthy of friendship, amiability and study, a man who himself sprang from that civilization which gave birth to the world's first parliament a thousand years ago (when China was struggling through chaotic years between the despots of the Tang and Song dynasties), Thor peering into the heart of China, listening to its beat, savoring its secrets and going out on the town with its college students. In other words, Bill Holm of Minneota, citizen of the world, spawn, of course, of Iceland.

Bill Holm is a man who loves northern lights and the shooting stars of August. His collision with China sets up sparks that illuminate the night prairie of Minneota.

Since the days of Marco Polo and the Jesuit Matteo Ricci, barbarians have been poking about the Celestial Kingdom and jotting down their impressions — China is a marvel, China is a cesspool of evil, China is an enigma. Bill Holm sets it down as a man of Minneota must — warts, wisdom, grit, jokes, horrors, adventures, love, tragedy, wit and insight.

Anyone who knows Bill Holm and his writings — *Boxelder Bug Variations*, for example — knows the sky-is-the-limit concepts that stem from a man whose feet are firmly planted in the real world. No wonder the men and women of the Middle Kingdom, particularly the younger ones, fell head-over-heels for Bill. He helped them see themselves as real persons, not as some kind of curlicued cut-outs from an ancient annal or a tired Marxist tract.

Bill Holm takes us for a delicious romp over the gray deserts that surround China's ancient capital of Chang-an, now so widely known as Xi'an. Tens of thousands of Americans, tour group after tour group, including that of Nancy and Ronald Reagan, have swooned over the terra cotta warriors on which China's first Emperor, the bloody Qin Shihuang, beloved by Mao Zedong, expended so much of his nation's time, talent and lives.

Bill Holm is a Minnesota marvel. So is his book. No one can read its pages without understanding acutely why Deng Xiaoping and his old comrades turned the machine guns loose in Tiananmen Square, delivering a deadly blow to China's future.

Coming Home Crazy is a title which Bill Holm took from the Chinese. Indeed, Bill Holm goes home crazy to Minnesota like a Minneota fox, and his words echo and echo in our hearts: "We gain nothing by playing ostrich except, conceivably, our own extinction. Either we remember and make conscious connections to the moral and physical lives of others, or we die."

—Harrison E. Salisbury

A FIRST WORD
开头的话

This is a book about what happened to an American in China, about adventures of daily life and on the road, and about what America looked like to me—both its inner and outer lives—after I got home. It is not a book about China, though most of the action takes place there. As any Sinologist will tell you by reading three or four of these pages, I don't know anything about China. But I do know what happened to me, and I can therefore be trusted to tell you the history of my experience. The point of the title, and of the book, is that I came home to an America that looked to me unwilling to know what our own experience has been, either as a country, as a community, or as individual citizens. The lessons of history had evaporated. The function of memory and understanding of its significance seemed to have been surgically removed from citizens without leaving a trace. Whether this is the effect of television, technological gadgetry or too much surplus income, I leave to others for speculation. But ask your neighbors and see. Test your experience. You will find out that Vietnam was a noble war, Richard Nixon was a great president, the Germans have been our friends for centuries, the Indians are all drunk, and the buffalo is a mythical beast invented by the park service and the U.S. Mint. Et cetera. This disconnection from history made me ask myself: Am I crazy? Have I missed something?

In China, I saw something else—a history so heavy and, in its consequences for daily life, so awful, that citizens had no choice but to acknowledge its presence. China is all the clichés a foreigner has ever heard—dirty, overcrowded, chaotic, oppressive, poor beyond imagining. These are not remarkable facts about China, though they are true. But China is also full of Chinese and, like almost every foreigner from Polo to Ricci onward, I came to admire, respect and take delight in them. Many, whom I came to know well enough without their language, I loved. They taught me with their humor, intelligence, courage, and failure, more about myself, my own home place of Minneota, Minnesota, and the whole of America than I thought possible. They fought like tigers, usually quietly because of police and Party bosses, to hang on to an accurate interior understanding of their own private history and the history of their country. Sometimes it cost them their lives and their personal freedom, as Americans saw on television in June 1989 — if they can remember back so far.

My Chinese students and friends gave me this book. They wanted me to see their lives, to hear their stories, to share their experiences. I first intended to name them all and send them copies. They said they would translate what I had to say and asked me only to be honest, to hide neither anger, ignorance, nor foolishness, mine or China's. That is easier said than done, of course. I have tried. Now, politics has changed the world so much so quickly that it is hardly safe to name them.

The experiences in this book came at me in a great chaotic mass, and, for a long time, I had no idea how to describe them with any coherence. I tried chronology but found, like Henry Thoreau, that time was unreliable and required reshaping by the imagination. One part of Chinese life that contributed to my "craziness" was the absence of orderly sequence — in Western terms. The Chinese language is not alphabetic, and thus nothing else is either. Why not impose, by will, an alphabet on this Chinese chaos and see what it looked like? This seemed at least as sensible as the casting of hexagrams from the *I Ching*.

This book sets forth the notion of "craziness" and then gives you an arbitrary alphabet of examples in the essays that follow. Nothing is proven by this method of examination; it is a *way* of doing it; there are many roads on the way; they all arrive at the same destination, wherever it is. The title of the conclusion is stolen from Samuel Johnson's history of a prince of Abyssinia, *Rasselas*. Dr. Johnson was a Daoist before his time. He was also Confucian.

I recommend, for clarity, that after reading the essay "Coming Home Crazy," the reader violate alphabetic sequence and read first "Xmas," a newsy description of daily life in China and what I was doing there; "Swiss Army Knife," the history of a trip and of preparations for China; and "*Waiguoren*," which will explain my reasons for making my own translations of Chinese words that I use throughout the text. Instead of using the usual polite official translations, I give the meaning understood by a Chinese citizen; thus, *waiguoren* is translated not as "foreigner" but "barbarian," and *lao bai xing* not as "common people" but "Old Hundred Names" (literally). Aside from that, the author's advice is to browse randomly until a subject or a letter catches your fancy. This was Dr. Johnson's manner of reading. It worked well for him.

Transliteration of Chinese names and words is a printer's nightmare. I use the new pinyin system for most names and places: Sichuan, Shaanxi, Beijing, *Zou houmen*, etc., but revert to the old-fashioned spellings for names already so familiar in English that their new forms are exotic: Yangtze instead of Chang Jiang, Canton instead of Guangzhou, Confucius instead of Kong Fuzi. The habit of calling the Chinese by odd nicknames: Old Fish, Old Two Noodle, Duchess, is not my invention. It is one of the pleasures of Chinese life. Icelanders do it, too: Onund Treefoot, Eysteinn Fart, Erik Blood Axe. I was frequently called Old Beer, Dry Uncle and Big Whiskers. Foreign noses have always looked oversized to the Chinese, and *Da Bizi* (Big Nose) is a favorite sarcastic description for foreigners. My nose was so thoroughly obscured by hair that the Chinese missed it, though they did not often mistake me for a native.

Many ideas in this book are influenced by Simon Leys, author of *Chinese Shadows* and numerous other books. He is the only writer on China who expected Tiananmen and who was not charmed by "capitalist" reform. Experience is not lost on him, though it seems not to affect several other famous commentators on China very much. When I gave students his books to read, they looked stunned afterwards: "This is a sad book, but this man is the only foreigner I have read who understands China. How did he learn so much?" By paying attention, presumably, and practicing a nice skepticism toward political dissembling, Chinese or foreign.

Inside China, I was grateful for fine reporting in the weekly *Guardian*, the *Herald Tribune*, and *Asia Week*. The Chinese revere Harrison Salisbury's books and, if they could get it to read, would think *Tiananmen Diary* a sharp account of their catastrophe. What China badly needs, now more than ever, is a newspaper that will provide a home for honest reporting. They are unlikely to get it soon. Liu Binyan, their best journalist, is in exile at Harvard, a gift for us, but a sadness for his fellow citizens.

It will be clear to the reader from the tone of this book that I loved my experience in China very much, primarily because of my dear, cherished Chinese friends. I watched the murders in Tiananmen Square on BBC while I was in England, and wept and raved. My hope is that readers will come to love these Chinese human beings, too, and be moved to work, in whatever way they can, to remove the nailed boot from their necks once and for all.

Bill Holm
Minneota, 1989

COMING HOME CRAZY
An Alphabet of China Essays

归乡喜若狂

Coming Home Crazy

COMING HOME CRAZY

归乡喜若狂

After a year's teaching in Xi'an, the ancient Tang capital grown into a grimy cement industrial city, it is the end of July and time to leave China. For weeks I have been fighting with bureaucrats, trying to get fellowship money and school visas for intelligent and ambitious students, only to bang into the granite bedrock principle of all entrenched bureaucracy: "pay your dues and wait your turn; I haven't got mine yet . . . " The lying, the fawning, the false smiles, the categorical *no*, the stifled anger, have worn me down. The call that never connects on the half-dead phone, the enervating heat, the army of flies, the endless bargaining over small potatoes, the chorus of *"mei you"* (not have) that sings out in reply to every request, whether for canned tomatoes, cold beer, or train tickets, has finished me off. I am exhausted and ready to go. I do not need a second opinion.

After a year in China, it is difficult even to remember America as a real country; it is a place created by your own imagination, where goods are available, service provided, language clear and direct, machines function with elegant efficiency, the food is clean, greaseless and served hot, the newspapers lively and truthful, and the weather an eternal southern California of the soul, helped out on rare occasions by Westinghouse and General Electric; in other words, a country with more than enough of everything, easily gettable everywhere, and because of that, no good reason to lie, hoard, or fail to do the job. I even forgot my old anger at American politics of the eighties and began thinking of the President as a benign old blatherer, silly but not capable of much harm in the long scheme of history.

Judge not my foolishness, dear reader! Every Westerner I met in China who was there for a long time invents his own version of this imaginary America. The old China hands who came in the thirties invented a bourgeois monster, and the foreign expert of the eighties invents a republic of pizza, good bourbon, T-bones, Chevrolets, and clerks who are happy to finger your credit card.

An anthropologist I taught with gave me an interesting insight early in my year in China. I'd complained to him that my cultural bolts were loosening, that living in a place without newspapers, television and cheese was all right; I preferred doing without them in Minnesota, but being enveloped by a culture which neither knew, valued, nor seemed to have any apparent use for Bach, Whitman, Samuel Johnson, Blake, Plato, Freud, Homer, Gustav Mahler, even Jesus, was discomfiting—particularly for someone like me who had staked his spiritual and intellectual life on those ideas and noises.

"In Asia," the anthropologist said, looking uncommonly wise and Confucian for a Minnesotan with a motorcycle, "you either lose your inner moorings, start to sink, go some kind of crazy, and just let it happen, or you will leave sooner than you expected and not learn anything."

"Impossible!" I fulminated. "My moorings are set in steel. I can't live without them!"

I woke up one morning three or four months later, crazy in exactly the way he described. I felt no panic, no fear; I was adrift and looking around, interested, even cheerful, in a manner that no one who has ever said the words, "Have a good day!" can begin to understand. It *would* be a good day; nothing would work, nothing would be available, and everything would go wrong differently than you imagined. Now I loved China. Now I was happy.

And now, for better or worse, I was leaving, curiously anxious to feel these two things simultaneously for a little while, the sharp new image of China while it was still fresh in me, and the old hazy daguerreotype of America, the yin and yang, the black and the white, the east and the west.

Scott Fitzgerald, in *The Crackup*, said he knew he was crazy when he became unable to hold two opposing ideas simultaneously. The experience of China means that you will never again see singly; the contrary of every idea in your life and culture looks as sane and reasonable as the idea itself. Your consciousness is bifurcated once and for all, so you might as well enjoy it. Every old truth is half a new lie, every perception half a deception. It's all right; be calm.

No Westerner ever really knows anything about China. It is too big, too old, too complicated, too unlike anything in our half-world made by Plato, St. Paul, and the British navy. Even the Chinese have a hard go of it to master their own civilization and, except for Party hacks, generalize timidly about China. But they at least start with the language. For a Westerner, literacy in Chinese means five years of intense drudgery and, without that language, nothing real can be known. But, after surviving a plunge into Chinese craziness, your mind opens in a different way to your own country, and having "seen" China, you are able to see what is in your own house or your own everyday life, with new "crazied" eyes. The view is peculiar and not what you expected.

My first view of China was the Shanghai airport at midnight, one lonesome planeload of late, sleepy passengers wandering around in a locked lounge, guarded at every entrance and exit by Chinese police — skinny teenagers in olive drab uniforms baggy enough to fit two or three of themselves. Jade imitations of old Chinese carvings glowed dimly in locked display cases. The water fountain told you not to drink out of it in two or three languages. Cicadas buzzed with such brazen violence that they vibrated the glass walls. Even if it was physically impossible, I *saw* the palpable heat pressing mushily over Shanghai.

Leaving China, I felt Shanghai in daylight for the first time in late July the next year. The heat was not a false image. Shanghai was three prairie scorchers squeezed together in intensity, plus the deep ominous humidity before a tornado, without any tornado arriving to blow it apart. Your skin, your shirt, your hair, were inseparable from the air. The old ramshackle houses (once home for a single Chinese magnate, now home to anywhere from fifty to one hundred, sans paint, sans toilet, sans windows) melted into it. The bricks and boards, damp, soggy, sweating, almost dissolved into the bizarre shapes of a Dali landscape. Through this heat moved more humans than you imagine on a whole planet, much less in a single city: humans loaded three or four to a bicycle, humans on foot, humans squeezed into rusty diesel buses, rich humans in air-conditioned taxis, humans underfoot, humans hanging out of windows, humans in limp uniforms in traffic kiosks, small humans, large humans, Chinese humans, foreign-devil humans, beautiful humans, grotesque humans, humans brought together with a single fundamental fact, the bottom of every fact in Shanghai — sweat — salty, acrid human sweat stuck everywhere in this vast, run-down, lively place.

I spent two days waiting for the plane to America in the Shanghai Jiaotong University faculty club — blessedly air-conditioned. Through the gray haze outside the lobby window stood an enormous bronze heroic statue of the Great Helmsman himself — Mao Zedong — right arm raised in salute, overcoat billowing in the nonexistent wind, face metallically noble, chin wart and all. Even the bronze sweats. Almost all these heroic helmsmen statues were pulled down after the Cultural Revolution, during which they pocked the landscape like teenage acne. The personality cult was now on the back burner, and though Mao's waxed corpse was still on show in Beijing, the normal Chinese citizen, tired of his recent political firestorms, could go off to work without the Chairman's wart observing his progress.

But here in this dank city, a big one survives: an anomaly, a contradiction, like so much else in Shanghai. Much more than on Beijing, the West left its hand on Shanghai: on the colonial architecture, the shaded boulevards, the magnates' mansions, the traffic roundabouts, the local taste for coffee, pastries, and dry wine, the signs in English and French, the overwhelming numbers of old people who manage European languages and speak to tourists openly, the clinging silky dresses on the women, the eagle-eyed, feisty urbanity of the Shanghai man on the street.

It is a strangely appropriate midway point between Xi'an, the ancient backward isolated provincial city, and San Francisco, my first destination, the Valhalla of twentieth-century mercantilism and lifestyle-itis. Shanghai is half-and-half, stewed in its own heat.

One morning I got up at dawn for a walk, hoping it had cooled. It had not. Night is black heat; day is gray heat; dawn is pink fuzzy heat, all the same temperature. I strolled over to the little grassy yard in front of the bronze helmsman, and, having lived in China for a year and gone crazy, was not surprised to find twenty or twenty-five old people out doing exercises. One old man in a wheelchair sat doing Taichi with his arms and his neck, the chair slowly turning in front of the Mao statue, as he waved, plunged, and wobbled in his seated ritual of half-fitness.

I sat down on the steps in front of the Chairman's toe and started sweating onto a notebook page, hardly knowing what I thought to say at leaving this odd, broken-down, magnificent place. As I sat there wordless and wet, an old man in a sleeveless T-shirt and baggy shorts ambled over and showed his missing teeth.

"You are a foreigner?"

Since I am around six-and-a-half feet tall and red-bearded, I thought this perceptive of him so early in the morning, and answered yes.

"You are coming to teach at our famous university?"

"No, I taught at another famous university, and am just leaving. I catch a plane this afternoon."

I knew the next question was coming; it is regular as the rotation of the planets.

"What do you think of our country? It is so poor and backward compared to your so rich and up-to-date country."

I also know what response was expected of me, but somehow on this last soggy morning in Asia, I couldn't give it. I asked him questions instead.

"Do you come here every morning to exercise?"

"Yes, I do." He swung his arms, and jogged in place, like an athlete winding down his body. "How old do you think I am?"

This was going to be twenty questions, and I was in no mood to play it.

"You are Chinese, and older than you look, I suppose. How old are you?"

"I am sixty-eight, but quite fit, don't you think?" He pounded his chest.

Indeed, he looked fit, short, compact, and tough enough to have survived the last impossible half-century of Chinese history.

"You speak English very well. Have you been to America?"

"I am from Shanghai before the Liberation. I worked with Americans and learned a little. My English is poor, don't you think?"

This was a thousand simultaneous conversations, every cliché I had memorized.

"It is very good. Do you teach?"

"No. I am a worker, but too old now. I hope my children can travel to your beautiful country someday."

He translated the Chinese word for America directly — *Meiguo* — "beautiful country."

"How old are you?"

"Forty-four."

"The hair on foreigners' faces, you know, makes them look to us . . . "

"Older. Yes, I know."

"And how many children?"

This was an inexorable conversation we were not engaged in, a verbal blitzkrieg. There was no stopping it.

"None."

"But you are a young man. Your wife can still . . . "

"No wife."

"Ah. Perhaps you need a Chinese wife! You foreigners can have many children. We Chinese only one. So many people, you see."

"*Bu yao!*" I answered, cranking out my primitive Chinese to bring this to a halt. He looked puzzled. Wrong tones again? Maybe not; this man speaks Shanghai-ese, entirely different noises for "not want."

"Do you know who this is?" He gestured toward the elephantine statue.

"Yes."

"What do you Americans think of him?"

"He was a man of great energy; some good, some bad. He brought China useful things, but much misery, too. Probably more misery. What do you think?"

"You are a welcome foreigner. I hope you come back to China. It has been very nice to speak English with you this morning."

As the damp sun began to slather over the helmsman's boots, we parted, my last spontaneous conversation with a stranger in China. The wheelchair was still at his calisthenics, waving his arms like a perpendicular windmill.

My only real errand in Shanghai was to repair a last piece of Chinese bureaucratic incompetence. For six weeks, I had asked for a reservation not to Minnesota but to Seattle, where I intended to reacquaint myself with bourgeois decadence by sailing in the San Juan Islands for two weeks. I patiently explained in slow "special" English, time and time again, that I did not, under *any* circumstances, want to fly to Minneapolis, that it was thousands of miles from Seattle, that I wanted an open booking, like round-trip tickets, an impossibility in China, ad infinitum, ad nauseum. When I got to Shanghai to pick up my ticket—impossible by phone or computer, possible only by standing in line, in person—it read SHANGHAI-SAN FRANCISCO-MINNEAPOLIS, all in one long consecutive marathon. Some Chinese bureaucrat knew only that I lived in Minnesota and could not imagine my deviating from a brisk return to my home work-unit. After all, had I gotten their permission to go sailing?

My anger exceeded language, so I silently pocketed the ticket, found a taxi, and asked the driver to take me in air-conditioned comfort to the booking office of any international airline in Shanghai that had a computer. My American Express card burned with rage in my wallet, ready to strike any creature that stood in its single-minded plastic way. I had wasted hours, days, months of my precious life, whitened a thousand hairs in my beard, raised my precarious blood pressure, all to have a simple booking made that, in a civilized country (so I muttered to myself), would have taken one phone call and ten or fifteen minutes. And I still had to do it myself! But, at least, I was in Shanghai, where credit cards meant business and, as it turned out, Northwest Airlines from my very home state had an office in an elegant old hotel, the Jin Jiang, complete with functioning computer, clean carpet, soft chairs, glossy brochures, No Smoking signs (the only ones in China!), and a beautiful Hawaiian agent who did her business briskly and cheerfully, albeit with a sort of melancholy look probably indicating that Shanghai was not her first choice for a lively work assignment. A few minutes and 114 dollars later, it was done. I was booked on a plane to Seattle two hours after I landed in San Francisco. I walked out smugly, thinking to myself, "Now that is the way business is done in civilized countries. Good to get home!" To celebrate, I went into the hotel coffee shop and treated myself to a tuna fish sandwich, potato salad, iced tea (with ice cubes!), cheesecake, and coffee, my first such lunch in a year. It was awful. I paid seven or eight dollars in hard currency and walked out into the Shanghai miasma. I have never much liked tuna fish, I thought to myself, and cheesecake once did in my gall bladder. Sweat poured out of more places on my body than a physiologist would think possible. I smoked my last chocolate-scented Phenix cigarette, found a taxi and retreated to the air-conditioned faculty club to read the *Herald Tribune* until the plane took off for San Francisco.

I left Shanghai in late afternoon at the still point of heat. Like every street of every city in China, the road to the airport was not a series of isolated, disconnected events, but a mass held together by the continuous presence of human clots. It looked almost as if the old western houses were ready to explode from the density of human life inside them. I made a mental picture of the million square miles of Chinese countryside stretching off in every direction but east, the numberless villages, the living room-sized farm plots, the stuffed buses weaving between mules, pedicabs, bicycles, and walkers, horns sounding a continual alarm continually ignored by the billion Chinese simultaneously out on the roads going about whatever their business might be; every inch of Chinese soil remodeled, refertilized, destroyed, rebuilt, destroyed again, rebuilt again, dense with six thousand or so years of corpses, ruins, tries, failures, secrets, catastrophes, treasures. China is a ruined place, spoiled by being used too long by too many, but it is ruined in the way that only human beings can ruin a place—with dignity, squalor, corruption, blood, foolishness, passion, and love. No animal did that, China says when you look at it, when you breathe in it. We did it, and that is what it looks like, and it will go on and on and on and on. Humans mostly do that, and, if nothing else, China is a human place.

From the air, the density of China's population is even clearer than from the road. Shanghai is surrounded and penetrated, not by farms, but by gardens, a green mist of countryside, not still, but shivered by the continual motion of the human mass moving over it. There is no real end to Shanghai and no beginning to the rest of China. It is of a piece. The plane moves past the estuary of the Huang Po and the Yangtze rivers and out over the open Pacific. How empty the gray water looks after China! I order Scotch and ice, pay with a dollar bill, open an *Asia Week*, take off my hot shoes, put on a pair of CAAC baby blue airplane booties to wait for my microwaved dinner. It is a breast of chicken in a bland sauce, potatoes, a hard roll, a chocolate cookie, and a bowl of iceberg lettuce with a chunk of cold lobster sitting on it. I am offered only a plastic knife and fork to eat with, so I do my best not to look awkward. The West begins early in the sky.

The plane lands for half an hour in Tokyo to disgorge passengers and take on fresh supplies. Narita airport looks like O'Hare, travelers in gray suits, signs in English next to the Japanese script, and twenty or thirty TVs to pass the time between planes. The commercial on television is selling Japanese Levis. I can tell without language. Pretty Japanese girls bounce around with their hind ends to the camera, wiggling red tabs. Bored Japanese businessmen slouch in front of the screens, their leather briefcases open on their laps so they can scribble sales reports between commercials. I go to the toilet and find it clean, a new roll of toilet paper waiting on its metal roller. Planters peanuts and Coke for sale at the snack bar. Tokyo or Chicago?

Soon the plane is off again over the long Pacific, the date line, the sun rising, the empty water. More salad, more chicken, more knives and forks, more Scotch. *Out of Africa* plays on the airplane screen. I watch without sound. English will begin soon enough. How pale Meryl Streep looks; how wooden and inexpressive Robert Redford's face. Kenya looks like someone's dream of romantic Africa, seen from six miles above the Pacific.

A standard Chinese traveler's joke, that CAAC stands for "China Airlines always cancels," was for once not true, so three hours before leaving Shanghai, I arrived punctually in San Francisco. The mysteries of the international date line are impenetrable, but they give you one day of your life twice. I had my second chance at the twentieth of July in the United States.

From the air, California looked like a travel brochure for California, or paradise (or in the opinion of some Californians, both simultaneously). Piercing blue sky, cliffs cutting up from a calm, dark blue sea, wooded green hills stretching back to wooded green mountains, the skyscraper tops of the Bay Area cities gleaming like polished crystal in the intense light, not a trace of air pollution in the crisp air, every landscape outlined sharp, clean, clear, the Golden Gate strung like a toy bridge over the bay, leading to the wilderness of Marin.

Wilderness, did I say? Space? As any schoolchild knows, the Bay Area of California is one of the most densely populated places on the North American continent, continually scrutinized for crime, crowding, and bad air. Realtors sell land by the inch, for more than most people can afford. Oakland, San Jose, Palo Alto, Santa Cruz, San Francisco, all teeming cities, jam together on a knot of rock. Auto exhaust fumes belch up by the ton into the ozone layer. And yet here was this clear postcard image of empty hills, trees, sun, small towns separated by open space. Tiny ribbons of road with sparse, harmonious traffic moving along to connect them, clean light and sea wind laving everything in sight. I astonished myself with the naïveté of my own perception, and yet, there it was, before my eyes, unaltered. I had flown into San Francisco from the east perhaps ten times and never seen it, never realized that it was a wilderness and not a megalopolis, and now for the rest of my life, I would never be able to see it from the air as other Minnesotans see it, as a big, exciting, corrupt, polluted city. It was, instead, a cultivated garden surrounded by almost empty nature.

The plane lands next to the terminal and I walk across the tarmac towards customs. It is seventy degrees, cool and brisk. The air smells of salt, lemon and pines, as if it had been professionally cleaned for my arrival. I hadn't smelled this for a year! Chinese air is dense with coal from factories and cooking fires and with human shit from open toilets and running sewers. Night soil's next journey is to a farm field, so even the countryside smells rich with it. Does no one shit in America? Where does it all go? Are there not enough of us to make a smelly dent in the pure air?

If you live with a smell for a long time, you become unconscious of it. Your nose, at first offended by what it is unused to, quickly makes private peace with whatever arrives in its capillary hairs—a bus full of those breathing garlic pickles after breakfast, the night soil wagon sloshing its overflow on the street, the fumes of a steel mill or of cooking wood pulp, the acrid pungency of chilies bouncing in rapeseed oil inside a blackened wok. It shocks the poor nose then, this sudden absence of smells long accommodated and befriended, like a new amputee missing the feel of his gone limb. I suddenly missed the old smell of China, without loving any less the lemony, bland, antiseptic smell of America.

I arrived in China with all my luggage (all!) lost for three and a half weeks, but now I was too tired from twenty hours on an airplane to sufficiently dread a repeat catastrophe. After all, this is America! I stand sleepily watching bags go around the gleaming steel carousel. I smoke a Chinese cigarette, forgetful that public smoking is now probably a capital crime in America. There are no police anywhere, no checkpoints; a few airport employees in crisp uniforms move about. Silence, calm, order, a clean, almost empty, room. No one shouts in any language. The baggage carousel whirs innocuously, as if it could keep going around forever and never break down or strand a bag. A voice behind me asks:

"You on the plane from Shanghai?"

"Yes," I answer, not looking.

"How long you been there?"

Obviously some friendly soul meant to wait for his bags with small talk.

"A whole year."

"Gee, what were you doing?"

"Teaching English to graduate students in Xi'an."

"Is that the town with all the old warriors?"

"Yes."

"They speak much English there?"

"They're very good, actually—the most interesting students I've ever had in my life."

"You buy much stuff?"

"You could buy out all of China, and it wouldn't amount to much here."

"You carrying any fruits and vegetables?"

At this question, I turned around. Here stood a small old gentleman in a gray uniform with a U.S. Customs badge.

"Welcome home," he said sweetly.

"Where do I go through customs?" I asked him. My bags had still not arrived.

"You already have," he said, stamping my form while he walked on to his next customer.

After a year of bitter fighting with Chinese bureaucrats, hearing sad stories of innocent Chinese savaged by their imperious power and rudeness, I almost knelt in front of the old boy and wept with thanks. Part of me knew he was not a fair symbol of American power and bureaucracy, but at least he was possible, and the gods conspired to have him on duty when I arrived.

This was all so smooth that I had two hours to kill as a consequence of efficiency, so I ambled to the Pacific Air counter to confirm the flight I bought in Shanghai. The man stamped the ticket and looked up at me.

28   *COMING HOME CRAZY*

"You want to go earlier?"

"I can?"

"Flight leaving in twenty minutes. I put you on it. Go straight to the gate."

I stopped at a newsstand on the way and fumbled in my billfold for the first twenty dollar bill I had fingered for a year. A gum-chewing girl sat at the cash register smiling at anything that moved and a great deal that didn't. The Chinese, like the Europeans, find the eternal smiliness of Americans false and cloying. Darkly, I imagine a McDonald's clerk hearing news of nuclear war with a big smile and a "What'll it be for you today?"

This brightly lit little newsstand, a bagatelle to an American, was an oasis, a palace, a grand emporium of commerce, a microcosmic Saks to me. A rack of newspapers! In English! Fifty different magazines! In English! Chocolate! Peppermints! Pistachio nuts! T-shirts! Nail clippers! Dried fruit! Aspirin! Flight bags! Salamis! Cheeses! Postcards! Paperback novels! Tums! Certs! Kleenex! Road maps! Key chains! Tampons! Calendars! Sourdough bread! Bic lighters! Camels!

Trying to look as if I were used to this, I bought a pack of Camels, peppermint Lifesavers, a Hershey bar and a San Francisco paper. "Anything else?" the girl asked, snapping her gum, smiling.

"Yes. Total immersion! Give me a *People*." She slipped my goods into a plastic bag, changed my twenty, and dropped a quarter on the floor. I thought I heard it ring.

"Are they silver again?" I asked.

"Huh?" she said. "Have a good day, now."

I grabbed my bag and trotted to the next plane. On time. Settled in on the way to Seattle, I ate my pasta salad, washed it down with a good Chardonnay as the long row of glacier-coated volcanoes led the airplane north. The young stockbroker in the next seat is a collector of foreign money, so I give him a *renminbi*. The engraving is of an idealized girl driving a tractor.

"Chinese money!" he says. "Gee, it's pretty." He misses the point that in Capitalist terms this is not currency at all, but that's all right. Almost every China survivor will tell you that everyone goes on missing the point, until you finally give up trying to make it and either go back to China or adjust in silence. This is what culture shock really means, either making your own peace, or leaving. Nothing is ever the same after you have gone "crazy." The anthropologist on his motorcycle knew this, but there was no way he could explain it to me until I knew it, and I can't explain it to you.

I reached into my airport bag, unrolled a peppermint, lit a Camel and opened *People*. I was not so isolated in China that I failed to be conscious of the main drift of American life for a year, but the *China Daily* gave a skewed view and the hard currency *Newsweek* finally seemed more trouble than it was worth to get. America would survive without my attention, I thought, and friends kept me up on the Jim and Tammy and Jessica show, surely the funniest news story of the year. Iran-gate, which I followed in outline, didn't surprise me, and I looked pleasantly forward to long prison terms for the Ehrlichmanns and Haldemans of the eighties. Ollie North, crookedly handsome marine and handsomely crooked patriot, stared at me from the cover of *People*. I flipped straight to Ollie. What is this? No prison for Ollie? He's a national hero? Ollie for President groups have formed? They're eating Ollie Burgers in Ohio?

Exhausted as I was, delighted with food, sun, efficiency and English in America, I began laughing almost hysterically. The alarmed stewardess stiffened. When I calmed down, I closed *People*, pushed the pasta salad to one side and began singing, in a well-modulated tenor, "America the Beautiful":

> Oh, beautiful for spacious skies,
> For amber waves of grain;
> For purple mountains' majesty,
> Above the fruited plain.
> America, America,
> God shed his grace on thee;
> And crown thy good with brotherhood,
> From sea to shining sea.

The stewardess came around, checking. "Need a drink?" she asked. "Aren't you the one who was in China for a year?"

"Yes," I said. "Yes, indeed."

"You must be real happy to be home, then."

"Yes," I said. "Yes, indeed. Bring whiskey. I'm going sailing. Shiver me timbers!"

中国文章的目录及附文

An Alphabet
of China Essays,
Plus a Few

ALPHABET

中国文学

We have all lived so long inside the alphabet that it seems to us nature rather than habit. God spoke alphabetically in the business about light, didn't she?

A cousin of mine who spent his life as a book editor and printer came to visit me in China. Since he is a genetic Midwestern Lutheran, he cannot be in the presence of squalor or chaos without improving it. Within a day or two, he was haranguing my students: If China would only give up its inefficient language and alphabetize, then it could be organized and modernized briskly. Libraries would blossom, computers everywhere, a real telephone book could be printed, things found and filed and found again.

Some one tried to explain the Chinese character to him, but it was useless. For him, as for you, the alphabet is not an invention but a theology, a matter not for reason but for faith. The universe is organized sequentially; it has a beginning, middle, and end; one event follows another in proper order; dictionaries, encyclopedias, telephone directories, and filing cabinets imitate the universe; imitation is praise and confirms the truth of what we already know without contradiction. It offends something deep within us that there should be a civilization without Jesus, Plato, or a properly organized dictionary. If we bring the truth, they will surely see it.

A Chinese dictionary is organized by the number of strokes the hand makes with a brush to form a character. It begins with one, *yi*, one stroke; two, *er*, has two strokes. A man, or a human being is a pair of running legs, *ren*, 人 . Beyond this, logic collapses, and with it, efficiency. You move into the hieratic world of radicals: fixed components of characters and the number of strokes added to give them meaning. To be a Chinese file clerk requires the quick intelligence of a mathematician.

Lu Xun, one of twentieth-century China's great writers, made, in the thirties, a cranky but spirited attack on the Chinese character, and thus on the whole foundation of the Chinese language, and, probably by extension, of Chinese history. Language is, after all, the only real news we have that something has happened.

Lu argued that the written language was too difficult: Old Hundred Names, the Chinese public, had never learned it. It was too conservative: the immense resistance to change inside the language (because of the weight of classical literary Chinese), confirmed the class structure and thus the feudal misery of modern China. Lu recommended Romanization—an alphabet. He wrote his argument in Chinese characters of great elegance.

If one thing does not follow another in proper order, we feel a great hollow space inside us. My friends Aagard and Zolynas know about hierarchy and the great chain of being. Things begin and they end. Alpha and Omega. But the Chinese do not practice eschatology. They are a civilization without closure, without the *Götterdämerung* implied at the end of the alphabet.

I felt that hollow space in China, too, when I asked for a telephone number and was handed a book without penetrable sequence, and therefore without use. It frightened me, as if I were a Stone Age savage watching an Oldsmobile drive into the jungle for the first time. A Chinese telephone directory is indeed useless, but for reasons much more complex and terrifying than the absence of an alphabet.

I mean here both to praise the alphabet and to use it, but not to mistake its randomness for divine order. There may indeed be a kind of truth inside that randomness, but it is not a truth that builds computers or temples, or files cards. I mean here also to praise living outside the alphabet for a while in some interior China of unknown sequences—even without sequence. If, in addition, you can manage to live in the exterior China for a while, too, that will help the imagination and give courage to your metaphors.

AIDS

艾滋病

I found this notice on the door of my room at the Barbarians' Guest House on December 15, 1986:

Notice

The Epidemic Prevention Station of Shaanxi Province kindly asks you to have AIDS test (blood sample taken) on Thursday, 18 December, 1986 at Foreign Guest house of Xi'an Jiaotong University. It is a new test given to all foreigners residing in China. The University Hospital issues this notice to you on behalf of the Epidemic Prevention Station. Your assistance is much appreciated.

Hospital of Xi'an Jiaotong University

I fumed. I raged. It was noon, so I went to lunch with my fellow Barbarians in the guest-house dining room. Four Canadians, three Brits, three Louisianans, a New Englander and another Minnesotan already fumed and raged over their three-shredded soup.

"I will not do it," I pounded the table. Eleven other fists pounded in tandem . . . and would not do it. It was an unlikely crew of revolutionaries, this last supper of mild Barbarians.

"Somebody should go tell the bastards," said the Louisiana Baptist. Driblets of three-shredded soup coagulated all over the table.

We found out later that sixteen Minnesota students had the same lunch rebellion, along with all the other Barbarians at other universities in town, all at their separate tables, all spilling their private soup, and venting together their private rage. That simultaneous rage was a united front. It worked like a Quaker meeting or Athenian democracy. It worked as democratic protest so seldom does, each citizen arriving at just truth and standing up for it, alone, together.

I informed the Barbarian Handler's Office of my decision. I refused the test; they had no legal grounds to compel me to it, and, if they insisted, they were welcome to deport me at their own expense, and thus terminate the exchange program with my university.

"But it is such a simple thing. No trouble really. Surely you are not one of those? . . . "

"I will not do it for three reasons, and what I am or am not is none of your damned business. First, I have seen the inside of a Chinese hospital. I have seen spit on the floor. I have seen a nurse give a shot, wipe the needle on her pants, and give the next victim a shot. My chances of contracting hepatitis from your test are greater than your chances of controlling AIDS by testing me. Second, I have seen a Chinese post office, and have seen your filing cabinets. The chances of my getting my own blood test results are probably fifty percent. If I happened to get the wrong one, my chances of buying any health insurance policy for the rest of my life are gone. Third, like every American, I grew up listening to stories of Nazi doctors. The rights of any government, yours or my own, stop at my skin. I will take no medical procedure under legal compulsion. If you want to test Barbarians for AIDS, make it a visa requirement, so that it can be done in their home country. My visa has no such requirement, and I insist that you live up to its legal provisions." I think I pounded on the table, spilling tea.

"You speak so fast, Teacher Holm. Here, you should sit and take a little rest. You are so red-faced. Smoke a Golden Monkey, very good local brand." I smoked. "Are you the leader and spokesman for the foreigners?"

"Barbarians speak for themselves. In this case, my guess is that you will have to listen to some version of my speech from all of them, but if you want to make sure, you can ask them yourselves. It's a free country." I failed to bite my tongue after that piece of rhetorical overkill.

Somehow, news of this latest Xi'an uprising leaked back to the Barbarian press, and when I got back to the guest house, one of the teachers was on the phone. "L.A. Times," she said. "Here, talk to them."

I gave the reporter a California version of my refusal speech. He asked if he could quote me. I asked how he had gotten the news of the AIDS test so quickly. A young Canadian from Xi'an had called her embassy in Beijing. It was a provincial experiment, and neither the embassy nor the Chinese Education Ministry claimed to know anything about it.

COMING HOME CRAZY

The embassy called Ottawa; Ottawa called Toronto; Toronto called Los Angeles, or some such electronic sequence.

"Is there anyone else to talk to?" he asked. At that moment Helen from Manitoba walked through the door. Helen and Oscar were in their early seventies, a retired school teacher and engineer respectively, and had come teaching in China, both for adventure and to be close to Chinese friends they had made in Manitoba. They were a scrupulously clean, neat, intelligent, kindly, decent pair, looking like the twinkly-eyed, high-minded, leftist grandparents everyone fantasized and no one ever had. Helen, hardly five feet tall, had snow-white hair, glasses on a chain, and the manner of your favorite third-grade teacher about to explain something with infinite patience to you for the fifth time. I handed her the phone.

"Yes. Where did you say you were from, young man? California? Yes. My husband and I are here teaching for the year from Manitoba. Yes. We are refusing the AIDS test, too. Yes . . . Well, we sympathize deeply, of course, with the Chinese people's worries over this terrible disease and . . . yes . . . . Oscar and I feel we're in the low-risk group." As Edith Bunker used to do, I stifled myself.

"Yes, young man. You may quote this so long as you don't use our names and so long as it doesn't appear in Manitoba. Los Angeles, did you say? That's in California?"

Since some version of the same scene took place at every university in town, the AIDS test was dropped and never mentioned again. Barbarian teachers coming for the next year were required to have the test at home and present evidence of a negative response before they were issued a visa.

The *China Daily* continued running ominous stories of the foreign plague and the danger of contamination through contact with Barbarians. AIDS, like cancer or tuberculosis, provides a fine opportunity for cautionary metaphors which, in China, assumed their classic xenophobic form.The language of contamination had for so long proved useful to the Chinese authorities in describing ideological deviation and class background that they fell naturally into it for a disease associated with black Africans, homosexuals, drug addicts and prostitutes. A place for everyone to project their brainless hatreds.

I doubt the Barbarian Handler's Office learned its lesson anywhere in China about tampering with private bodies, but the Barbarians' behavior cheered me. It was braver than America's spineless capitulation to the swine flu vaccine a few years before. Maybe there was still hope for Jefferson's democracy.

When Helen and Oscar returned to Manitoba a few months later, they were met at the bottom of the airplane exit ramp by their little granddaughter who leapt into Helen's arms and asked with wide eyes: "What's a low-risk group, Grandma?"

BANKING

银行

On Christmas Day, 1986, I go to the Bank of China. Devaluation rumors float around, and I sit on 1,500 of the people's money, *renminbi*, mostly in stacks of ones, twos, and fives, the preferred cash salary payment for my "foreign expert" teaching job.

This weighs in at three pounds of currency, which despite its heft, is "soft," and therefore must be disposed of before its value sinks. There is one international bank in this city of two and a half million, and I have been in China long enough to take a Chinese factotum with me. English disappears at the speaker's convenience here, and my baby Chinese doesn't make much of a dent in that inconvenient habit.

It is a gray, dusty winter day, just above freezing. Coal smoke, diesel exhaust, and an unknown combination of noxious and gritty factory fumes coagulate the air. Visibility is one hazy block through the man-made fog. Farther away, the world disappears behind an opaque gray scrim — the slums of Dickens's London, one hundred and forty years later.

Liberation Road swarms with humans. "Swarm" is not a whimsical metaphor, not a literary verb, but a fact, a photograph. Every ten feet of sidewalk is inhabited by fifty or sixty moving human legs, an endless flat escalator in an eternal, slow rush hour, an undulating body with a thousand heads of black hair weaving, eating, talking, gawking, never speeding, never stopping, swarming toward some non-existent destination, which is only the same sidewalk, the same store, the same noodle stand, a half-mile, or a mile, or a thousand miles, or a hundred years, or a million, down the same street through the same gray grit that fills the air like the brine that packs a jar of pickles.

Though it may be purposeful from the inside, to an outsider this swarming seems an aimless streaming towards nowhere particularly different from where it is now. It is a thing by itself, whose only purpose is itself, is motion. It leads to the bank.

The Bank of China, a seven-story, gray cement building, rises over its low neighbors. A Hong Kong bank is whimsical and ostentatious, an architectural emblem of the savage and good-humored greed that permeates that strange space station of a city, but a Chinese bank, like a Chinese hotel or block of flats or university classroom or train station or public toilet or provincial office, is proof that though Stalin is dead, Stalinist concrete still weighs down any country touched by his ghost.

In this city of gray socialist cement, the Bank of China distinguishes itself only by sticking up a couple of extra stories into the swirling airborne grit.

Inside the bank, the swarming stops. Two customers stand at one window; Xiao Zhang and I make four. An empty room in Xi'an! We go to the teller's window. I'm wrong—this is not an empty room at all. Behind the glass: a roomful of desks, bank clerks waiting on a slow day. We hand the money through the slot in the window.

After a minute, the teller looks up from his newspaper. "Wrong window," he says, failing to indicate which is the right one. We line up behind the other two customers. One is a very pretty girl in a bright red jacket. I practice the oriental virtue of patience and content my mind with various imaginary scenes starring the red-coated girl.

After three cigarettes and twenty minutes of low mental exercise, I notice that none of the four of us has moved. A few employees have filled tea cups, turned to fresh pages in the newspaper and lit new cigarettes. Lunch, and the two-hour closing time for the Chinese siesta approaches rapidly. On the customer side, the clock reads 11:15; on the employee side: 11:30.

Given this evidence, I'm ready to bet that their lunch arrives before mine. Matching the bank clerk cigarette for cigarette, I light my fourth on the butt of the third, and inquire of Xiao Zhang whether we shouldn't try another window. A scholarly-looking young gentleman doodles away on an abacus with one hand, but without missing a click, picks up my money-changing form and says, "Stamp on seventh floor . . . " He resumes his abacus clicking in something like a samba rhythm and stares abstractedly off in the direction of the employees' supercharged clock.

Seventh floor? No elevator, so we find the stairs, and, dodging various debris—sawhorses, overturned chairs, two-by-fours, water buckets, and plaster chunks, we bound upwards. The floors are not marked, and

40

most are blocked off with plastic ropes. "Is this the seventh?" we inquire of each other, nearing the fifth and beginning to sweat.

Finally, we top the building. No sign of an office, but, behind a heavy quilt (there is no heat in the bank) is an unmarked door, and inside sits a girl at a desk reading a newspaper. She looks up calmly, examines the forms for a few minutes, gives them a red stamp, and resumes the editorial.

Remembering that the employee clock is hyperventilating well past Greenwich Mean, we bound back down the stairs. No need to rush. The same two customers are still at the same window. The public clock now reads 11:30, the teller's 11:45. The clocks face each other down, like dueling views of history.

No need for suspense. The man gives up, the girl disappears to another window, the teller examines the forms, fingers the passport, pours more hot water in his teacup, and tells us to go to another window. The girl stands in front of us, red coat gleaming, glossy black hair cascading over her collar. Falling temporarily out of love, and by now mightily impatient in the classic American manner, I decide to count employees and see why it has taken an hour of my life in an empty bank to do a three-minute errand. I walk back and forth in the big cement room, counting aloud in English.

Fifty-four human beings are on the job behind the glass. Sixteen read newspapers, seven or eight read books, ten or twelve get fresh tea water out of the thermos, nine are gossiping (judging by sound and hand gesture), two quarrel, four play with their abacuses, though in no purposeful way, five or six seem to be fingering piles of forms, three stare off into space or at the clock which now reads 11:52, customer clock, 11:37, thirty-nine are smoking, and one is sound asleep.

These fifty-four employees make an average of seventy cents American per day, and are worth every penny. They have managed in one hour of working time to service three small and routine transactions.

I was sorry, for just a moment, that I was not born Chinese, not assigned that bank job. I am sufficiently both lazy and uninterested in the progress of money and international business to have managed a career there with considerable style. God knows how many poems, outrageous political ideas, and entertaining sexual fantasies went through those fifty-four human intelligences in that one hour. If I worked in that bank, I would regard myself as having permission to write, on company time, novels that would dwarf Dostoyevsky's.

The right clock now reads 11:55, the left one 11:40. Xiao Zhang and

I exit with my small stack of newly bought American dollars and follow the brilliant red coat out into the gray noon.

It's lunch time. The Liberation Road Dumpling (*Jiaozi*) Parlor next door is crowded, smoky, noisy and jolly. The air steams with hot boiled dumplings. Chopsticks clatter. Inside every dumpling I find a marble of spicy meat, tasty and unexpected.

The table is covered with the customers' white surgical masks, taken off only long enough to eat dumplings. The Chinese, too, notice the coagulated grit in the air as for thousands of years they noticed idle bureaucrats. The Chinese noticed everything, long before I did.

BLACK HAIR

黑头发

After a whole year of looking at me in the hallways of the Barbarians' Guest House, the Chinese girl who answers the phone at the front desk can't hold back any more. "Why is your hair red?" she asks. In China that's not such a bad question.

I say, "It's my mother's fault! I'm not guilty! I've got no responsibility for this red hair!" She scrunches her nose and looks puzzled. I continue: "And why is yours black?" This is too much for her. She breaks into a giggle, and her almond cheeks turn the color of my hair.

Humans have black hair; aberrations have red. Her evidence is conclusive, based as it is on large experience, a vast sampling of humans. Watch Chinese bicycle traffic: a human merry-go-round of black hair, bobbing up and down, down and up, unpunctuated (except at tourist spots) by red, or brown, or blonde — or even much gray. The Chinese dye almost till death.

Hair science tells us that there are about 125,000 hair follicles on a human scalp. Demographers tell us that there are 1,200,000,000 Chinese in China, and at minimum, another 100,000,000 genetic Chinese elsewhere. Mathematics tells us that $1,300,000,000 \times 125,000 = 162,500,000,000,000$. That is a lot of black hairs for one small-sized planet in a medium-sized out-of-the-way solar system. Also a lot of zeros. Consider also the Japanese, Malays, Polynesians, Africans, Arabs, Australian and North American aboriginal stocks, Tibetans, Mongols, Thais, Kazakhs, Burmese, Indians, Pakistanis, Afghans, Turks, Eskimos, Pygmies, Hawaiians, Greeks, Italians, Spaniards, Portuguese, Lapps, a majority of French, Welsh, Irish, Jews, Belgians, and Slavs, a healthy percentage of Germans, Scandinavians, Brits, Finns, and Dutch, and various mixtures of the preceding tribes. The weight of evidence is therefore conclusive: black hair is human; red maybe, maybe not.

* * *

A few weeks after I arrived in Xi'an and started teaching, I heard an unexpected knock at my door late one afternoon. It was my student, Hu, who said: "There is a lecture at 5:00 on post-Cultural Revolution poetry by a hot young critic and poet. Would you like to come?"

"Very much. Is he lecturing in English?"

"In Chinese, of course, but no worry. Hu will translate. Good practice!"

We sat on chairs set up close to the speaker's podium, half facing the main body of the audience. The hall was packed, some students even perched in window ledges. This was a polytechnic campus, with no programs or degrees in arts or humanities. I was astonished at the full house and said so to Hu.

"Much more interesting than reinforced concrete," he said.

A young, slightly built man stepped to the podium, set down his ashtray and tea cup, and began lecturing. He discussed the new experimentalism Chinese writers felt free to indulge, the loosening of literary reins since Mao's death, the new freedom not to make phony heroic images of proletarian saints, to monkey creatively with language and dreams. Hu translated wonderfully in my left ear and I cupped my hands under my beard, looking out now and then at the crowd of rapt scientists, some taking furious notes. The lecturer shifted to a cautionary warning that some young writers, in their enthusiasm, violated simple common sense to make metaphors so outrageous as to offend both truth and propriety.

"For instance," he said, "a few writers are carried away with odd adjectives in their metaphors: green love, green feeling, green sky. It's all right sometimes, but you must be careful. One writer called a woman's eyes green, thus insulting her by describing not human eyes but the eyes of a wolf." I heard giggling and shuffling and looked away from the speaker, realizing to my horror that half the audience starred fixedly at me. Not at me, perhaps, so much as at my green eyes.

I complimented the speaker afterwards, while we exchanged signed books, a world-wide writer's ritual, even though neither of us read the other's language. He apologized for his remark about green eyes. "For Chinese audiences, you know . . . "

"Don't mention it," I said. "Besides, you were probably right. I always suspected there were wolves on my mother's side."

* * *

On trips with Chinese students, we frequently rented cheap dormitory-style hotel rooms and slept together in a gang. One night, getting ready for bed, a student came over and asked shyly if he could pat my belly.

"Of course," I said. "In fact, I would be happy to sell it to you, very cheap, two *fen* maybe. Do you want it?"

He giggled, a little embarrassed, as he tenderly patted twenty-five years of butter and cream. "It's a wonderful belly," he said. "I admire it very much." He weighed perhaps 120 pounds, and I could have numbered his ribs.

Unlike red hair and green eyes (which, considered biologically, are a genetic inside straight, but an unalterable fact), nevertheless, something can actually be done about a belly. And China did it — shrinking my belly back inside my belt.

The few of us on this planet without black hair should spend less time complaining about our bad luck, and get on with the business of trying to be human in other ways.

BOOK SMUGGLING

书籍走私

One of my highest functions as a Barbarian teacher in China was book smuggling. On a rest and recreation trip to Hong Kong, I took along a carefully disguised sheet of Chinese characters. I had no idea what they meant. They might have been a laundry list, or Deng Xiaoping's address, or some old baseball scores. Their presence in my billfold gave it weight, and a sense of intrigue, as if I were smuggling letters from Jews out of Germany in the thirties.

I went to a Chinese bookstore in Hong Kong, smiled sweetly, and gave my list to a young girl on duty. Two minutes later, she handed me a red, hardbound book and said, "Forty Hong Kong dollars, please." I gave her my American Express card, and within moments it was over. So easy! In my plastic carrying bag, those regime-toppling pages burned and vibrated between scarlet covers.

How to get it past customs? Easier than expected . . . walk past. The customs man smiled benignly, looked over my bottles of duty-free Irish whiskey and said some equivalent of "Have a nice day in China . . . "

A few days later, I passed the book on to its new owner. Resisting the impulse to draw drapes, lock doors and windows, start water running, play loud rock and roll, and converse only in Icelandic, or perhaps classical Greek, I asked simply, "What is this dangerous book I have risked my life for? An exposé of corruption, some Chinese Solzhenitzen?"

"It is a novel."

"A new dissident novel by one of the Democracy Wall writers?"

"No, an old novel, *Jin Ping Mei*, from a couple of dynasties ago. I don't know quite how to translate the title. Only a few high cadres and professors—big potatoes—can get this book. It is about a woman, a courtesan . . . "

"Good God, is it *The Golden Lotus?*"

"Yes, that would be right. Have you heard of it?"

"Heard of it? I read it when I was fourteen years old in the Grove Press translation I bought for $2.95 at Berge's Book Land in Marshall, Minnesota. There are three copies on my shelves in Minneota, one in Norwegian. Why have I just smuggled one of the three or four most famous Chinese novels into China? This is a little like smuggling *Huckleberry Finn* into Missouri, or *Oliver Twist* into London."

"Impossible to get. Very dangerous book. Only on locked shelves in special libraries."

"You will shortly see how dangerous it is. Have a good read," I said, confident that I had not shaken this or any other regime to its foundations by introducing a slightly spicy story about a courtesan's shenanigans, bawdy in an archaic way, to a descendent of the tribe that imagined it and a native speaker of the language in which the Golden Lotus first had her adventures.

But not only as a smuggler did I prove useful to young Chinese in obtaining books. I visited one of my students in a small town in rural China and went out to stroll the streets with some of his middle-school students, admiring the local sights. Suddenly, apropos of nothing, one of the young girls turned to me and said, "Would you like to see the church?"

"Of course," I answered, having had enough experience in China to answer all odd questions in the affirmative. Something interesting will usually happen, and not always what you expected. We turned up a narrow alley and went through a cement arch marked only with a small, almost invisible red cross. The old doorman stopped the Chinese girls with a flurry of language, but when he saw my pink face and beard, he brightened, smiled, pumped my hand and asked whether I would like to meet the bishop. "Of course," I replied. A few minutes later, out came an eighty-year-old man with hooded eyes, an ironic mouth, a week's gray stubble, and perhaps the most intelligent face I have ever seen worn by a human being. He addressed me first in French, then inquired after my Italian, and with a slightly disappointed look took my arm and guided me into the church where for fifteen minutes we spoke softly in English. I have fallen among Catholics before, but this old bishop rose above party denomination, above religion. After a few sentences, I quickly understood that this was no ordinary religious functionary. The old man breathed silent rebellion. He seemed to me a human astonishment, full of irony, courage, and brains. This man would be dangerous to bureaucrats wherever he lived, Washington or China. This was the first time these girls had even seen this legendary old man or been inside his sanctum. We went out, met another man whose function was clearly to keep track of the bishop for the local authorities. The conversation took a bland turn to "How do you like the weather, the food, etc.?"

While blathering with the bishop's watchdog, I saw out of the corner of my eye a tug at his sleeve by one of the students, heard a little burst of modulated language. The bishop scurried agilely off to the side while I discoursed engagingly on the subject of Minnesota being somewhat colder than central China. A few minutes later, the bishop came back, passed a book to the student, and rejoined the conversation to make pleasant goodbyes. We all shook hands, swore eternal friendship between countries, whatever the winter temperature, and I soon stood in the street being thoroughly ignored by several lively Chinese girls who passed back and forth a square burgundy book as if it were the sacred sweet potato.

I have been used, I thought to myself, nothing but a pink Icelandic tool, but how pleased I was! Having for years made skeptical and sardonic remarks about Bible salesmen, and hotel-room Gideons, I became the modus operandi for a Bible transfer. For us, the Bible is a book more prattled over, or used as an instrument of abuse and intolerance, than it is read or understood, so I was oddly moved at the delight and fascination on those girls' faces as they fingered that Hong Kong Bible. A little danger and persecution do wonders to make Christianity a more humane and useful institution.

Some books even a Barbarian can't find. Like millions of old sixties Americans, I read the *Dao De Jing* in college, and loved it. It seemed a relief from the pious certainties of Lutheranism. It was (and is) ironic, paradoxical, witty, modest, brief, and probably beyond comprehension. Every commentator makes something slightly different of it, surely one of its chief charms. It was an anti-war book in the sixties, a California self-actualization book in the seventies, and an anti-business book in the eighties. It is all and none of those things, and both considerably more and less than that—to use its own language. Thoreau admired it, a substantial recommendation.

Among perhaps ten or fifteen translations of it in my house, I threw Witter Bynner's into my China bag. I remember almost taking it out, thinking that carting one of the two most famous Chinese books (Confucius' *Analects* is the other) ten thousand miles to its place of birth was a little like carrying coals to Newcastle. But no, I thought, it will be interesting to compare Bynner to the Chinese translations, and left it in the bag. Good thing I did, since there was no local competition. Perhaps the Chinese, busy building hydroelectric stations and writing tractor operas, haven't had time to get their own new translation out. Since I always like to own a favorite book in its own language, in a cheap edition that a local citizen might read for pleasure or carry in his pocket, I had someone write down the Chinese characters, which I then carted into bookstores. Here's the conversation:

"*You mei you Dao De Jing ?*" (Do you have *Dao De Jing?*)

"*Mei you.*" (Not have.)

"*Mei you?*" (Not have?) Rising astonishment.

"*Mei you.*" (Not have.) Finality.

The next logical question is "*Zai nali?*" (Where?) Not in China, probably. And so the next: "*Weishemma?*" (Why?) It is feudal. We do not read it in the new China.

How can anyone understand it well enough to figure out what is feudal (whatever that means) about the *Dao De Jing?* It might as well be a sort of paradoxical Marxism. In fact, some of Mao's poems and his more cryptic remarks read like debased versions of the *Dao.* There are no answers for any of these questions, except, as usual: "*Mei you.*"

What is available in China if *The Golden Lotus* has to be smuggled in, the Bible passed off in the presence of foreigners, and the *Dao De Jing* is *mei you?* China is, after all, the oldest literate civilization on earth, and still a nation of compulsive readers. People must read something!

They do. Students read (for lack of any alternative) Chen Jia's *History and Anthology of British Literature,* a set of books that whitened thousands of hairs in my beard. I arrived in China with all luggage gone, including books, still in a foggy state of jet lag and dysentery, was told I was teaching British literature, and handed Chen Jia. By the time I finished looking through his anthology, I was afraid the dysentery had moved from my lower intestines to my frontal lobe. This was not the British literature I remembered or had read.

Chen Jia has one idea, and either he is convinced of its truth or something convinced him that it is politic for this to be the true idea. Neither alternative offers the innocent reader much consolation as he looks into a table of contents without Donne, Herbert, Marvell, Sterne, Smollett, Boswell, Smart, Clare, Hopkins, George Eliot, Arnold, Conrad, etc. There is one page of Dr. Johnson, twelve lines of Yeats, and one edited chapter of *Sons and Lovers,* unaccompanied by the information that Lawrence might have written other books. On the other hand, the reader finds large doses of Cobbett, Ernest Charles Jones, John Watkins,

William James Lindon, Gerald Massey, Thomas Frost, Elizabeth Cleghorn Gaskell, Lewis Jones, Ralph Fox, J.B. Priestly, and most curious of all: twenty-five pages of Robert Tressell's *The Ragged Trousered Philanthropists*, next to "The Lake Isle of Innisfree," where Yeats' contribution to English poetry is described in two or three sentences, one of which reads:

> Tired of the life of his day, Yeats sought to escape into
> an ideal fairy land where he could live calmly as a hermit
> and enjoy the beauty of nature.

Indeed, Dr. Chen, and have you read "Sailing to Byzantium" or "The Wild Wicked Old Man" lately—?

But it is useless to beat a dead horse! Let Dr. Chen speak for himself. He announces that he will make his judgments

> from the viewpoint of historical materialism,
> giving proper places to each writer in accordance
> with the roles, healthful or otherwise, that they
> play in the progress of social history.

This is an interesting, if somewhat Procrustean, bed into which to trim a literature almost none of whose skilled practitioners would have had the slightest idea of what Dr. Chen was talking about. Here are some samples on *Beowulf*:

> With the disintegration of tribal society and the
> appearance of class divisions, professional singers
> or narrators of these stories emerged.

Class divisions would, I think, have amused Grendel. Book IV of *Gulliver's Travels* is an

> 'exposé' of the vices of the upper classes in
> England, who are compared with the Yahoos.

The working class should be grateful to Dr. Chen for getting them off Swift's hook in Book IV. Most readers seem to think Swift had the whole human race in mind, which, for better or worse, includes Dr. Chen. Charles Lamb writes charming prose but

> betrays his petty bourgeois idiosyncrasy of wishing
> to have free time to indulge in his little whims.

Enough, enough, enough.

Dr. Chen parrots Russian books from the forties and fifties, which tried to create a British literature so simple-minded that Stalin could enjoy it. It is almost always the only university book available and was thus foisted off on the next generations of Chinese intelligentsia. Some had the courage and humor to resist it, but I also received piles of papers (from otherwise intelligent people) full of watery versions of this nonsense that the sole purpose of literature was to describe the history of the class struggle. Beware the single idea. There is a loaded gun inside it, anywhere on earth, pointed directly at your head.

Here are three pieces of evidence about the importation and circulation of books in modern China. On arrival, each tourist is given a customs form that prints, in English, the regulations for prohibited items, among them: "manuscripts and printed matter detrimental to Chinese political, economic, cultural, and moral interests." Without definition, that sentence can cover a lot of ground in the hands of an imaginative customs agent, under the right circumstances.

There are large libraries in China, but entry to them is based on a complicated system of authorization that bears some resemblance to a State Department security check. The *China Daily* loves statistics and, announcing construction of the new National Library in Beijing, boasted that with 175,000 hectares of floor space, it is second in size only to the Library of Congress. What it doesn't mention is that ninety-nine percent, or more, of the Chinese population will never have authorization to read its fourteen million volumes, while I can walk in off a Washington street and monkey around in my national stacks.

In the same issue of the *China Daily* appears the headline "ATTACK ON ILLEGAL BOOKS" and on underground publishers "producing 'unhealthy' and illegal books . . . featuring stories about sex, superstition, murder and other crimes," such "malpractice serving to contaminate people's minds," whereas publishing houses are "encouraged not to make profits but to help educate the people and foster scientific development." The language in this sentence is interesting. Notice that the list of unhealthy subjects can be made to include *The Golden Lotus*, the feudal *Dao De Jing*, and most of Dostoyevsky for good measure. Notice also that the true metaphor in that piece of journalistic prose is that books are a sort of potential communicable disease, a public health problem that must be dealt with by knowledgeable doctors and methods of quarantine: "unhealthy . . . malpractice . . . contamination . . . ." Dr. State will make sure that no nasty intellectual germs hatch any inconvenient epidemics of ideas.

It doesn't profit the west much, however, to pat itself on the back for its liberality and tolerance. The locked Chinese library stack is only an eastern variation on the Vatican Index, which at last report still included Laurence Sterne and Charles Darwin, Freud and Marx. The Chinese imprint of public approval, "translation and publication by Panda Books" (the state printing house) is only an oriental *nihil obstat* and imprimatur. No Beijing propaganda minister could be any more vigilant about protecting morals by disposing of books than Jesse Helms' fundamentalist troops. It is no surprise to me that the Chinese bureaucrats and the Jesuits admired one another for such a long time. They shared habits.

Foreigners who love books have always idealized China for its part in the invention of printing, paper, and movable type, for its ancient and magnificent literary culture, for the marvelous books of poems, stories, and ideas that have come out of it for thousands of years, and for its elevation of the scholar, the learned and bookish person. So, when they discover that China, too, practices intolerance, Puritanism, bullying, and smug ignorance in its official cultural life, their idealism is wounded. Mine is, at any rate.

But be assured, at least, that a culture this tenacious cannot be damaged for long by forbidden novels and brainless censors. There is a kind of Shavian comic opera quality in it; if the Norwegians have not sunk into debauchery from admiring *The Golden Lotus* or being confused by the *Dao*, surely the Chinese can resist it. They are, after all, still a nation of passionate readers, and in America, where everything can be published, who has any assurance that anything at all will actually be read by anyone?

I went on smuggling books and haunting bookstores. My favorites were the foreign-language bookstores, wonderful microcosms of this classless proletarian society. There is always a closed section for Panda Books, tourist coffee table books, postcards, *Newsweek* magazines, dusty translations of the former Chairman's thoughts, foreign currency only, no Chinese allowed. Your foreigner's big nose gets you in. This section is usually only a few feet from the FOREIGNERS KEEP OUT! sign. This is the floor for stolen editions, and here your nose keeps you out. A Chinese bookstore is about as classless as an old friend's description of the state colleges of Virginia: "A place for everybody, and everybody in his place." But as the *Dao* says,

> A sensible man
> Prefers the inner to the outer eye:
> He has his yes, he has his no.

Good reading to you.

BOUND FEET

缠足

In western Minnesota, even houses without books owned a Bible, a hymnal or a missal, a few *Reader's Digest* shrunken books (which are to real books what the small heads of enemies are to Borneo hunters), and a turn-of-the-century picture book on the world and its wonders. I suppose I first saw images of China in such a book.

Two main details of Chinese strangeness stayed with most readers forever: the Great Wall, and the bound feet of women — the one unnaturally large, the other unnaturally shrunken. When I came back from China, I showed pictures and told stories of my adventures to groups in small Minnesota towns. The audiences were intelligent and curious people and wanted to know something real about China, but they had begun life with the same books I read and were haunted by the same details, so the questioning always began with the big Wall and the small feet.

"The Wall," I said, "is not worth seeing. It is only piled rock, now full of tourists and souvenir stands. It was the greatest make-work project in any history, built by a mad paranoiac emperor who feared everything and whose passion was to box and freeze the world. He standardized the axle length and the scale, and with the Wall, tried to standardize an entire continent. Like all defensive boondoggles, it never worked. The Mongols and the Manchus simply bribed their way through the gate and conquered China. There are plenty of walls to see in China without going north of Beijing: city walls, temple walls, guarded walls around the houses of leaders, walls crowned with broken bottle shards around the concrete flats. The walls are only metaphors for the invisible walls between the Chinese and between China and the world. Power loves walls; people ought to hate them and tear them down. If the Great Wall is all you can see of human labor from the moon, we will not be judged sympathetically by creatures who have the power to watch us." Silence usually followed. I doubt that any prospective tourist marked the Wall off an imaginary itinerary.

Then another voice: "Do they still bind feet?" I carried with me to show to audiences a little pair of lily-foot slippers that I bought from a Muslim souvenir peddler. The tiny oval foot under the silk brocade boot is perhaps three inches long. Mutterings around the room: "Monstrous! Barbaric! Unbelievably cruel! Stupid!"

"No, merely human," I said to them. "The Chinese fancied a tiny foot, thought it beautiful and erotically arousing. Even Chinese women came to see unbound feet as ugly and awkward. It was fashionable, and fashion is not reason, either there or here. Did the Chinese invent the hourglass corset that had to be strapped on by a servant? Did the Chinese wear girdles or four-inch stiletto heels? Do the Chinese blister and darken their skin under artificial light? Do the Chinese strangle themselves with knotted cloth at the neck on boiling summer days? Obviously humans find pain and suffering for fashion gives them sensual pleasure, otherwise (whatever pieties they might deceive themselves with), they would not so universally endure them."

Someone in the audience usually waited patiently through the fulmination and then asked again the question I neglected to answer before.

"No, whatever else the Communists did, they stopped that. A bound foot was useless for labor; it created, in women, an artificial leisure class. Women deserved liberation for more fashionable socialist pursuits like class warfare and factory work or, in the case of Jiang Qing, governing China."

The movement against foot binding began in the last century. The great novelist Ding Ling's mother was among the first women to publicly unbind her feet. As a teenager, she went to a school that had gymnasium classes, but was forbidden to take them with the other girls because of her feet. She came home and undid the bindings. Her feet stank of rotten meat, the bones already partly crushed. She scandalized her family by this disgraceful unbinding. Walking was immense pain. But she washed the feet, found new shoes, and walked awkwardly into her gym class. Her daughter grew up to be a great revolutionary, a passionate and gifted writer.

Xi'an was full of old ladies with bound feet. I would guess the youngest were in their sixties. In the countryside, it was impossible to marry off a daughter with big feet, and farmers are stubborn about being improved by progressive ideas.

54   *COMING HOME CRAZY*

Many of my students had grandmothers with lily feet. Some lurched on heavy wooden crutches, some on two canes, some on one; some, still agile, moved with amazing speed on their own power, in the sort of awkward mincing gait that Chinese husbands found so stimulating. At Xingqing park on Sunday afternoons, grandmas went strolling with their broods, leaning on the arm of a son or grandson, clopping along on their tiny semi-stumps. At the outdoor market where I shopped and snacked, the old lady who checked bicycles had lily feet. I often stopped at the *baozi* stand next to the bicycle park, had a steamer or two of dumplings, and when I finished, smoked. The old lady always smiled, and then clumped over to bum a cigarette from the red Barbarian. She liked it when I had been to Hong Kong and had Camels, but always settled gladly for a Golden Monkey. She sat down on the next stool, lit up, and we talked, she in fast incomprehensible Shaanxi country dialect, and me in nods and um-hums. We were great friends. She once corrected my table manners, refusing to let me eat sour cabbage out of a plastic bag with my fingers. She lumbered to her feet, found chopsticks, and jammed them into my hands, pointing at the cabbage, and speaking sharply. "Now, there! That way!" was what she said, even if I couldn't understand it. I sometimes had a hard time not staring at her feet.

One of the favorite Chinese leisure sports on Sunday afternoons is to walk up mountains. Half the considerable number of mountains in China seem to have perpendicular stairs cut to the top. Some mountains are pilgrimages, some merely pleasures. All are steep. I often went with students who assured me that some little mountain would be a short, easy stroll. Since I am middle-aged, fat, and one of the last living smokers in Minnesota, I frequently got halfway up some three or four-thousand foot "ascent," huffing, sweating grandly, and thinking to myself, "What madness!" While I paused to wheeze, a student looked at me sadly as if to ask whether this mountain was perhaps too steep for Icelanders. Meanwhile, an old lady with lily feet grasping the elbow of an arthritic eighty-year-old on crutches would lurch past, moving inexorably, though slowly, to the top. "Oh, the hell with it," I said, and puffed onwards. "Excelsior!"

Bound feet and the Great Wall share some unexpected qualities. When you bind the foot, you crush the bones so that, as in a bonsai tree, you make an artificial shape, something never seen in nature. For better or worse, only humans either imagine or do that to a foot. If you wall a country or a civilization, you misshape it, too, as certainly as if you strangled it with bindings. You have built the wall not just outside but inside, and what you have walled up will be grotesque and stunted, whether you look at it from the moon or elsewhere.

Maybe Deng Xiaoping was right. Maybe the Tiananmen demonstrators were the new Manchus, storming the north gate of the wall, and the only solution is to rebind the mental foot and crush the bones until it stinks and shrivels into the fashion you have imagined. You don't want that foot to be able to walk upright as an adult, without your help.

CHINGLISH
中式英语

I found this note on my door one afternoon at the Barbarians' Guest House:

XIAO ZHANG STOLE YOUR TYPEWRITER!
FORGIVEN ME!

I forgiven . . . and I saved the note. Pure poetry!

Later, the same Xiao Zhang, returning the typewriter, stopped to tell a story about one of his friends.

"He is . . . can you say a "norrible" man?"

"You can, but I don't know what you mean."

"My English is so poor."

"Nonsense. Your English is wonderful. How do you understand the word?"

He paused and thought. "Partly he is a noble man, and partly he is horrible. Both together . . . is there an English word that says those two things?"

"Now there is."

Later, Xiao Zhang borrowed the typewriter again. He loved monkeying around in English on that typewriter until the small hours of the morning, and this time he forgot to return it for several days. When he brought it back, he looked contrite and said, "How thinkless of me to keep it so long."

"Pardon?"

"It was thinkless of me. Did I make a mistake?"

"What do you mean?"

"I did not think well. I forgot the typewriter. If you do not think, then you are thinkless, right? Like a man who does not harm is harmless?"

"Right. You were thinkless, but I didn't need the typewriter anyway."

"Good-good," he said, translating straight from Chinese, which so often says things in pairs: *haode, haode.*

The Chinese, at least until last June 1989, were obsessed with learning English. It was the national pastime: English lessons on television, stores piled with self-help English books, streets full of English practicers poised to swoop down on any nose that looked like a native speaker, reserved corners of public parks where only English could be spoken. It was my excuse to be in China, teaching in a program to train Chinese teachers to teach English. It made it well nigh impossible to learn any Chinese myself when half the billion-odd Chinese seemed to regard me, and others like me, as a walking textbook and language lab.

Chinese courtesy and ritual modesty demanded continual apologies for poor grammar, bad accents, mistakes. More often than not, the Chinese had, in fact, done a remarkable job of attacking English and, unlike many foreigners, were fearless and creative in using what English skills they had for what they were meant: to communicate. With gestures, circumlocution, and astonishing linguistic inventions, their English got the job done. You sometimes had to listen creatively yourself (not a bad skill to cultivate), but almost always you could grasp the point. Xiao Zhang's inventive English is only one of the myriad examples any Barbarian in China could give you.

Whatever the xenophobia of the government, the Chinese like odd people and are curious about them. Unlike the Japanese, they really are not an introverted culture. What good are words if you can't say them to other humans?

The university language programs are, however, another matter. They sink under the weight of the age-old Chinese obsession with memorization and "correctness." Every morning, walking past the university fountains on my way to class, I heard a hundred mumbling student voices on the benches or under the trees, memorizing their lessons for "intensive reading." That course is the foundation of Chinese language teaching, and despite the pleading advice of almost all Barbarian teachers and linguists to give it up, the Chinese universities cling to it as to a life raft in a raging sea. Intensive reading consists of assigning a page or two of English, and then going over every word, every phrase, every punctuation mark, every sentence, ad infinitum, ad nauseum to find the "correct" explanation.

I was hounded from beginning to end of the school year by a middle-aged woman who taught intensive reading with fiery, single-minded intensity, a sort of Euripidean fury of practical linguistics. She had a thick black notebook of study questions and a deadly finger-jabbing technique. She cornered me almost daily.

"Now, I will read you three versions of this sentence and you will tell me which is correct for a native speaker." She read the three sentences, usually slight variations of one another.

"They're all O.K."

"But which is *most* correct?"

"They're all correct."

"But one must be more correct than the others."

"Not at all." I sighed, girding up for another *Reader's Digest* condensed version of descriptive linguistics. "I understand them all. A native speaker could say all of them. They all get the job done. They are all fine. Some people say it one way, others another."

"Then I have not put the question right if all the answers are correct."

"I would say you've done a good job. There's no such thing as a single correct answer to most language questions."

The index finger worked full time now, almost sweating, if fingers could sweat. The black notebook trembled. "That is not possible! There must be a correct answer. I will ask another American."

Poor lady! I'm afraid I was no help either for her hypertension or for the Four Modernizations, the current propaganda campaign to push modernizations in agriculture, defense, industry and science.

The Chinese called their occasional butcheries of English: Chinglish—mispronunciations, gaucheries, garbled verb tense or number (Chinese has neither), wrong pronouns, direct mental translations from Chinese idioms. I found these mistakes sweet, comic, interesting, creative, and no impediment to communication—*urally*. . . . I did not misspell that word; it is the shibboleth of Chinglish. The Chinese native speaking tongue has an awful time with that buzzed "s", so *usually* came out sounding something like *urally*, and was not an adverb describing a mountain range in Russia. Reagan urally came out Leagan and I liked him that way, insofar as I could be said to like him at all. Since Chinese has only one syllable, "ta," for all gender pronouns, beginning speakers made wonderfully comic sentences like "My wife, he is a very good cook." I had a feeling that both Gloria Steinem and Mark Twain's German coach might have approved that one, so I never corrected it. It was no barrier to the passage of information.

I asked the students in a writing class for scientists to describe in a page some spot on the campus that they fancied. This gem arrived:

Beside the big fountain there is a beatiful [sic] garden on the right, and the other one stands on the left. In both of these there are screwing paths among the lawns. During intervals or after supper, many students go there for fun.

I'll bet they do, urally . . . . The poor fellow needed a word he didn't know and was led astray by a thesaurus, down the well-known screwing path. A girl asked me to write a recommendation for some Chinese award. "What tone should I take?" I asked.

"Sugar the letter," she said. Chinese prose, and thus its English, is full of old-fashioned Victorian sugaring—long verbal sighs, clutched body parts, and grand exhalations of feeling. The Chinese are, after all, like the Italians, an operatic culture. They are not Swedes, thank God. Student papers were full of these gestures that sometimes went magically wrong: "I think of you from my deep heart"; "Writing to you now, tears are full of my eyes."

Chinese is a monosyllabic language; Chinese sign-painters, like Dutch typesetters in the Renaissance, frequently have never heard the words pronounced and don't understand the language they are reproducing. Every tourist has seen beauties like this:

ARE YOU FOND OF THESE ARTS
WE ARE SURE THAT IT WILL MAK-
E YOUR GUEST ROOM BED ROOM M-
ORE TASTEFUL FOR YOU TO PICK
OUT AND BUY SOME OF THEN FOR
DECORATION. IN ADDITION, IF Y-
OU WANT TO SEND PRESENTS TO
YOUR FRIENDS WE ARE VERY HAP-
PY TO PROVIDE YOU WITH THESE
PRECIOUS ARTS. WHAT MAKES
YOU GLAD IS THAT WE ALSO SER-
VE YOU WITH FOLLOWING ITEMS
   1: TO DRAW PORTRAIT FOR YOU
   2: TO DRAW SOME KINDS OF AR-
TS ACCORDING TO YOUR REQUIR-
EMENT OR TITLE. WE WILL SA-
LE IT TO YOU IN THE PRICE TO
YOUR SATISFACTION AND THAN-
KS FOR YOUR PARTRONAGE.

Chinese commercial packaging is also a rich source of Chinglish. Here are directions from a noodle package:

Cooking put it into boiling water and stir it tightly
until it becomes soft and then you can choice it in
any way you like. May serve in Chinese and Westen [sic]
style sweet and sadly.

This noodle writer will either be improved by intensive English or will write the Chinese *Finnegan's Wake*.

These examples are funny, of course, but they are also brave. China was closed for thirty years; during the Great Proletarian Cultural Revolution (GPCR), speaking or reading foreign languages, particularly English, was counter-revolutionary, ground for beatings, humiliations, exile to prison or the pig yard in Qinghai; English books were burned—both from libraries and homes. I met Chinese who had been afraid to speak English for twenty years. A seventy-seven-year-old man, fluent, even elegant in English, inquired what was new in the English novel since 1957. I asked one of my students who taught at a college on the Siberian border in Xinjiang, not just miles but light years away, how he picked up his refined and old-fashioned British accent. He learned English pronunciation from 1947 BBC language tapes. He had never met a foreigner or heard a native speaker. He found my accent difficult because it didn't sound like London in 1947 to him. Another student who graduated with an English degree in 1966 had his books destroyed and was sent to work in a lumber factory for sixteen years. In the mid-eighties, the state decided it needed his language skills and put him back in front of a classroom. He spoke perfect English with painful slowness, like Rip Van Winkle first opening his mouth after the long sleep. Even after the Cultural Revolution, the only available language texts consist mostly of brainless propaganda. A twenty-five-year-old woman from western China lent me her English text, where I found this gem:

WE LOVE CHAIRMAN MAO

We love Chairman Mao,
We love his writings, too.
His writings give light to our minds,
And strength for all we do.

Great and wise is Chairman Mao,
His writings are our guiding word.

They point to a bright and broad road,
Along which we march forward.

Seriously study his works,
On applying them be intent.
Solemnly we pledge our word:
Carry the revolution through to the end.

We love Chairman Mao,
We love his writings, too.
Heartfelt thanks to Chairman Mao,
To him our happiness is due.

That's not language teaching; it's hagiography with fangs. It's possible that the madness now rising again in China could make English not the path to visas and prosperity but, once again, a kind of death warrant.

Americans have never understood either the passion to learn or the usefulness of other languages. We teach them badly to each other and don't feel much guilt over it. We think foreigners will understand us if we just speak a little louder. Generally, that works, because it is an advantage to understand English, but perhaps it will not always be so, and then the great language teacher, necessity, will improve us briskly.

I have two ideas about why we are less brave than the Chinese about languages. Great numbers of us had grandparents or parents who spoke broken English, who gave up their own language, culture, and half their soul, to come here and suffer humiliation and scorn for mastering this new language and culture badly. Having gotten the language readily ourselves, we extract a kind of psychic post-mortem revenge on our own grandfathers' persecutors, by refusing to hear or understand anything that deviates from television English. Paradoxically, we not only join, but *become* those persecutors, but that is, of course, the unconscious cycle of American history.

Second, Americans are used to being powerful people, in control, feared and humored, if not respected or loved. We abhor dependence, the appearance of weakness or need. When you begin learning a language or try to use a new one, your adult power and resourcefulness slip away, and you sound to yourself, and to others, like a drooling child or an idiot. In a new language, you are first a baby, then a little child; then, if you work hard, a badly educated teenager with a low IQ. If you start to learn a foreign language as an adult, you will probably never really become an adult in that language unless you are both tenacious and clever.

COMING HOME CRAZY

When the Chinese make mistakes in English, they seem comical, but they exhibit a kind of courage that we don't have. A sense of humor and a dose of stubbornness doesn't hurt in language learning either. Finally, it requires a Daoist resignation to the great "WHAT IS," relaxing into the language and letting it swirl around you, understanding that you do not understand, that some enlightenment will occur in time if you are patient with yourself. It is as if your personality were being absorbed into a different layer of consciousness.

I learned a little of that in Iceland when I went to a non-English-speaking farm to work for three months. There I was, an oversized intellectual, a teacher, a writer, a man who used language as his major weapon in the world, reduced to mumbling "yow" to questions I only vaguely understood, sitting silently in the midst of talk when I was used to dominating it. After a while, I came to like being stripped of my weapons, to sit defenseless in the middle of a language I couldn't conquer. I wrote a small poem about that feeling:

LEARNING ICELANDIC

For a week I say nothing,
understand only a little.
Without words, I'm lighter,
float around more
than I have for years.
Give me an order . . .
I'll walk the other way,
over the cliff, smiling.

Xiao Zhang, the poet of "norrible," this brave cliff walker in English, went on a short holiday to climb Mount Emei in Sichuan, one of China's great sacred mountains. When he got back, he came up to my room with gifts, a bamboo cane, and a natty cigarette holder carved from a tree root. "What was it like?" I asked him.

"It was good-good; wonderful mountain. I have not enough English to say . . ."

"Of course you do."

"Well, it was like this . . . ," he paused. "Monkey, monkey, monkey, temple, monkey, monkey, temple, temple, bamboo, monkey, bamboo, bamboo, monkey, temple, temple, top!"

I leave you to imagine the gestures yourself. If that is Chinglish, it is also poetry.

DUMPLINGS

饺子

No book is complete without a recipe, so you shall have one. A cultural virgin in China expects to eat rice, but I arrived in wheat land, the country of the local noodle. We were served rice in the Barbarians' Guest House, but my students called it "pig rice," dirty and full of stones, fit only for livestock or Barbarians. I lost three old fillings in that rice, biting stones, and went three times to a Chinese woman dentist who laughed ironically at the delicate teeth of Barbarians. The Chinese are more accustomed to eating stones in hard times.

"For real rice, you must come to Hunan," said one student.

"The pigs in Sichuan eat better rice than the Hunanese," said another.

"Oh, the rice in Suzhou," sighed a third.

"In Xi'an you eat *jiaozi*-dumplings," said the Shaanxi local man with finality. And so I did.

Jiaozi, like Norwegian lutefisk, Virginia Brunswick stew, Stearns County bouya, and Belgian hutzapot is not really food; it is a ritual—an affirmation of community, not private nourishment but public celebration, food not for the body, but (to steal a fine word from American black cooking) for the soul. But since China is, if nothing else, a practical country at table, eating *jiaozi* is pleasure heaped over duty like rich gravy. Tasty morsels, these dumplings.

When the Chinese invite you home for dumplings, they have adopted you as a friend. You are now caught in the fine skein of Chinese obligations and mutual favors, of shared defense against official life. You do not merely eat dinner; you are part of the dumplings.

Do not undertake to boil dumplings lightly or alone. Dumplings, like military campaigns and the Four Modernizations, require strategy, central planning, and division of labor. No one human will show equal talent for all the jobs in dumpling assembly. The fun is in assigning various work units their dumpling duty. Though this essay promises a recipe, it will not be exact. There are as many dumpling recipes as there are cooks in China (that approaches a billion), or as there are occasions to eat them. The recipe depends on Chinese history, the state of the economy, the latest Party directive, mere chance, whim, fate. Do you have grain tickets for enough flour? Is meat available? How much and what quality? Has rain fallen in the countryside? Are the right vegetables and spices in the market? How hard can you bargain to get a sufficient quantity at a good price? Is there enough coal to keep the fire burning long and hot enough to boil the dumplings?

For the dough, you need flour and water and labor and time, the two simplest ingredients and the two most precious. You need a dumpling stick to roll the dough. An American will go to the mall and ask for a genuine Shaanxi wooden dumpling pin. A Chinese will unscrew a wooden handle from a broom or a shovel, or empty a quart beer bottle. A dumpling pin must be round and hard and able to press dough. Use your imagination, not your Visa card.

Roll the dough out as if you were making a long snake. When he is as big around as a broom handle, cut off his head and hack the body into end-of-your-thumb size pieces. In your enthusiasm, do not hack your own thumb. You have only two, they are opposable, and you will need them. Don't mistake metaphor for flesh; politicians do that. Turning and flattening the pieces as you roll, make a skin about three inches in diameter, the size of the palm of a Chinese hand. Make hundreds of pieces of dough. There is no point doing this in a small way, and you will be hungry from the labor of dumpling making. Since you are Chinese now for a while, you will not insult your guests by feeding them skimpily or cheaply, though you will say to them many times in the course of the evening that that is what you have done. They will then say to you many times that you are a good and generous host, and ought not to have gone to so much trouble for such unworthy guests. The point of a ritual is to repeat it. And repeat it.

The filling begins with meat — pork, of course, the meat of humans, of civilization. You will not need much, but take care of its quality. Go to the pork butcher; establish the price; have him cut two *jin* (about a kilo) from the loin with only a little fat; have it ground finely, and watch the grinding. Do not grind the meat at home; remember "from each according to his talents." The butcher will remark that you seem likely to make dumplings, will wish you well and wish that he were invited. Compliment the butcher on the fine pork. The state of pork is the state of China, and you have made a patriotic gesture. Two *jin* of pork will feed two Americans on a barbecue grill, along with martinis, tin foil potatoes, and something chocolate. You will feed ten or twenty "full to death" (as they say in Chinese) on dumplings alone, with a little wine and tea and a few peeled apples and pears and some melon seeds. The true genius of civilization is its economy, not its opulence.

Go next to the vegetable market. You will need a head of cabbage, a couple of handfuls of green spring onions, a few handfuls of garlic shoots (long, rough-textured spears of green aromatic garlic), a piece of ginger root half the size of your fist, a skein of regular garlic buds tied in a dry reed, a good-sized bunch of Chinese parsley (coriander), and a handful of some magical herb that looks like quack grass and whose name in English, I never found. You have soy, vinegar and "essence of smell" (MSG) at home already.

Make sure the cleaver is sharp. Put your guests to work chopping vegetables; they will enjoy it. When the blade goes into the garlic shoots, parsley, and "quack grass," your house fills up with the dense, acrid perfume of the Chinese countryside. This smell is thousands of years old and always fresh. Mix the chopped vegetables and pork by hand. A spoon will not do. The vegetables want to be touched and will not mix harmoniously without your hands. No violence here; be patient with the pork and garlic shoots. They blend in good time.

Now you are ready to stuff dumplings. Pour tea for everyone and settle them on stools and boards. This will take time. Dumplings are individual as snowflakes, and reveal your character. No two humans stuff and fold in the same style, and no single human can conceivably stuff two perfect duplicates. A skilled dumpling stuffer will create the illusion of order and harmony, of unanimity, of perfect rows of symmetrical dumplings, but he knows that every dumpling has a mind and soul and secret of its own. There is a political metaphor in this that frightened the current regime enough to call out its tanks.

I am a poor dumpling stuffer. My work shows the flaws in my character and in my life: impatience and greed for meat. I use too much filling and seal the dumpling carelessly. My dumplings fall apart; they are too fat. Call my dumplings extreme extroverts. An extreme introvert uses too little meat and pinches the dough too tightly. His dumpling is dry and tastes like boiled flour. Balance and moderation in this, as in all things; a good dumpling is fat enough, holds together well, and keeps its precious juice inside until the right time. A well-made human stuffs a well-made dumpling.

Start water boiling in a big pot. When the filling or the dough runs out, you are done stuffing and ready to cook. An economical cook plans these two events to happen simultaneously and remarkably enough, they always do. Keep the water at a rolling boil, and feed the dumplings in a few at a time. They must not touch. They will bounce and jiggle, bob and weave—children playing in a bath. This is good; an active dumpling develops muscle, thus flavor. Bring the water back to a boil three times. When the dumplings get too foxy, slap them down with a dose of cold water, back to a boil, then another cold slap. Only on the third rising are they finished. This is the revolution of rising dumpling expectations that you must three times discipline sharply. This is training for Chinese life. The bubbling water turns cloudy with starch, and after hundreds of dumplings have gone swimming in it, it is thick and aromatic. Don't throw it away; this is your soup, the last course, as is proper in a Chinese dinner.

On the table, set bowls of soy and dark vinegar and hot red pepper, either dry or fried in an oil emulsion. Set each guest chopsticks, a small bowl to mix sauce, a tiny glass for *baijiu* (strong white liquor), and another glass for wine or beer or sweet orange soda. Set the bowl of *jiaozi* in the middle. Take and Eat! "*Gan bei!*" Bon Appetit!

There it is, one dumpling recipe! But don't imagine you have exhausted dumplings so easily. Dumplings are not only individual as snowflakes but also equally numberless in variety of pastry, decoration or stuffing: sweet, sour, hot, mild, fried, or steamed. I described the Old Hundred Names dumpling of Shaanxi, but Shanghai, Sichuan, Canton, Mongolia, Hunan, and Beijing all offer competing theories of dumpling. Beyond that, there is a whole language of dumpling, a poetry of dumpling.

Dumplings are best eaten in a Chinese home with friends, after joining in to make them yourself, but restaurants and snack stands sell them too. Indeed, the best restaurant in Xi'an is a dumpling house. The first time I went with a Chinese friend, I asked for a translation of the sign over the door. He read: "Liberation Road Polite Person's Dumpling Parlor." This two-story building was, like so many Chinese institutions, a tangible concrete metaphor of the Chinese class structure. Old Hundred Names—the common people—lining up below for dumpling tickets, buying their one choice—plain dumplings—by the half or whole *jin*, and eating at communal tables on a cement floor. Upstairs, the Barbarian bourgeoisie, a rug on the floor, a gold-buttoned uniformed waiter to serve, a tablecloth, a bill at the end of the meal rather than a ticket to eat, beer and wine for sale (downstairs bring your own), a hundred different hand-rolled dumplings in their individual bamboo steamers, and for the final course, a flaming Mongolian hot pot of Dowager Empress dumpling soup.

I ate in both classes and loved them equally. To make a judgment between them resembles asking a father to choose his favorite child: one grew up to be rich and elegant, the other, poor and honorable. The Chinese authorities for forty years howled at their citizens the question: what is your class? I always wanted to answer that question as Woody Guthrie answered the hospital admitting nurse who asked him his religion:

"All."

"You can't do that, Mr. Guthrie," she told him sternly. "You must choose—in case of emergency, you know."

"All or none," he said. I stand with Comrade Woody.

I often went downstairs with my friend, Xiao Zhang. He held the opinion that Chinese citizens required at least a *jin* of dumplings at a sitting once a week to sustain life and courage. We made a nice contrast: he a sleek handsome fellow of about one hundred and thirty-five pounds; I, a disheveled and corpulent two hundred and forty pounds. Dumplings went for about two *kwai* (fifty cents) a *jin*, and could be purchased in half *jin* lots.

He said: "A sturdy fellow like you should eat two *jin*."

"Only one," I said modestly. The lines were perennially endless for tickets, and the restaurant manager, seeing my large foreign nose in his line, invariably came out and tried to move me to the front, or find out if I had made a mistake on my way upstairs, where I belonged. Xiao Zhang assured him that I was where I wanted to be and that I refused to budge from my proper place in line. After a flurry of Chinese, he shrugged his shoulders, turned, and went back to managing the restaurant. Chinese officials want you in your place. They do not subscribe to Comrade Woody's catholicity in class or religion.

Unlike most state operations, the Polite Person's Dumpling Parlor was, indeed, well managed. The floors got swabbed and swept continually, the lines moved briskly, the dumplings arrived promptly and were succulent as Grandma's. After buying tickets, you sat at round, communal tables set with soy, vinegar, pepper and a chopstick dispenser. After a few minutes, a huge steaming dumpling cart wheeled through the restaurant and delivered your bowl, *jin* or half *jin*, and a bowl of the starchy dumpling broth to wash it down. A *jin* of dumplings is not a serving of food; it is a mountain, a dinner party, close to gluttony if not all the way there. I watched amazed as Xiao Zhang ate his way through

Mount Dumpling, chop sticks working like a hyperactive steam shovel. I got halfway through the dumplings, as death from explosion approached.

"What! A sturdy fellow like you with such little stomach!" exclaimed Xiao Zhang, picking his way through the remains of my dumplings. They were delicious. I ordered a half *jin* on my subsequent and frequent visits.

Upstairs, a princely price and God's plenty of dumplings. Almost certainly the Chinese customers were either Party big potatoes, or export business types. The price, fifteen *yuan*, about four dollars, was beyond university professors, students, factory workers, or Old Hundred Names. When I took students there, I paid the tab, and in retaliation invited them to take me to dinner downstairs where they could use their eloquent Chinese to fight off the manager in the ticket line.

Dinner arrived in three acts. First, a round of cold dishes to warm up the chopsticks and get the stomach juices flowing: pickled lotus root, tiny shrimps, thinly sliced ham cured with honey, chicken wings, smoked mutton, hundred-year-old eggs, fried peanuts, cubes of dried bean curd, the first round of Chinese beer, and sweet orange soda. The Chinese don't generally booze much at dinner; the wicked toasts for "Rixon" and "Leagan" were, can you say . . . , performed for the nose?

Then a parade, no, a royal processional of thirty dumplings arriving each in their own bamboo steamer, one dumpling per guest at the table, set down with a great flourish, and an announcement in Chinese — and sometimes English — of the dumpling's name, each dumpling differently folded and decorated in the shapes of hats, stars, moons, bird nests, faces, animals, fish, jewels. You watched a poem of thirty images being written at your table — with one succulent bite and a sigh between each line, as if to let the language (and the dumpling) resonate down into the body. A new line came before the last idle chopstick was laid in its little porcelain stand. More images lay in reserve in the kitchen, but here are the names of part of a single evening's dinner, a dumpling poem:

> Fragrant Duck
> Wish You a Great Fortune
> Making Dowager Empress Happy
> Cherry Lotus
> The Emperor's Hat
> Gold Coin Fish Maw
> Black Pearl in the Imperial Kitchen
> Double Flavor Shrimp

Eight Treasures for Longevity
Black Dragon on White Snow
Steamed Jade Belt
Xian Gu Mushroom Magnolia
Steamed Sesame Jam
Double Flavor Baby Chicken
Steamed Quartz
Hot Pot Golden Fish
Five Seasoned Eel

Before the last act, a little pause for smoking and meditation, then the Mongolian hot pot arrives. The waitress lights it. Flames leap wildly across the table, the aromatic broth begins steaming, while the server tells the story of the soup. When the Dowager Empress was ill, she could eat only tiny bites of food, only the white meat of chicken, but she hungered for dumplings (she *was* Chinese, after all . . .), so she ordered the imperial chef to make dumplings so tiny they would not irritate her heavenly throat. Thus, the Dowager Empress dumpling soup. Chinese nostalgia for the Dowager Empress resembles a bunch of old Jews telling stories about Hitler days. I always found it comical to hear this tale in a "people's" restaurant. In 1987, it showed sanity, a sense of humor, of putting the past in its place; if the soup is good, eat it, tell the story, and to hell with the Dowager Empress. I wonder if they still tell that story on Liberation Road. . . .

Beside the soup, a bowl of tiny *jiaozi*, the size of thumb nails. When the squid and chicken broth comes to a boil, in go the dumplings and down goes the Dowager Empress. Afterwards, should you still be hungry, a big bowl of Old Hundred Names dumplings arrives (a reminder of the other world still turning underneath you), and a plate of peeled apples and pears.

So there, dear reader, is a recipe and a restaurant review for you. Should history be kind and the gates swing open again to a more humane China, go yourself. Plunge into the great dumpling boiler of the east and see what poetry inside you comes of it.

ERHU

二胡

Xi'an is the last Chinese large-walled city. The wall survived the fifties madness to destroy vestiges of old China more through neglect than design. The city was too poor and out of the way to bother with. Now it is a tourist attraction, so it is probably safe for a while from new binges of socialist reconstruction.

This is not the original wall that circled Chang'an in the Tang Dynasty when this was the greatest city in the world. That wall was much vaster; this is the Ming wall of reduced expectations. Even as a symbol of decline, it's a majestic wall, maybe thirty feet thick, with crenelated battlements, impregnable-looking archers' towers, a deep, wide moat, and four narrow, arched entrances at the compass points, impediments to modern traffic but protectors of the ghosts of history.

On pleasant afternoons, I went walking on top of the wall, reciting Li Bai, Bai Juyi and Du Fu to myself, not in my poor Chinese, but Englished by Arthur Waley. On rare clear days, I could see the jagged crests of the Qin Ling mountains twenty miles south, outside the wall, and the noble silhouettes of Big and Little Goose pagodas, now dwarfed by belching factory smokestacks and square gray concrete blocks of high-rise flats. Looking north inside the city wall were the last old Chinese neighborhoods: low, enclosed courtyard houses with upturned tile roofs, an ancient Confucian temple with gardens intact, and the liveliest old-fashioned street market in town. I'd stare into this now ramshackle labyrinth of twisting lanes and sagging roofs, listening to the noise of bicycle horns and loud bargaining in Shaanxi farm dialect, trying to imagine what Chang'an looked like when the great poets were alive, bargaining for vegetables in the same markets, in the same language, lost in thought about courtesans, plum blossoms, and crazy-quilt court politics.

One day, I looked over this scene and saw a crowd gathered in the grassy park just under the wall. What they watched was invisible to me, blanketed by black hair, but what they listened to ascended up the old stone walls. Two piercing falsetto voices singing in dialogue, harsh and loud, accompanied by a string instrument that sounded sawed rather than bowed. I clambered down the stairs to join the crowd. Six-and-a-half feet of height was a great advantage in most Chinese crowds; by standing on tiptoe I could see from behind, thus not becoming part of the spectacle myself. Two old men, bald under black skull caps, wearing shabby, gray, padded jackets, sat on stools facing each other, singing a dialogue in high-pitched nasal twanging voices that sounded petulant to me. They sawed away with their bows at small wooden cylinders with upright handles and what looked like two strings each. They cradled them in their laps like babies, rocking back and forth as they sang and sawed. No human infant could have slept to that music. A well-dressed gentleman at the edge of the crowd sidled over to me and asked, in English: "Do you like this music?"

"I've never heard anything like it before."

"It's Shaanxi opera. They are playing two women arguing about a lover. Old people like this music very much."

"What is the instrument?"

"There is no English word for it, a sort of old-fashioned violin."

""What is it called in Chinese?"

"A kind of *erhu—a banhu*."

I told the story to my students the next day and asked if any of them played the *erhu*. A girl in the front row confessed she did.

"It is old-fashioned now," she said.

"Then why do you play it?"

"My grandfather taught me. During the troubles, many young people got sent into the countryside away from their families. My grandfather said I should spend less time studying foreign languages and practice the *erhu* instead. He told me old people in the countryside still loved tunes from before the liberation played on *erhu*, and that they would like me and give me better food to eat if I could please them by playing."

"Was he right?"

"Yes. They liked it. Would you like to hear *erhu* music by the greatest old player? I have a tape."

"I would like that very much."

And I did. She gave me a tape of music by Liu Tianhua, dead in 1932, and of Blind Ai Bing, dead since 1950, evidently China's two most famous *erhu* composers. I had wearied of the eternally cheerful bouncy loudspeaker and television music, all smiles and socialist optimism, thumping away with an electronic beat for the Four Modernizations or some other propaganda campaign. Even American supermarkets and elevators had not quite prepared me for the deadening effects of music played in public against your will, judgment and taste, music as a deadly weapon against the life of feeling and intelligence. I understood now the glazed expressions of so many Americans listening to their Walkmans playing loud thump-thump. You could commit any atrocity you wanted in their presence as long as the batteries didn't go dead.

But this *erhu* music! It was the most human stuff I had ever heard — the *erhu*, a weirdly accurate representation of a human voice, most often sad and thoughtful, but also capable of anger, comedy, playfulness, great virtuosity and heartrending simplicity, the sound of wind, grass, running water, candle flames, domestic quarrels, funeral wails, bawdy ballads, owls, larks, and aspen leaves. I didn't understand Chinese, but I understood this music. And all on two strings, on a relative of that primitive-looking contraption I saw under the city wall! I put on a tape of Bach's unaccompanied "C Major Violin Sonata." It was magnificent in its way but sounded glassy and hard compared to the immediate humanity of the strange and beautifully quavering *erhu*. I vowed to see and hear one played live by a great player.

As with all Chinese musical instruments I saw, the *erhu*, over whatever thousands of years it evolved, arrived at great simplicity and elegance of shape — not like some complex machine that grew and altered through mechanical experimentation but like something discovered or improvised by a musician monk alone on a bare mountain with only a few stones and trees, something closer to nature than to art, so obvious that it is subtle, like a musical purloined letter sitting before us for years until we look, see, say "ahh . . . ," pick it up, and bow the strings.

The sound box of an *erhu* is a hexagonal cylinder of polished wood, about half a foot long and a third of a foot across. At one end it is closed by a rose carved of lighter wood — bamboo or balsa — and, in the front, by stretched python skin. An *erhu's* voice, its soul, depends on the fineness of the snake. In buying an *erhu*, one should hold it to the light and look through the bamboo rose at the back of the python. Light should come through the translucent skin brightly and evenly. The texture of the scales must be close and fine — a rough python for coarse music; an elegant python to sing love songs.

The shaft comes up about two and a half feet and curves at the end. It is often decorated by a carved ivory ornament, a dragon perhaps, to guard the snake's ghost. Two pins, usually wood, sometimes brass, hold the strings. In the old days, *erhu* strings were made from wound silk. Mine are metal. I suppose great players use gut, perhaps even the old silk. The two strings are tied together at the top of the neck by a piece of kitchen string that holds the horsehair bow inside. No grand sweeping bow strokes for the *erhu*! The player cradles the instrument upright, pushes the bow towards him for the bottom half of the scale and pushes away for the top.

The *erhu* players I saw rocked and swayed continually as they bowed, a kind of musical tidal action. You mute the *erhu* by putting a piece of cloth between the bridge and the strings; one of my students used a red farmer's handkerchief; another used an orange rag he picked up on the street. And yet this simple two-stringed contraption is capable of virtuosic chains of trills, glissandos, high harmonics, pizzicati, and an almost human singing tone.

It is, of course, impossible to describe musical sound in its physical absence. Explain light to the blind! The closest instrument in sound is the saw, played brilliantly. One of my father's neighbors, a seventy-year-old burly Norwegian farmer from Cottonwood, played the saw with wonderful delicacy and feeling, always sad, usually slow old Scandinavian folk tunes and salon pieces like "The Shepherd Girl's Sunday" or "The Last Spring." The wavering vibrato of the saw was like the voice of a great contralto, perhaps Kathleen Ferrier or Marian Anderson. How gently old Henry coaxed music from this plain saw, barely touching it with the bow clenched in his raw, work-scarred hands! That is close to one of the sounds of the *erhu*.

Though an *erhu* is capable of almost anything when played by a virtuoso, most of the music I heard was romantic and inward, often evocations of nature, and of melancholy meditative psychic states. Here are some awkward translations of a few titles of Liu Tianhua's *erhu* pieces: "Singing in Sickness," "Moonlit Night," "Trembling Red Candle Shadows," "The Sound of Emptiness," "Beautiful Night," "A Walk in Bright Sun." He also has a famous stunt piece, "Played on One String Only," that recalls the legends of Paganini's similar exploits. "Birds Singing in the Empty Hills" resembles Messiaen in virtuosity, though in spirit it is closer to Couperin's nightingale. Even when the Chinese dazzle you, they like to remain calm. Here is a Chinese description of the piece:

> The title comes from a poem by Wang Wei in the Tang Dynasty.
> "Empty hills, not a soul in sight." The work has five periods along with
> a prelude and a coda. The prelude describes the idyllic scene of woods
> and hills with echoes of birdsong singing in the valley. Then enters the

main theme of man, a rather brisk and dynamic melody which runs throughout the work, now alone, and then in harmony with the chirping birds. The performer is especially proficient with the Aliquot [sic] tones in long phrases. As well as the imitation of singing birds.

How Chinese this union of art, nature, and humanity! No old painting is without a poem inside it. Wang Wei was equally famous as a painter. This music on two strings is a sort of Chinese *Gesamstkunstwerk* in which you use everything at once. Considered from the right angle, it is all one thing anyway, variations on the *Dao*, the ground of everything.

For years, my friends have complained that I knew too much about music. They expressed simple pleasure in a piece, and I'd give them a small lecture on Bach's fugal technique, Bruckner's modulations, Ives' polytonality, or harpsichord construction in the eighteenth century. They sighed, and expressed hope that I still felt some joy in music after reading all those books. Of course I do. I feel no shame for a passionate interest in the minutiae of scholarship. But my introduction to the *erhu* shamed me and taught me something about human parochialism and the limitations of Allen Bloom's jackass notions of education.

When I came to China, I had never heard of an *erhu*, much less consciously listened to one. I suppose I had heard tapes in Chinese restaurants of orchestras that didn't sound to me like the Minnesota Symphony, but my head was full of Bach or Jelly Roll Morton and I didn't actually hear them. Music was Luther's hymns, and philosophy was Plato and Aristotle. But China is not just another culture; it is another planet, intellectually. None of "us" makes any difference to "them." "Them" imagined the *erhu* without Stradivarius and evolved sophisticated technique without Paganini. Almost all Barbarians from Polo and Ricci onward suffered the same shock to consciousness when China became partly apparent to them, but I add my testimony. It is one thing to read abstractly that you are not the center of the universe, and that truth, divine or otherwise (if such a distinction is possible), was not dropped exclusively in your lap, for your personal amusement and salvation. The lesson to be learned from these shocks is to cultivate modesty and curiosity and to eschew evangelism and certainty. We do not need more fixed ideas but more experience, more *erhu* music.

FRIENDSHIP
友谊

Hermann Goering always reached for his gun when he heard the word *culture*. A jack Mormon farmer in Utah told me he kept his hand on his billfold when his pious neighbors began talking *mission*. Thoreau left the room when someone announced that they intended to do him *good*. In China beware *friendship*.

Beware not the thing, but the word. Real Chinese, one at a time, are geniuses at the art of friendship. If you have been lucky enough to make Chinese friends, it will both bring you and cost you more of yourself than you imagine. Chinese literature and history are full of this sort of friendship—a bond in the soul that the turnings in your life will not bend.

Every Chinese town with tourist trade has a Friendship store. It takes not "people's money," but Barbarian exchange currency, Barclay and American Express cards. In Xi'an, it is next door to a real Chinese department store. The Chinese store is dirty, chaotic, unheated, full of the kitschy, shoddy goods that Old Hundred Names can afford. Its crowd of customers spit, haggle, stare, mill around, and if they are children, piss in the stairwells. What you want is frequently "*mei you*"; what you get frequently doesn't work. I liked its jolliness and shopped there often.

The Friendship store is air conditioned, carpeted, relatively orderly and watched by a security guard. His function is to keep Old Hundred Names out, firmly, if necessary. This store is for you, friend with the foreign nose. It sells Scotch, cognac, Marlboros, Silk Cuts, good wool rugs, tiny ivory sages, jade Buddhas, silk dresses, furs, gold and silver jewelry, and gigantic reproductions of the local tourist attraction: the clay soldiers. The clerks, if they can be roused to speak at all, can speak English, and probably Japanese, but they don't seem to like you very much. If pressed insistently, they will take your money, if hard. Barbarian teachers in China were issued "white cards" enabling them to spend soft "people's money," but if they tried it in a Friendship store, it was hurled contemptuously back in their face, law or no law, and the clerk nastily demanded foreign exchange certificates—hard stuff.

Towns with tourist attractions usually have a Friendship hotel, the only place that will officially take Barbarians for the night. Often you can talk your way into a much cheaper and more pleasant, if dirtier, Chinese hotel simply by going next door. The Friendship hotels are, not without reason, famous for their surliness and overcharging.

Dinner in a Chinese home is generally a sweet and joyful occasion, full of comedy, affection, verbal hi-jinks and flying noodles. Beware, though, of formal banquets with high officials, at which set speeches and toasts are delivered. The officials in charge probably neither like nor trust you very much but will deliver honeyed speeches to friendship between our two nations. Humans are friends; nations have things in mind which are seldom friendly, though they may be advantageous. Try to do something friendly at one of these banquets, such as either offering or soliciting a genuine opinion, or being playfully contrary. The weather in the Midwest or the ingredients of the next course suddenly rear up in the conversation and, after that, silence. What William Blake said is as true in China as in Minneota! "Opposition is true friendship."

Poor language! It means to say something, often simply or plainly. Then history, politics, religion or commerce get their hands on it and wring out the juice until it is frail and desiccated and has no strength to rise and stand on its own meaning.

GOLDEN FLOWER

金花

The Golden Flower Hotel in Xi'an is, so states its advertising copy, a "miracle in the heart of China." As a genetic Lutheran and evangelical Transcendentalist, I do not take the language of miracles lightly, so I decided to investigate. The hotel was within a couple of miles of the Barbarians' guest house, an easy stroll past shish kebab carts, bicycle repairmen, street markets, wine shops, dead rats, smoking and gossiping old ladies, sidewalk pool games, rows of bamboo bird cages, night soil barrels, domestic quarreling, black market money peddlers, monkey circuses, and an occasional leper. It was a ten-minute bicycle ride, an accelerated version of all those sights — not really two miles away, but two light years.

Amidst blowing dust, coal-fired haze, flickering alcohol burners and dim bare light bulbs, there it stands, a brilliantly lit, eight-story glass rectangle with a curving drive and a sizable car park, all protected behind high iron gates, a sort of elegant prison fence. At the front, the guards stand at eternal attention, two clay, eight-foot reproductions of the dictator Qin Shihuang's terra cotta army soldiers, bow strings bent and ready, mailed fists clenching sword hilts, next to two of real flesh with gold epaulets, stripes down their trousers, crisply starched white shirts, and Windsor knotted ties. The flesh guards open doors for you, if you come with a proper nose, and bid you welcome in your own language. The private generator hums all day, all night, providing dependable electricity for this bright glass box glowing in the semi-darkness of the Chinese unelectrified night.

Inside, on marble floors, stand more warriors next to potted plants lit by brilliant light. To the left, a curving staircase to the bar and a shop full of Colgate toothpaste, Nivea hand cream, Alka-Seltzer, *Time*, *Newsweek*, *The Asian Wall Street Journal*, silk bathrobes, and smaller warriors to take home. The American Express card machine stands at the ready. To the right, a big oval pool and fountain, lit from underneath. In the middle of the pool, a beige marble island sporting an ebony Japanese grand piano. A Chinese girl in an evening gown plays Chopin's "A^b Impromptu," a transcription of Schubert's "Serenade," Beethoven's "Für Elise." There are restaurants on either side of the pool, tables covered with heavy, crisp linen, fresh-cut flowers in a little vase on each, a wine rack with French and German bottles, a dessert cart loaded with tarts, glacés and mousses.

Step in. Your place is set with a goblet of ice water. A knife and fork. A menu in English printed on heavy paper in a leather binder. Coquille St. Jacques, rack of lamb, tournedos of Shaanxi beef with Perigord truffles, Beef Lindstrom, an appetizer of Danish herring garnished with sliced beets, onions and rye bread. A hamburger with pommes frites. An entree preceded by a small appetizer would cost a Chinese cardiac surgeon a half month's wage. In theory, a university professor could buy two bottles of wine; a bus driver, hamburgers and beer for two. In actuality, none of them can buy anything because they don't have hard currency and can't legally get it and couldn't get in the front door to spend it if they were not guests of mine or someone who looks like me. But I can. I'll have an iced martini with a lemon peel, this Danish herring for a starter, the boneless chicken breast Florentine, and a hazelnut torte with whipped cream, please. Thank you very much. Do you have a nice dry house white, maybe a Bordeaux?

Upstairs in the bar, a black Kawai grand with a Filipino woman in a low-cut blouse playing and singing "Somewhere Over the Rainbow"; in another room, a disco thumping behind a closed heavy door. All you can hear is the regular thudding of the bass notes. A cognac, please, and an espresso.

The bar customers are of two sorts. Middle-aged men in business suits drink heavily and distractedly, looking like traveling executives from Boeing, Sylvania, GE, Janssen Pharmaceutical, Phillips, Johnson & Johnson, AT & T and, of course, they are—the joint venture gang, biding their time in the hotel where many live and all drink. They are invariably losing money, suffering insane snafus with Chinese bureaucrats and longing for their next excuse to go to Hong Kong on business. I eventually got to know many of these businessmen and came to like and admire them. They were doing their best under awful circumstances. Many kept up an amazingly high standard of tolerance, good humor and cultural sensitivity. But they will almost certainly return to their western jobs with damaged livers—and if I wore their wingtips, so, probably, would I.

The second sort are tourists, generally American, sometimes British, German, French, Scandinavian, Italian. China is expensive on the travel agency tours, which always include Xi'an. Fly in, eat at Golden Flower, one night in the bar, tour of terra cotta warriors, one handy pagoda, free time for shopping and fly on to Guilin for "good view" scenes. If you can afford this and like it, you are probably not young and probably do not subscribe to left wing magazines like *Harper's*, or vote for Democrats. I do not understand this paradox, but such tourists invariably speak with loud New Jersey or Texas voices. I don't know where they really live, but one never suspects that they live in Seattle, or St. Paul, or Charleston, or quiet towns in the Vermont hills. Words like "dirty," "cute," and "cheap" drift in and out of their conversation. The Barbarian teachers and students who drank in the Golden Flower bar sidled away from them to corner tables, pretending no comprehension of that English.

The horror of seeing your own countrymen on the road is universal. Germans, French, British, Scandinavians alike recount their shame at seeing their fellows, loud, arrogant, drunk, and/or whining at resorts everywhere; presumably Japanese feel it too. The son of a friend who has lived in Japan for a long time wrote me confessing that whenever he heard American voices in the Tokyo subway, he skulked away, ashamed, started a conversation with someone in Japanese, or hid. He is six feet tall and blond, an unlikely "salary man." Perhaps those brash, touristing countrymen are a mirror in which, as Swift says, "we see every face reflected but our own." Perhaps, to any other ear, that is our own Dallas twang sounding in the bar.

The Golden Flower Hotel was, indeed, a miracle, an island of Omaha in the middle of Chinese squalor and disorder. Partly financed by Swedes, it was entirely run by Scandinavians: a Norwegian manager, a Swedish chef, big blond Stockholm girls with names like Inger and Kirsten running the housekeeping—thus the herring, the rye bread, the Beef Lindstrom, the relatively squeaky-clean interior. But it was not The Plaza. It was a Holiday Inn in the Midwest transported east, cheap vulgarity in the decorating and overpriced, though botulism-free, mediocrity in the restaurant. The drinks in the bar were watery and the Kawai slightly out of tune. But in the land of "*mei you,*" it functioned, owned its own generator, and for a hundred dollars a night provided the illusion of home, if you wanted to be there.

I had real need of it once. I returned to China at Christmas in 1988 to see friends. After a stretch of no electricity for three days a week, no hot water, a non-functioning toilet, no heat and bone-chilling cold, I was exhausted, dirty, full of bronchitis and diarrhea. On the day before Christmas Eve, I walked to the Golden Flower, gave them my American Express card and collapsed. I ordered coffee and a ham sandwich from room service. It came. I showered under steaming water for an hour in a clean bathroom. I used my plastic envelope of shampoo. I toweled my body dry with large white towels and fell into a queen-sized bed with crisp sheets. I ordered a hot brandy from the bar. It came. I read *Newsweek* under a bright bed lamp. I slept. The next morning I got up, showered again, had coffee and left. Back out of the miracle, through the iron gates, into the real China. The bill was around 150 dollars. That is nine months' salary for a Chinese high school teacher. Such comparisons are unfair, make no sense, and prove nothing, but I defy any human being, Chinese or Barbarian, to resist making them. If I had not gone to the Golden Flower, I would have coasted down into serious illness, so one night to recover was cheap, if undistinguished. I could afford it and I did it. My Chinese comrades could not.

I once lost my temper at the Golden Flower. For my students, that walled hotel represented something mysterious — even miraculous — dancing, bright lights, gaiety, fashionably dressed people, elegance, freedom, the unknown world of the West, Hong Kong itself shrunk to half a city block and visible through the iron fence. So, one night, since they loved "disco" music and were marvelous ballroom dancers (one Taiyuan charmer spent the year trying to teach her old clubfoot teacher to tango!), I decided to take a bunch of them out for a night on the town. We even got a taxi. There were stares of disapproval from the Chinese doormen as I trooped past the fake terra cotta warriors with a half dozen obviously local students, the Old Hundred Names of the university. But my nose and brusque demeanor protected them at first. I started a tab at the bar, bought drinks, mostly Cokes and a few cheap tap beers (Chinese students are not boozers and are perfectly capable of a good time sober), shoved them into the disco lounge and sat down with Boeing and Sylvania, to hear business complaints and drink serious bourbon. It was "cowboy night" in the cocktail lounge with a crock pot of "Montana Chili" steaming on the bar. The waitresses were dressed in plaid pearl-buttoned shirts, cowboy hats and admirably snug Levis. The Filipino girl at the piano was singing Engelbert Humperdinck and Kenny Rogers songs: "Please Release Me" and "You Picked a Fine Time to Leave Me, Lucille." New Jersey and Dallas thought it was "cute." After a couple of hours, during which I sloshed down a good deal of bourbon, and even danced a few in lumbering style, one of the hotel staff came up snippily demanding that I either get the forbidden Chinese out or pay an outrageous cover charge for them.

"No cover charge for me?" I said.

"Of course not. You're a foreigner."

I lurched to my feet, knocking the chair over. "Listen, you son-of-a-bitch! Those people are my guests. They are your countrymen, but they are my guests, and I am paying the bill for them. They will dance and you will treat them civilly and not insult them or me, or I will knock your god-damn face in." It was later reported to me that I broke a glass. I stood there like a boozy gorilla about to spring; a little pink foam came out of the corner of my snout. My students calmed me down, got me home and settled in bed. "*Mei guanxi,*" they said in the Chinese fashion, with shrugs. It doesn't make any difference.

But it does, of course. I often thought that if there were an elegant hotel—a "miracle in the heart of Minneota"—and I were forbidden to enter it, had to press my envious nose between the iron bars to watch the lights, I would storm that hotel and loot it of its treasures. That would be useless, of course, without changing something underneath that hotel, indeed under the whole civilization. Otherwise as Yeats says, "The beggars on horseback change places, but the lash goes on."

Now, two years later, after the Tiananmen massacre, the multitude of Chinese luxury hotels are empty of foreigners—no Swedes, no Boeings. I had a call from an old friend and I asked her about the hotel business now. "The Golden Flower is open to Chinese," she said, "and we can spend renminbi and go to the disco, but there's nobody there."

"Do you go?" I asked.

"They haven't lowered the prices. We still can't afford it." Maybe that's the miracle in the heart of China.

HARD SEAT

硬座

In train tickets, first class, second class, third class reminded the old Chinese Marxists too much of the bourgeois class structure. The rich rode in cool leathery elegance while the poor sat jammed together, sweating, with their chickens, pigs and croupy children. So, in the style Barbarians have come to value so much from watching television, the language-crafters decree that if you do not say a thing, it will not be so. Keep the fact intact, change the language, but exile or shoot everyone who remarks on the difference. "Language management," a university catalog might call it and it would be a required course for everyone interested in careers as beggars on horseback, whether their line was politics, religion, finance or literary criticism.

In a Chinese train station, you find not orderly British queues but wavering surges of flesh, different surges for different destinations, frequently a special Barbarian window. It will take hours to make your way forward through that line and, having done so, you have no guarantee that you will arrive at the "correct" window. (Correct, "*dui*," is a favorite Chinese word. "*Bu dui*" means "not correct." Chinese life is a continual examination. It is not graded on a curve. You are in danger of failure at every moment.)

At the window you have a theoretical, though not an actual, choice. Soft sleeper, soft seat, hard sleeper and hard seat are available at eight wildly variable prices, one for each grade and a double set for Barbarians and for "people." In fact, only hard seat is ever available, unless the circumstances are "special." If they are indeed "special," you probably haven't stood in line. Such tickets arrive only through the "back door."

Here you are at the window, perhaps a foot-square opening manned by a bellicose invisible voice that clearly doesn't like you, doesn't think you deserve or have legal authorization to go anywhere and can either shut the window on your hand or holler "*mei you*" (nothing available), thus setting off a Chinese shouting match. That window is a verbal gun embankment, and you have clawed your way through the muddy trenches of those lines, but you have no grenades, no weapons, nothing. You wait only for the gun to swivel. You hope for luck at best, mercy at worst. This is "classless" life on the way to the people's own train.

Soft sleeper is a closed compartment with four bunks, lace doilies, and tea cups; soft seat is an American-style train car with four padded arm chairs across. Only foreigners or Party officials ever ride these posh classes. You can be certain any Chinese you meet there is an important person, a "big potato," and did not stand in line to get his ticket. Hard sleeper is an open car with three tiered bunks, your own quilt, one toilet a car, sinks to wash in and a line to hang your towels and socks to dry. The steward comes around and refolds your towel if you have done it badly. This is the jolly Chinese class, reasonably comfortable if public, full of smoking, card playing, arguing, noodle eating. This is what you travel if you have a little extra money, factory business to attend to or a close relative who works in the ticket office. Then there is hard seat — Old Hundred Names' class — the "people's" class, the dictatorship of the proletariat made visible.

Theoretical "seats" exist in hard class, but your chances of having a home for your butt are soon mitigated by the most obvious fact of Chinese life: 1,200,000,000 humans. There is no limit to the number of tickets sold for your car. If it is only stuffed when you first arrive, it will fill up later. Be patient. There is no escape. Hard seat is hard, a narrow board thinly upholstered with green plastic; the back is perpendicular. The human body does not sit comfortably at a ninety-degree angle. No slouching or reclining, please.

There are perhaps a hundred seats to a car and by the time you arrive wherever it is you go, another hundred and fifty will have joined you with all their bags and goods, gunny sacks of grain, cages of chickens. The Chinese have two peculiarities (only two . . . Barbarians have more); they mistrust cold water and moving air. No matter how hard you try to keep the windows open, whatever the season or temperature, someone is going to close them and seal that car hermetically. Two hundred and fifty humans and a few animals breathe that enclosed smidgen of oxygen over and over. Those humans squat to shit and piss in one rolling *cesuo* (toilet) that opens onto the tracks under the car. Some are sick. The car is full of bronchitis, hacking, phlegming, spitting. Probably a little tuberculosis too. They sweat and fart. You too. It is nine hours until

COMING HOME CRAZY

those doors open and the bum's rush for freedom begins. An old farmer has fallen asleep standing up, his forehead whacking against the wall as the train pitches and rolls over the wobbly track. His arm has fallen on your shoulder. His hand is heavy and wrinkled, with liver spots and knotty knuckles. You want to pat it, assure him that this will soon be over, that the Four Modernizations will lift his burden. Meanwhile we Old Hundred Names must suffer, bear the misery.

We? My red hair, Icelandic nose and hard money would get me out of this hell in ten minutes, into a clean, closed, probably air-conditioned compartment, with a bed and a tea cozy. The new freedom for Barbarians in China was to choose misery. The Chinese thought them crazy and half admired them. Misery was cheap and got you there.

But there was another side to hard seat travel. Here surfaced the Chinese genius for making do, for trying to have as good a time as possible under appalling circumstances: starting a lively card game; having a sing-down with alternating satiric verses of popular opera tunes (this helped to drown out the "good thought" loudspeakers); opening the window at short stops to buy food from local vendors on the station platform: warm hard-boiled eggs, fruit, bread, local noodles, sometimes whole roast chickens, thus magnifying the floor piles of cigarette butts, bones, fruit peels, candy wrappers and spit. The train steward came around with steaming kettles of boiled water, filling up pint jars and covered tin cups, reactivating old tea leaves or dried noodles. The steward also swept up now and again, hurling the garbage out of the rolling train, fertilizing another small parcel of the Middle Kingdom. The best conversations with the most interesting Chinese always happened in hard seat (or hard sleeper, if you were lucky). The demonstrable evidence was that, no matter how awful, you would live through this experience and remember it.

An unexpectedly attractive Barbarian quality surfaced in China. Recognizing the monstrous hypocrisy of the official pretense that no class structure exists in Marxist China, many Barbarians refused to be protected and thus isolated from Chinese life behind the comfortable screen of privilege. It was useful for these Barbarians to see the rough handling Old Hundred Names got from official China. It might protect them from taking their own political leaders at home as anything other than a continual threat to their own private humanity, something not to adulate or admire but to guard against, to hold at arm's length and to watch carefully.

A student of mine came from Urümqi in Xinjiang—Chinese Turkestan—three days by train from Xi'an. He was a college teacher, with no influence and no money to spare; when he went home, he sat hard seat, night and day, for seventy-two hours. "For a week before I travel," he said, "I am sick with terrible headaches from dreading the misery that is to come." Then he paused: "But my girlfriend is there. She is very beautiful, and I miss her night and day. And the food in Urümqi! This Shaanxi slop is not fit . . . "

That humans are indeed human, even after what has happened to them, is to me one of the great wonders. Nothing really human fits comfortably into a class structure — or probably any invented structure at all, praise be to the oversoul! We will all go out sitting hard seat, sharing a boiled egg, whacking our foreheads on the wall in sleep.

COMING HOME CRAZY

ICELAND

冰岛

Being an Icelander has been useful to me at odd moments in my life. I am not, in fact, an Icelander at all, but a proper American citizen born in Minneota; like other Americans, I have endlessly humored myself with the fiction that I have some connection to my grandfather's life and blood. All my "*ætt*" (as the Icelanders say) came in the 1880s from the northeast corner of Iceland, mostly from around the weapon fjord, Vopnafjord. This is the most remote section of the most remote island in Europe. It is, in fact, only marginally Europe and my grandparents' farms, only marginally Iceland. Iceland itself is only marginally civilization, only marginally habitable at all. And there are so few Icelanders—either in their marginal homeland, or elsewhere—maybe 300,000, including half-breeds, alive on the planet now.

I liked being a "margins" man, a side viewer, someone who could ignore the center as inconsequential. Being Icelandic removed you from taking sides in small American quarrels.

"Are you Catholic or Protestant?"

"Neither . . . Icelandic."

"Democrat or Republican?"

"Icelandic."

"Black or white?"

"Icelandic."

To be Icelandic was, of course, to escape the pigeonhole of definition, to stand outside the ring, disengaged, as American actions whirled in front of you. If you are an Icelander, you are your own man, something no one else ever heard of or cared about, a group of one, as humans at their best are supposed to be.

That deliberate detachment from feeling quite a part of the United

States comes in handy when you travel. Intelligent travelers, leaving the country for the first time, usually surprise themselves by feeling two powerful and contradictory, even paradoxical, reactions. First, the smug attitudinizing ignorance of their own countrymen appalls them: loud complaints about dirt, disorder and spicy food, and equally loud jingo political and religious intolerance—"We shoulda gone in there and let the Marines finish those buggers off, by God!" But simultaneously, they hear themselves making patriotic speeches defending the unlikeliest parts of American life from attack and denigration by foreigners—the French engaging in self-righteousness about American racism or Vietnam, the Brits getting snippy about the vulgar manners and accents of Yanks. We can make those attacks, but not *you*. *You* have no right. How can you take seriously the judgments of a nation that pushes mushy peas onto the back of a fork with a knife blade? These contradictory reactions are troubling. However, if you play at being an Icelander, you can remain, in a lofty Olympian manner, above this pettiness: "Of course, Americans do that . . . "

This disguise worked well for me until I went to live in Iceland, where this slippery defense is not only useless but landed me in even deeper trouble, since I am, of course, not an Icelander at all. The Icelanders had a special category for me: Western Icelander. Since my genetics were impeccable, they couldn't quite dismiss me as a garden-variety "plaid Bermudas and git-over-next-to-that-there-geyser-for-a-pitcher-honey" type. Yet, I was clearly not one of *them*. An eleven or twelve-year-old black boy, presumably the son of an Icelandic mother and an American soldier, sold newspapers on the street corner in downtown Reykjavik and had the real equipment to be an Icelander: the history of his whole life in a place, a voice that hollered *Visir!* and *Dagbladid!* with proper intonation, with reserves of slangy Reykjavik boy-talk under it, and a competition with other Icelandic boys who wanted to beat him up, steal his street corner (the best in town) and sell their own papers there. Genetics be damned; history, language and chance make you what you are, and that, for better or worse, is what you are going to be until the day you die.

It surprises and saddens Americans who go off to Norway or Belgium or Wales or Poland or wherever, to realize that Grandpa's folks are not interested in you, Grandpa, or your ethnic quest for a new identity. When they think of immigrants at all (and that, seldom and cursorily), they think "good riddance . . ." Your grandpa was, after all, rubbish, one who couldn't take it, and his exit to America solved all sorts of problems—it cleared land, houses, jobs, wives, groceries, for the *real* citizens. Those citizens of any homeland watched the immigrant boats sail west with a sigh of relief, and they still do. When you, the descendant, arrive back, bring plenty of hard currency, don't complain, and hang on to your pre-booked return ticket back where you belong.

When I left for China, America was into the sixth year of Reagan: the poor had gotten poorer, shooting each other in subways and whacking joggers on the head for a few dollars; the Business section of any newspaper was twenty times the size of Arts; college students were sunk in an abysmal, whiny passivity—"Jist gimme a job; I'll do or think anything you want" whistling out of their noses. Racism and fagbashing were fashionable again in the best circles; Grenada was safely invaded, Libya safely bombed, and North was doing his best for the brave Contras; Evangelical Christianity that would cause Mencken's grave to rumble was rich, televised, respectable and venomous; citizens debated only two live public issues, smoking and abortion, and arranged themselves into armed, facing camps, playing sanctimonious canned tapes at each other at top volume; "access" was a verb acceptable to Lutheran ministers; and professional education types said "learner outcome" in public without being beaten up. I wanted out. I couldn't swim any more on the margins of this soup which sucked everything into the vortex of its whirling maelstrom. I was drowning in America; playing Icelander couldn't save me anymore.

I found myself unaccountably in China—teaching American literature, giving little lectures on American life, and being simultaneously feared and heroized for being a symbol of something I wasn't even sure I could stomach any longer. Chinese officials feared (and still fear) Americans because they imagine them spreading discontent and disobedience. What a joke, I thought; the only thing that could goad a real American to rebellion is canceling the Super Bowl, and yet, here we all were—imaginary pink Nat Turners to the Chinese authorities!

Chinese students, starved for any real experience of America, except for the "Voice of America," "special" English broadcasts and old Walt Disney cartoons on Sunday Chinese television—imagined a country populated by the happy rich, a few dope peddlers, murderers and thugs, and a President everyone adored.

"But I'm not really an American," I said. "I'm an Icelander from Minneota."

"A what from where?" they asked, puzzled.

I described empty prairies, cranky immigrant farmers, cornfields, haybarns, disagreeable relatives, graveyards of Belgians, Norwegians, Icelanders. Probably I described Minneota in 1947 rather than today, but it was all news to them. To be Han Chinese is to be born into the world's largest club, whose billion-odd members are shackled to each other with heavy chains of history and family. I explained that being American was a mere accident, somewhere Grandpa went because it was *that*, starvation or prison. Being born an American didn't make you automatically rich, nor did it obligate you to like being one. "Why are you so disrespectful to your leader, President 'Leagan'?" they asked.

"Because he is an idiot, and because his ideas, insofar as he is capable of having them at all, are venal, contemptible, and inhumane. Besides, I didn't vote for him, and I am not compelled to like him or any other damn fool politician." This shocked them some.

"We would not say those things about Deng Xiaoping — not in public. It would not be respectful."

"Respect is to be earned. It is in the human, not in the office. An accident of geography should not turn you into a liar — either to yourself, or to others."

"You Americans talk so freely . . . "

It occurred to me that, in a way, I did sound American when I talked like this — though like a theoretical rather than an actual American. Jefferson, Thoreau, Henry Adams and Mencken would have approved of this verbal savagery, maybe even joined in it insofar as any of them were joiners in anything. The actual America liked Leagan and kept electing him or his clones.

Margins depend on surplus, and it is the vast American surplus that makes life there possible. The demands of Chinese life are more immediate: eat, smoke, hoard, go, lie. Poverty is a maelstrom that sucks you into the stomach of its reality. Think of the frightening poverty and violence at the center, the heart of any American city. The economic margins men move to ever more distant rings, hoping for peace, silence, harmony, escape from the real America. Meanwhile, the center whirls at great speed trying to suck them back down inside. The suburbanites clutch their villas and their Volvos like life buoys, praying that no wave will wash them back. Every morning they attach themselves to the many-laned concrete lifelines that descend into the maelstrom and are reeled back to the margins every night. China sucked me often into the center of things, away from my imagined detachment from everything I had come to dread in America. It was a hard place to play at being an Icelander.

A real Icelander arrived to show them that, at least, I hadn't completely fabricated my disguise. An old friend from Reykjavik buried her mother after a long illness, during which she functioned as nurse, lawyer, accountant, counselor and breadwinner for her family. When it was over, she realized that she was exhausted and needed to be, for a while, as far from Reykjavik as planetary travel permitted. She looked at a globe, and remembered letters from her old friend teaching in . . . Xi'an. That is as far away from Reykjavik as you can go in this solar system. She planned to arrive via Hong Kong and Canton and go back through Beijing about ten days later.

My students, now friends, were curious. "What do Icelanders look like?"

"Like me. Or like you."

"Is it always frozen in Iceland?"

"Not so frozen as in Xi'an in February, indoors."

"Isn't Iceland a socialist country governed by a woman?"

"Unlike China, there is a little real socialism in Iceland, and no one can govern the Icelanders except perhaps their mothers. They govern themselves one at a time. Vigdis is president; she is a very nice and intelligent woman. She lives in an unlocked house, and if you visit Reykjavik, you can probably go have tea, more likely coffee, with her."

"What shall we do to welcome Comrade Wincie on Tuesday?"

"Do you want to sing in Icelandic?"

"Yes!"

We made huge red signs in Chinese and Icelandic reading:

WELCOME TO THE MADHOUSE, WINCIE, FROM ALL US
MANIACS FROM MINNEOTA AND CHINA.

In China, I almost never referred to myself as an American: I was a citizen of a considerably smaller republic: Minneota, Minnesota.

I taught them to sing an old Icelandic folk song about the boy Olaf riding into the kingdom of the elves.

> Olaf rode along the mountains,
> lost in the night.
> The elf pack lived in the rocks there,
> and their flames burned bright.

Imagine training a Chinese chorus to trill Rs! The Mongolians had an easy time of it and thought Iceland must be a province of Mongolia. We rented a van and drove to the airport on a typically dark, grimy night, and were still rehearsing when the plane landed, only four or five hours late. We stationed chorus and signs outside the customs house where the luggage arrived. Someone spotted a tall blonde woman coming across the tarmac. We broke into incomprehensible Icelandic song and shivered our signs. Wincie half wept and half giggled.There had never been a welcome like it.

The students introduced her to chopsticks and Chinese beer, while Wincie brought Icelandic treasures out of her bag: hard fish (dry cured fish, the consistency of cardboard), Icelandic blue cheese, English mustard, Akureyri chocolate and a precious bottle of Brennivin, the Icelandic schnapps affectionately known as "The Black Death." Wincie fumbled with her chopsticks; the students politely nibbled tiny pieces of blue cheese and tried to avoid the Brennivin. The next morning I found a potted plant in my room fertilized with crumbs of blue cheese, discreetly disposed of when the Icelanders weren't looking. Cheese, of any variety, smells to most Chinese like baby vomit; a taste for it is a sure symptom of being a Barbarian.

Wincie Johannsdottir is the daughter of Johann, a schoolmaster, and Winston, an American, and a school teacher, too, so she did the logical thing. She became a teacher of English as a foreign language. I drafted her into the Chinese classroom the next day, where she charmed the students completely, preaching fearlessness and joy in the speaking of English. Damn the torpedoes and full speed ahead! Don't worry about mistakes! Charge! Practice! Carry on! This was nothing like their intensive reading classes.

They wanted to know about women in Iceland. Wincie described the new Women's Alliance whose rules allow men to fold letters and seal envelopes but not run for seats in Parliament. China is, of course, run by doddering old men who don't run for anything.

They asked about teaching in Iceland. The Icelandic teachers were either on strike or about to go out on one. Wincie was a union potato. "You have to stand up and tell them off," she said. "Otherwise they'll never pay you or respect you." Not advice to warm Deng Xiaoping's old tender heart.

One girl asked Wincie after class about the relationship between men and women in Iceland. She told the story of her parents trying to coerce her to marry a fellow she didn't think she loved.

"Tell him to bugger off if you don't love him," said Wincie. "It's your life, and it doesn't belong to your parents or anyone else."

The girl's eyes widened. "I must learn from Comrade Wincie," she said in an admiring voice.

"You must think for yourself," said Comrade Wincie.

This, to my Chinese students, was a real Icelander—despite being half Alabaman: someone who stood up brusquely for herself, carried on in her own way, loved adventure and risk and didn't care very much for money. These qualities are not, of course, shared by all Icelanders, but if these Chinese students had a small sample of experience by which to judge Americans, an Icelander may as well have been a moon creature or one of the elves that Olaf meets on the mountain. *Bing Dao* (Ice Island) was the margin, not just of the planet, but of the known universe.

China and Iceland, in an odd way, are *nether* images of each other and, like all opposites, share some amazing resemblances. The first point of comparison is in the numbers: there are over a billion Chinese on the planet, a couple of hundred thousand Icelanders. China is among the poorest, most desperate places on earth; Iceland, at the moment, but not always in its history, one of the wealthiest, a country without true poverty, where everyone lives well. China is buried in dirt, grime and pollution, an ecological disaster; Iceland is the cleanest inhabited place on earth. There is one factory, few cars, a tiny population, lovely air and the sweetest, purest water you can drink. The Chinese jam together in brutal concrete flats without paint, plumbing, or humanity; the Icelanders, like all Scandinavians, live in spotless, orderly, spacious houses, full of light, flowers, paintings and finely designed wooden furniture. In a Chinese store, there is nothing to buy but cheap kitsch and machines that fall apart. Bad taste or bad workmanship is almost illegal in Iceland; anything not in quietly understated good taste is not imported, much less manufactured, therefore unavailable at any price. Machines are usually imported from Germany or Sweden, and no more need be said about them.

China is the worst governed place on earth and has been for thousands of years. There is no such thing as a good emperor or a useful bureaucrat, though the Chinese, idealists to a fault, go on imagining that the next one, the best one, is around the corner or will appear tomorrow. The massacre in Tiananmen is remarkable not because it was unexpected but because it was part of a tedious routine thousands of years old. The Chinese have lived with a boot on their necks through five Egypts, three Romes, and twelve British Empires, and the heel is still ground in for the foreseeable future. Iceland invented parliamentary democracy with the *Althing*, and is still, arguably, the only real practitioner of it in the world. It is a place where things are counted one at a time and have names. The complete welfare state is an accomplished fact. There is no army, few police (mostly for drunks), and a waiting list to get into prison. There are only a few spaces, so you have to stay home for months, even years, waiting your turn to serve your sentence. Five newspapers representing five political parties howl at each other daily, but all warfare is verbal. In Iceland, it is probably illegal to strike someone with the back of your hand, much less hang a criminal. In China, as the world saw on television, you are given a summary trial after the judge has determined your guilt, promptly shot in the back of the head after you have been paraded through the streets, and your family is sent a bill for twenty-five cents to cover the cost of the bullet.

What could these two countries conceivably have in common? Everything important. They are both held together by a stubborn language and almost nothing else. They are the two most literary places you can imagine. Poetry is no public disgrace in either of them. Even Mao wrote it, badly. All Icelandic presidents turn out rhymes, though not so skillfully as the farmers.

Iceland, for most of its history, was even poorer than China and stayed that way until well into the twentieth century. I thought of the meanness of my grandfathers' lives when I saw Chinese peasants. Life at the edge of starvation was normal; dinner was remarkable, when possible. The country was so worthless and marginal, economically, that it was hardly worth the trouble for the Danes to oppress it for five or six hundred years, though they did. Habit dies hard in empires.

Iceland was certainly the poorest literate country in the western hemisphere, but it was both poor and literate with a vengeance. It invented one of the great European literatures of the Middle Ages, during the Sung dynasty in China. While the rest of Europe sacked ancient libraries and burned manuscripts, the Icelanders busily turned out poetry, novels, short stories, histories, the only books with real information about the old destroyed religions, codes of law, genealogical tables, translations out of Latin and other languages, manuals of seamanship, and much, much more poetry. When the culture began sinking under the weight of its poverty, those magnificent books buoyed it up, along with the Icelanders' fierce attachment to their archaic, impractical old inflected language, so fierce that they have almost managed to stop the inexorable steam roller of language change for over a thousand years, and kept their linguistic Model T intact and running. It saved them, and they feel some just gratitude to it.

If Icelandic is a Model T, the Chinese character is a horse and buggy. More than one Barbarian, driven mad by the difficulties of mastering written Chinese, has demanded a new language. A modern, alphabetic, logical, orderly language without all these damned pictures and hen scratches, one that Barbarians can actually learn. (The same complaints are made about the intricacies of Icelandic grammar.) The Chinese smile stoically—even inscrutably!—and point out that the characters were all right for the Tang poets and The *Dream of the Red Chamber* and that

COMING HOME CRAZY

a billion Chinese seem capable of using them without complaint, but, of course, Barbarians with their more limited intelligence and capacity for human language . . .

Dating from the oracle bones, Chinese characters are probably humanity's oldest try at written language. The oldest poetry, the oldest novels, the oldest histories, the oldest philosophy, the oldest type faces and printed books exist in them. The Communists tried to modernize those characters by fiat, by central plan, but the old people only nod their heads and wait. Those characters are older and tougher even than politics, and outlast all the emperors.

The Chinese, even after forty years of propaganda about the feudal past and censorship of the classics, adore the grandeur of their own literature. And well they should. In size and (the Chinese modestly assure me) in quality, it dwarfs all European literatures combined. The most miserable exile in a Xinjiang pig yard, if he is literate, has that literature in his head to remind him that the current emperor is not all there is to China, that this ramshackle old civilization, this vast slough of misery and poverty, is the home of perhaps the most extraordinary flowering of human ingenuity, and that there will yet be life enough for it to survive. Who knows? Even prosper.

So Chinese and Icelanders share an archaic impractical language, and an old literature. They are tribes of poets, not machine-tool technologists. That poetry gets them through the poverty with at least part of a soul intact and gives them insufferable pride, self-centeredness, even arrogance, that they also share. I was discussing political chaos in Reykjavik with a seaman once. He said, "It is very difficult to govern a country inhabited by 200,000 gods." Westerners have, for over a thousand years now, had the feeling that the Chinese (even the poorest and meanest of them) don't quite regard them as fully evolved human beings. Sing a poem by Du Fu for someone Chinese. That might jack you up into the higher mammals.

* * *

Wincie spent a week traveling in the countryside, going to the Golden Fish Ditch (a magnificent mountain valley and lake) for a student picnic, visiting temples and grimy little restaurants with brilliant cooks, being invited to a Chinese doctor's flat for dinner, eating dumplings, sitting up all night arguing and telling and listening to stories with a parade of Chinese friends. She didn't want to go home, and the Chinese, who had by this time fallen in love, didn't want to let her.

But duty waited. Before leaving Reykjavik, she'd had a call from the mother of an Icelander in China, a Reykjavik girl who answered an ad in *Morgunbladid* offering a scholarship to learn Chinese in China. She had been in Beijing for two and a half years, and her mother wanted to send her hardfish and other Icelandic soul food. Off we went to Beijing on a hard sleeper train car, clutching packages of smelly fish to deliver to Bryndis Dagsdottir, the only real Icelander living in the vast Middle Kingdom.

Bryndis was easy to track down. Go to the dormitories of the biggest university in a city of ten million in the most populous country in the world and ask for the *Bing Dao ren* — Ice Island person. Margin types come in ones. Bryndis turned out to be a small, auburn-haired woman, with a quiet temperament, but as the Icelanders say: *nautheimskur* (something like "stubborn as a bull"), and decently fluent Chinese. These last two gifts came in handy for me.

She was happy to get the hard fish, of course, and to hear from her mother, but her greatest delight was simply speaking Icelandic again. She and Wincie chattered away, hurling trilled Rs at each other. Since no one in China spoke Icelandic, Bryndis confessed that, in addition to picking up Chinese, her Danish and English had improved immeasurably. She used them every day with other Barbarians in town and with Chinese anxious to practice. We wandered around Beijing with Bryndis for a day or two, always astonished at Bryndis's power to manage Chinese in daily life with ease and fluency.

Finally, it was time for both Wincie and me to get back to work, she to London and then Reykjavik, me to Xi'an. Only one problem: I had to buy a ticket. This involved going to the CAAC office downtown, standing in mulish-tempered lines for two or three hours, getting to the window at last, asking for a ticket in my poor Chinese, hearing a sharp, impatient voice snap "*mei you*" at me, then the window slamming shut. I didn't have enough Chinese to argue or even to bribe. I was doomed.

On the third day of this charade, I asked Bryndis to help me out. We stood in line for the usual two hours. At the window, I made my plaintive request.

"*Mei you.*"

The next customer was about to nudge me out of the way and begin his personal ticket psychodrama when Bryndis swung into action. Standing on tiptoe, she peered in at the man behind the counter, giving the ticket seller a fierce green eye, speaking to him in a sharp tone. He winced at the sight of this marginal women hollering at him in Chinese.

The argument went on, *tutti fortissimo,* for about five minutes. He handed Bryndis a piece of paper and she turned on her heel to leave. I followed her out meekly.

"What happened?"

"He gave me a voucher for a ticket this afternoon. There are plenty of seats on the airplane."

"Why didn't he sell me one two days ago?"

"He didn't know who you were."

"I'm not anybody. What did you tell him?"

"You are a foreign lecturer, the guest of the government and must be in Xi'an to deliver lectures at a famous university. If you are delayed, the foreign office might hold him responsible."

"As my friend Howard Mohr says at a time like this: 'Whatever'— Thanks for the Chinese."

"That was nothing."

But indeed, it was something—a magnificent battle of languages between two old and stubborn tribes, both marginal in their peculiar ways, the one by virtue of geography and lack of consequence, the other by choice, the fruit of walling itself up like a cask of Amontillado.

Two years later, I am back in America, still trying to live on the margins. Most of the old Icelanders I grew up with are dead, and I've had to invent new kinds of margins in order to detach part of myself from the rage and disappointment I still feel at America. The new margin might be Minneota, an ugly harsh place far from anywhere, where no sensible American (other than a farmer) would choose to live. Television is the vortex of the maelstrom in America, so I prefer to live without one. Presumably Jack Paar and "Gunsmoke" are still on the air, but they may have changed for all I know. Does Ed Sullivan still have that show with the young British boys on now and then?

But, in some way, this hiding on the margins doesn't work. The more you try to shun the center from disgust, to live safe from the Defense Department, rock and roll Walkmans, and the Dow Jones, the more American you become. Walt Whitman says:

Apart from the pulling and hauling stands what I am,
Stands amused, complacent, compassionating, idle, unitary,
Looks down, is erect, or bends an arm on an impalpable certain rest,
Looking with side-curved head curious what will come next,
Both in and out of the game and watching and wondering at it.

But later he says:

I am not an earth nor an adjunct of the earth,
I am the mate and companion of people,
    all just as immortal and fathomless as myself,
(They do not know how immortal, but I know.)

Both Chinese and Icelanders love and respect language more than we do, and now the Chinese are suffering from it more than we can imagine. Think about the interminable and compulsory political meetings at which the "true" story of Tiananmen Square is being repeated again, and again, and again, like some perverse mantra from the kingdom of lies. Yet real language survives in the brains of the Chinese who remember even a few lines of their great poetry. Nien Cheng, the brave woman who wrote *Life and Death in Shanghai*, saved her sanity and kept her courage during her long torture and imprisonment by reciting mentally an old anthology of Tang poetry she memorized as a girl. There are lips moving silently in political meetings all over China today.

For a while in the election of 1988, I didn't think Whitman's noble American language would survive the brutal onslaught of "card-carrying liberals, Willie Horton furloughs, and a thousand points of light." I wanted someone to throw up in public, for a reporter to walk away, disgusted, from a press conference. None of this happened, and the country slides on, asleep at the wheel.

"I am a Minneota Icelander," I whispered to myself, "I am going back to China. I live on the margin. None of this has anything to do with me. I will cultivate my garden here on the margin of everything and play Bach late into the night." This, too, was a mantra of sorts. Then I remembered Walt Whitman again, our great poet of margins:

Then I will sleep awhile yet, for I see that these States sleep, for reasons;
(With gathering murk, with muttering thunder and lambent shoots we all
    duly awake,
South, North, East, West, inland and seaboard, we will surely awake.)

We will, old Walt, we will! We will!

JESUS

耶稣

In Xi'an, as she did in small western Minnesota towns, God wisely divided Christians into Lutherans and Catholics and let it go at that. She saw no need for Baptists, Methodists, or Christian Scientists.

Though seldom curious about Lutheran churches in the United States, this accidental parallel between Minneota and Xi'an so pleased me that I decided to go to church and investigate. As a genetic Lutheran, probably a Sunday school contributor to Chinese missions, and semi-retired church musician, I was lonesome for hymns.

One of my fellow Barbarian teachers attended church every Sunday. For him it was a powerful and resonant experience. Joe's father, a Louisiana Baptist, promised God in the trenches of World War I that if he survived the shelling, he would go to China for the rest of his life and preach. He did, for almost thirty years, and his family were almost the last to board the escape boat in 1949 as Mao's victorious army moved through the Shanghai streets toward the docks. After 1949, missionary-ing in China was temporarily washed up since Mao had his own church to evangelize. Joe and his brothers and sisters grew up with street Chinese as a first language, listening to their father preach in formal Chinese. They arrived back in the United States as grown children to a culture shock greater than I can imagine. Their father vowed to wait out the Communists and go back to China. Though he lived to almost ninety, he didn't quite make it. His son came back instead, thirty-nine years later, an artist in his fifties, to teach and to listen to sermons that must have contained the ghost of his father's voice.

Shortly after he arrived, Joe tracked down the details on the survival (or rejuvenation) of Christianity in Xi'an. There were two churches, Catholic and Protestant, the latter descended from an old Lutheran mission church, now generic "Chinese Protestant," both of them carefully monitored and supervised by the authorities, but lively and active again after their more than thirty years' sleep. In 1985, the St. Olaf Choir even sang here! Imagine their specialties, "O Day Full of Grace," or "From Heaven Above," two old Norwegian folk hymns in treacly harmonizations, sung by a clump of blond hair—a gaggle of Petersons and Andersons—in a dusty Chinese Lutheran mission!

On a bright Sunday in October, I went looking for the church. I found it well disguised in the courtyard of an alley off a main shopping street, marked only by a discreetly small red cross on the gate, and guarded by an old lady standing next to it checking bicycles. I still suffered considerable paranoia, maybe justified: did the red cross mean Party-approved? Did the old lady check names as well as bicycles? I waited, intending to arrive late and, I hoped, inconspicuous. Barbarians in China, particularly large hairy red ones, frequently become the quantum particle that changes Chinese occasions. Instead of watching an event, they become the event. I wanted only to sit quietly and listen, the invisible Lutheran.

No luck. A black-suited usher spotted me, grabbed my arm, led me through a crowded courtyard into an old barn-like stone building, up the aisle past the packed congregation. He saw the front row already full of Barbarians, moved two elderly Chinese ladies out of their second row seats, and with a great flurry of "*huanyings*" (welcome), sat me down. Every eye in the place gawked at the back of my neck, by this time pinker than usual. Had I known enough Chinese then, I might have explained to him that genetic Lutherans prefer the back row. It would have done no good.

Someone played "*An die Freude*" on an out-of-tune piano, meandering through the melody with no Beethoven rhythmic snap, the harmony underneath a continual tri-tone drone. When the piano was last tuned, sometime before the 1911 revolution, that interval probably sounded a real fifth. I looked around; this was a room full of old people in drab dark ragged clothes. The up-and-coming in Xi'an had discovered a little consumer fashion—western suits and neckties, snappy blue jeans, colorful silk blouses. But not here—here sat the poor and the old, who had waited faithfully for thirty years to be Christians again, suffering ostracism, criticism, persecution. No university slots for Chinese Christians, no cushy jobs, no party memberships, no "*guanxi* (influence)."

And then, the Great Proletarian Cultural Revolution . . . Many of these old Chinese must have been converted, educated, and preached to by people like Joe's father, and had their simple and harmless version of Christianity cost them almost everything. Like most Chinese, they probably went on revering Buddha, Confucius, Lao Tze, even Mao himself as well as Jesus, but the western taint cost them almost everything in the kingdom of the single truth. They understood sacrifice better than any comfortable Barbarian who mouthed well-intentioned words every Sunday while feeling virtuous about loading the collection plate for foreign missions. I am half a cynic about missionarying, but the other half was moved by that room full of brave old human relics.

The choir filed in: sixty and seventy-year-old women in white smocks. The service began with "Holy Holy Holy!" Joe turned around and handed me a Baptist hymnal in English. I bellered out the words in an aggressive tenor. The tri-tone drone still sounded under it, the only harmony. Chinese volume defeated me. There exists no noise on earth quite like a bunch of Chinese women singing at full throttle—nasal, harsh, high-pitched—the sound of fan belt whine heard through a megaphone. I thought of Charles Ives' father's reply to complaints about the harsh loud monotone of old John the stonemason at Danbury camp meetings: "Don't listen so hard to the sound or you'll miss the music." This singing would have defeated the Red Guards and made the tanks pause in Tiananmen. It was spirit and praise incarnate! This was music! Damn the ugliness!

The choir sang an anthem. Ushers passed the collection plate. I dropped in the equivalent of two and a half dollars in foreign exchange currency. Everyone in the row stared at it. The sermon began. The minister had a solemn humorless face—a rarity among the Chinese (except in officials)—and the local version of a crew cut. Someone brought him tea in a blue-flowered cup. Tea steam curled up in front of his face as he talked. I was afraid this tea would give him strength to go on. He spoke a kind of train announcer, exaggeratedly sing-songy Chinese. I followed almost nothing. The words *Meiguo, weiguoren,* and *erzi* drifted in and out: *America, foreigner, son.* For his sermon text, he took the parable of the prodigal son. I got out my notebook and began writing discreetly. The Chinese looked intently at my left-handedness. The old gentleman next to me nudged my elbow. He wrote in a notebook, too, elegant spidery characters with his right hand. We admired each other's notebooks and smiled, writers together. He whispered loudly in my ear, "I am a visitor here too, from Hanzhong. You are American?" I nodded. We both continued writing, while the sermon droned on. And on. And on. Forty-five minutes on the *erzi* . . . One of the only sentences I know that is always and everywhere true, in Minnesota, in Kenya, in France, in China, and knows no cultural or historical limits is: "The sermon is too long." It is a touchstone of absolute truth in a world of shifting perception. You could found a church on it; many have already.

Before the benediction, the congregation sang: "What a Friend We Have in Jesus." It was accompanied by the same dissonant drone. My seatmate, correspondent and comrade handed me his Chinese hymnal.

"All our sins and griefs to bear . . . Take it to the Lord in prayer . . . " in characters. I held the hymnal, probably upside down, took a deep breath and sang it out at the top of my lungs in English. No one cared. They couldn't hear me for the noise of their own praise.

I went to a Lutheran church again when I got back to Minnesota. Here was a roomful of scrupulously clean, prosperous Scandinavians, a first-rate well-played pipe organ, a congregation of pleasant voices singing in accurate parts, a humane and reasonable sermon on grace and stewardship (it was too long . . .), a watery liturgy out of the watery new green hymnal, signs about caring and sharing, a watery handshake followed by watery coffee. There was a vague feeling of self-congratulation in that room full of clean people acting out the demands of history and respectability. No one paid anything other than money to be there.

KINDERGARTEN

幼儿园

Like every Barbarian in China for the last thousand years, I complain a lot. Dirt, spitting, smelly squat toilets, rude bureaucracy, overcrowding, noise, bad wiring, worse plumbing, nasty store clerks, appalling safety, broken-down machines, cold gray cement buildings, grim apartments, no hot water, no clean air, drab clothes, dust, garlic pickles, greasy meat, surly service, on and on and on, blah-blah-blah, ad infinitum, ad nauseum. After a while, it begins to disgust and bore even the complainers. Our voices begin to sound like an old warped 45 disc of "Ballin' the Jack" ·played at 33–1/3 on a crooked turntable.

Enough, I say; let's have some praise!

Today I went to kindergarten. It was the first day of true spring in Xi'an, April 7. After a long, bleak winter, lilacs exploded, sycamores budded, flowering crabs flowered, and fifty other bushes and shrubs showed their colors. On such a day, even cynics feel benevolent toward the failures of their fellow creatures.

I've lived next door to the kindergarten now for seven months, seen children carted in and out of it daily, looked inside the gates and passed on to my little cement apartment in the Barbarians' guest house. Who, after all, really wants to go to a kindergarten? Probably not even the kinder.

My friend, Xiao Zhang, decided to take pictures of children for a Chinese photography contest, so I offered to go along and watch. Physically, the kindergarten is one wall away from the hotel . . . spiritually, ten thousand miles. It is another planet. There's a bird cage inside the gates, full of brilliant parakeets—the first bright-colored birds I've seen in Xi'an. The bird cage had been cleaned within the previous three hours. This is an important detail.

We walked down quiet, clean sidewalks lined with hedges and

shrubs, lilacs, plums, cherries, all green and blooming. The leaves of the hedge had been hosed down in the morning and shone in the spring sunlight.

How do I know they had been cleaned that day? Xi'an is a city constantly full of dust and coal grit. A white shirt left outside for a few hours turns into a gray shirt. Every bush in the neighborhood is caked with grime — except these. In contrast to the gray cement outside the walls, the buildings were freshly painted pink and brown, decorated with old Chinese flower patterns.

It was the end of nap time. The rooms were mostly empty, windows open, pale curtains blowing. We snooped. Classrooms alternated with nap rooms down long corridors facing into a garden with lots of play equipment.

The classrooms were brightly painted green or blue or yellow, lined with painted shelves covered with neatly arranged colorful toys, games, books. The room itself was big and airy, with ceiling fans, good sturdy radiators covered with wire grates for safety, three or four sinks for washing, clean towels neatly hung above them.

Big tea kettles sat ready to boil on gas stoves. A western-style toilet and washroom was connected to every classroom, scrubbed down with disinfectant. The linoleum squeaked. The room smelled sweetly of spring flowers, jasmine, and soap. It smelled clean. Why is a simple, clean airy classroom so worthy of praise? Because it is unlike any public room I have set foot into here in Xi'an, or elsewhere in China — unlike the Beijing airport, the Forbidden City, the University Library, the Provincial Government Hall, any luxury hotel, or my own apartment.

That room smelled and looked simply and unostentatiously clean, gay, practical, affectionate, cared for. The machines worked, the paint was fresh, simple details of safety and comfort had been tended to. Things had been scrubbed down and tidied up with attention. No foreign delegations were expected; this was done for the children. This is a civilized room, full of love and intelligence, it said to anyone who walked in.

The nap rooms have perhaps twenty beds, all covered with colorful and different silk quilts, the headboards painted with tigers, dragons, and rabbits. Under the quilts, twenty little heads of black hair began to stir. Three or four teachers, mostly pretty young girls, helped the children get up and dress. The room was almost silent. It was a lovely calm silence.

Parents dress Chinese children brilliantly in layer after layer of bright colors: pink, lavender, orange, red, yellow. No proletarian blue for the kinder! I watched one little girl being dressed; her tiny pigtail held up by a red ribbon, she watched me with immense calm as three or four peacock layers covered her tiny body. Xiao Zhang spotted a little boy with a particularly photogenic face getting dressed on the other side of the room, and set his camera. The little boy broke into a grin and posed shamelessly, his eyes huge and fascinated in front of the strange camera. Soon forty brown eyes peered out of their silk quilts at the big Barbarian. Still no sound. I swear to God, black-hearted cynic that I am, that I could have adopted every child in that room. The beauty of those eyes, that sweet silence, the kaleidoscope of color in those quilts, that calm wind moving spring air into the blue curtains almost made me weep with joy.

Xiao Zhang's true purpose was to take a picture of the Chinese child's famous open-butted pants that enable his whole vast country to survive without a single smelly diaper pail. He moved the little boy into the classroom, found him a toy train and set the camera. The little boy behaved like a professional fashion model, squatted to open his pants, fondled the train car, and looked engagingly back toward the camera. A prize-winning photo for sure!

Our mission finished, we left, thanking the teachers who smiled pleasantly and waved us out. Children had begun to gather in the playground now, and at the sight of my red beard and outsize body, they called to me in Chinese, "*Lao Yeye!*"

"I'm the foreign devil, I suppose," I said blearily to Xiao Zhang.

"They are calling you 'old grandfather!'" said Xiao Zhang. "It's a term of respect."

"Some respect . . . " I said. "Maybe I won't adopt the little devils after all."

"What?" he asked, not having followed my sentimental moment in the nap room.

That kindergarten is a wonderful place. It is safe, warm, bright, airy, clean and lovely. At six, those children graduate to cold rooms, dangerous wiring, no plumbing, dirt, drabness and discomfort. They stay in that world until they get to bring their own children to kindergarten. At the moment, in China, they die in the second world. China's work is to make the whole country into that kindergarten, and it will take more than money. It will take a new psychology of human life.

Americans and Swedes, for instance, have plenty of money, and must still do the same work. Even in America, the richest, most powerful country in history, we still do not have enough rooms like that kindergarten — either for children, for the old, or for all of us.

Preparing those rooms is humanity's work, if it manages not to exterminate itself before the next century. If we succeed, we will all deserve some praise.

LAWRENCE IN CHINA

劳伦斯在中国

I became a college teacher because I couldn't think of anything else to do. To confess that your professional life has been based on a failure of imagination is neither so embarrassing nor so unusual as it might seem. Give truth serum (or three or four whiskeys) to any college faculty and you will see what I mean. If you are an administrator and a teacher tells you that he does his job because he wants to "help," to "improve" his students, fire that teacher on the spot. He is either lying, or a fool, both sane grounds for dismissal. A teacher does his job because he is able to and because sometimes, against all odds, remarkable and unexpected circumstances occur, even in universities.

I loved to read, to talk and argue, to scribble, and to have long stretches of privacy. Blood, legal jargon, paying attention to money and farming all seemed tedious, a waste of perfectly good loafing time. Therefore, I taught literature. If there had been an ocean close at hand in Kansas or Minnesota, I might have become a seaman. Failing that, the university seemed at least partly an honorable living.

Yet, for the better part of twenty-five years, I felt discontented with teaching in America. This is not a country that reads much, nor believes that the little it is required to read has anything to do with the world of banks, cars and missile silos. We are practical to a fault, clean mental machines, so Thoreau, Whitman, and Mark Twain go in one ear and pass out the other, frequently without impediment, loss of speed, or any notable effect. On the other hand, books changed my life and, God forbid, even my opinions. They gave me courage when I needed it. I joked for years that I was a fundamentalist Transcendentalist, and worshiped regularly at the cathedrals of St. Walt, St. Hank and St. Ralph. The yawning of the business majors irritated me as profoundly as Mencken or

Shaw would irritate Falwell, Bakker or Helms if they could read them. So life in the "Introduction to Literature" classes was not always easy. Since I am, at least, partly a realist, all I expected was a little curiosity about the unknown and an openness to ideas and feelings, a willingness to see and, in the best of all possible worlds, a sense of humor. What I got, often, was either bored passivity or whiny resistance to any un-received idea or language. What I did not get was passionate curiosity about the world.

I started teaching at a black college in the middle of the Vietnam war and the civil rights eruption. There was plenty of political interest, but even there, not much sense that books had anything to do with "real" life. When the war ended and America sank into Reagan, the sleep of reason and the complete evaporation of any connection between history and rational discourse, things, needless to say, did not cheer up in the literature classroom. I was back in the Midwest, one of the black holes of obedient passivity, the cathedral of the practical. I would stop in the middle of a sentence, and ask myself, silently, "why?" I hurled questions into the silence and in response heard only the buzzing of fluorescent lights.

I approached despair, ready to give it up and go to sea, when the universe dropped China in my lap. "Of course I'll go," I said. "Where from and when do I leave?" I went, like Ishmael, with a sense of adventure — the idea that whoever was not curious to see and experience China gave clear evidence of death and should be embalmed soon before he perfumed his own house. But China had an odd side-effect: it saved my faith in teaching, and certainly in the power and majesty of language.

I taught in Xi'an at Jiaotong (Traffic) University — an old polytechnic college established late in the nineteenth century to train Chinese engineers to run railroads. By the 1980s, it had become the Chinese equivalent of M.I.T., or Cal Tech, a premier engineering school, in Chinese jargon, a "key" university that recruited students by examination from all over China. As a result, it had a bright lot of students, mostly engineers.

I taught in the foreign-language department, a program primarily to train students to teach English to scientists. Officially it was called "applied linguistics," but the curriculum dictated a couple of literature classes, which were my job. I taught first and second-year graduate students and a special class of "teacher trainees," a one-year graduate program for victims of the chaotic and inadequate universities of cultural-revolution days. The students varied in age from nineteen to their mid-forties and came from the far corners: Xinjiang, Qinghai, Hunan, Manchuria, Suzhou. Some had Chinese accents so exotic they were forced to speak to their classmates in English most of the time.

The one common thread, I quickly discovered, was their distaste for applied linguistics and dread of a drudge life teaching engineers to translate technical articles. They cared passionately about history, anthropology, poetry, political journalism, translation, almost everything but hydraulic systems. Chinese students, of course, have no choice. Mother State determines where they will "serve the people," and off they go. It's the only step into a better apartment, better *guanxi*, the chance to change jobs later. But it meant they were eager for whatever had nothing to do with technology and party dogma, and I was lucky enough to be their teacher — a kind of deliverer from the tedious and the practical that they had served up to them everywhere else.

My first quarrels with the department authorities were over textbooks. A Chinese English literature survey class lists the "main" writers, gives birth, death, publication dates, names "important" books, gives "main" ideas, and offers three or four sentences of canned social criticism to pigeonhole the writer safely in the official scheme of things, then a page or two of carefully edited text. A Chinese teacher in a literature class read the canned stuff aloud, wrote "main points" on the board in Chinese and English, broached no questions and held no discussion about a text he may or may not have read himself. For the examination, the students dutifully memorized this material and wrote it down exactly as teacher and text had agreed on its being said. The irony, of course, was that the class, and sometimes even the teachers, were voracious readers of everything they could find, even on the black book market; the more dangerous and forbidden the text, the better.

I demanded that the department duplicate an abridged Norton anthology so that the students would have some accurate texts to argue about. The department refused, then agreed, then did nothing, although the university had its own print shop with the latest equipment that turned out mostly public relations fluff and party directives.

Finally, I stormed into the office, and demanded to know why nothing had been done. "Perhaps," said the functionary, "the students perfer Chinese style texts?"

"Nonsense!" I fumed.

"But," said the functionary, "we are so short of money . . ."

I took out my checkbook, wrote a check for five hundred hard dollars and threw it on the table. "Pay for it with that," I raged, "and never mention it to me again." I had done the one thing necessary to win the quarrel: I had threatened the department with a loss of face. They declined the check, and the texts were completed a few days later. The students cheered and applauded when they arrived. We were off on a course of pure sedition.

While half of me raged at Chinese bureaucracy, the other half exulted. I had just lived through years of listening to the American student's nasal whines of: "Do we have to read the whole book? It's so-oooo expensive if we're only going to be tested on half of it." At last, I was teaching human beings for whom books meant something besides furniture and an intrusion into their beer money! So this was why humans taught school.

We were off! Blake, Dr. Johnson, Whitman, Thoreau, Yeats, Auden, Sherwood Anderson. It was all candy, all delight. Here are three examples of what it was like to teach in China.

Melville was almost entirely unknown. There was a summary of *Moby Dick* in the official literary history and a few lines of critisim about his bourgeois individualism. We read "Bartleby the Scrivener." Bartleby, to refresh your memory, is the drudge from the dead letter office who "prefers not to . . . " The story is wonderfully enigmatic, and having defeated American literary criticism, it defeated the official Chinese passion for a "main point." The students loved arguing about why Bartleby "prefers not to" and began seeing parallels to Gandhi, Taoism, and the history of Chinese bureaucracy. I tried to cut off discussion after three days and move on to Stephen Crane. Life is short and art is long, but having opened this Pandora's box, I had some difficulty closing it.

I taught that class from ten until noon, and invariably I ran overtime. This always produced a great clattering of rice bowls and spoons. It was lunch time. The military music blaring from the loudspeaker outside the window announced to those students that they had better move briskly to the lunch lines or there would be no meat left. Chinese students carried their own bowls and utensils to the people's lunch line — if you want to eat, bring a dish; if you want tea, bring a cup and bring tea. After lunch came *xiuxi* — naptime, the one inviolable law in Chinese life. China comes to a halt for two hours; citizens lunch perfunctorily and then doze till 2:00 p.m. (If the Pentagon plans to invade China, they should do it after lunch. It adds the element of suprise since the People's Liberation Army is probably sound asleep. Notice that the Tiananmen massacre did not take place after lunch. Some things are sacrosant, after all.)

I, too, came to treasure my nap — two hours of absolute privacy. But Bartleby undid Chinese courtesy. Two or three days running, a knock sounded on the door after lunch.

"Yes," I called sleepily from under my quilt. Students came in two or three at a time and pulled up chairs next to the bed.

"We are sorry to disturb your nap, Comrade Bill, but we have been studying more of Bartleby, and we think we have found the true reason he prefers not to. Is it because . . . ?"

The best I ever did for them from the kingdom of half-sleep was a "maybe" or a "that's possible" before shoving them back into the Middle Kingdom. I was half outraged by the invasion of my nap and half exultant. I don't ever remember being gotten out of bed by an American student to settle an argument that started in a class, although I have been called in the middle of the night for a grade, or with a third dead grandmother of the semester as an excuse for a missed paper or exam.

I began teaching Emily Dickinson with trepidation. My students had good workable English, solid understanding of prose and comprehensive vocabularies. Furthermore, they had read a great deal of this literature in Chinese translation. Emily D., though, with her mordant irony and her dense peculiar English struck me as untranslatable, either in culture or language. But I carried on; nothing ventured . . . When was the last time an American teacher went into a classroom piqued by pure curiosity about how students might respond?

I began with a little lecture about Emily's odd life. I explained hymn meter and sang a stanza or two of her work to tunes like "Duke Street" and "Amazing Grace." I asked if she was at all known in China. A hand went up in the front row from a young woman with a Chinese opera face and an infectious giggle. When I first read her name, I asked her if it meant Small Vinegar. She giggled, "You don't read Chinese characters."

"No," I said. I had made a silly pun—the two sounds in her name meant small vinegar but they meant fifty other things, too. Whenever class went slowly, I crossed my eyes at her or made a monster face. She couldn't resist laughing magnificently and loosening up the whole room. She had one of the most lively and immediate faces I've ever seen, which murdered with one stroke the cliché about inscrutable Oriental faces. It is American academics and politicians who so often have the stony, shifty faces.

She answered me this way:

> I'm Nobody! Who are you?
> Are you—Nobody—Too?
> Then there's a pair of us?
> Don't tell! they'd advertise—you know!

> How dreary—to be—Somebody!
> How public—like a Frog—
> To tell one's name—the livelong June—
> To an admiring Bog!

I was not quite speechless. "Wonderful!" I said. "Why did you learn it?"

"She is my favorite poet and my namesake."

"Your namesake?"

"My English name is Emily. I took it from Emily Dickinson and Emily Brontë, two of my favorite writers."

Some teachers insisted that Chinese students take English names. I refused this custom and fearlessly butchered their true names in Chinese. We had a little talk about how this poem might connect to the secrecy and jealousy endemic in Chinese life, how this manifested itself in a passion to be anonymous, to be in no one's files. Nine or ten other students knew Dickinson poems by heart, too. The next day they brought in Chinese translations and read them to me. We found mistakes, translations out of inaccurate editions, misunderstandings of New England idioms, misread ironies. We did "scholarship." I gave them a few ideas out of Freud about Emily that the Party had neglected to mention. They all wanted to learn to sing Emily to a hymn tune, so I rehearsed them on "Because I Could Not Stop for Death" to "Amazing Grace." No American class except an Elder Hostel ever demanded singing from me.

D.H. Lawrence was the hardest case for the Chinese literary pigeon-holers. Having hatched the notion that British writers are almost entirely bourgeois (true) and reflect bourgeois values (sometimes true), they were stumped by Lawrence. A true man of the working class, he hated capitalism—so far, so good. But he hated socialism too—equally as much. And insisted on the business about sex. Orwell's description of Big Brother's attempts to destroy and pervert sexual life is exactly and literally true. Change the names and it describes China. Change them again, and it describes any institution like China; name your own preferred church or government. Chinese translations of *Lady Chatterley's Lover* sold on the black market at prices ranging from seven to twenty *yuan*, ferociously expensive, but not enough to keep readers away from its dangers and delights.

I started Lawrence gently by giving them a few small poems. We memorized them and said them aloud. Since Chinese students were used to memorizing whole books on demand, these tiny poems were no trouble. The first was:

> The youth walks up to the white horse, to put its halter on
> and the horse looks at him in silence.
> They are so silent they are in another world.

How like an old Chinese poem, they said. How smart for a Barbarian to do this! Lao Tze's countrymen still understand silence and other worlds.
The next was:

> I can't stand Willy wet-leg
> Can't stand him at any price.
> He's resigned, and when you hit him,
> He lets you hit him twice.

How well Lawrence understood us, they said. We are too passive, too obedient. We are a little like Willy wet-leg. This was two years before Tiananmen. It was clearly not Willy wet-leg standing in front of that line of tanks.

At last we came to "The Horse Dealer's Daughter," the story that happened to be in the Norton anthology I had duplicated. I grew up Lutheran in a small Minnesota town in the fifties, so I understood repression of erotic life, but I had never imagined so thorough and cynical a manipulation of human feeling as that in China. Young Chinese grow up with a horror of touch, a fear of their own eros. There are to be no marriages before age twenty-five, no touching in public, no mention of sexuality except to condemn it as counter-revolutionary, no "dating," no acknowledgement that humans might have duties to themselves different from those owed to the state. Every political campaign wrecked families and marriages. Chinese job assignments kept husbands and wives thousands of miles apart for decades. My Chinese students existed in a state of sexual suspended animation. The ones in their twenties reminded me of naïve junior high students in America. And yet, underneath this mad repression, I sensed that many Chinese are hopeless romantics, doors waiting to be opened. Real sexual energy is a genuine threat to political authority. The moral Stalinists are not wrong.

I asked them to read the story aloud, a paragraph or two at a time, to practice their oral English. How wonderful that story sounded in a grab bag of Chinese accents, voices, and sweet mispronunciations, steadily more full of feeling as the story progressed! Lawrence tells the story of a woman who lives with three loutish brothers and decides to give up on life. She walks into a pond with no intention of walking out. A typically constipated young British doctor, a friend of the family, who admires Mabel but is too reserved and frightened to act, sees her. He walks into the brackish waters of the pond in order to carry her out, waterlogged and unconscious. He takes her to the house, lights a fire, undresses her and then wraps her in warm blankets. She revives. She first thinks herself dead, then realizes she is naked and that the doctor is there:

> For a moment it seemed as if her reason were going. She looked
> round, with wild eye, as if seeking something. He stood still with fear.
> She saw her clothing lying scattered.
> "Who undressed me?" she asked, her eyes resting full and inevitable
> on his face.
> "I did," he replied, "to bring you round."
> For some moments she sat and gazed at him awfully, her lips parted.
> "Do you love me, then?" she asked.
> He only stood and stared at her, fascinated. His soul seemed to melt.

From this point on, two thirds of the way through the story, the room charged with erotic energy, as if each woman were Mabel, naked, damp and wild-eyed by the fire, and every man Dr. Ferguson, speechless, astonished, frightened, his soul sliding away underneath him. Insofar as I have ever had a mystical experience, I had one in that classroom—the right work of art telling the right truth to the right people—an absolutely impossible concatenation of events, a violation of the laws of probability, happening before me. And the room drenched in feeling, as soggy with eros as Mabel's damp clayey dress, as the doctor's sodden tweeds, and all palpably alive.

He touches her.

> A flame seemed to burn the hand that grasped her soft shoulder.

The classroom trembled. The doctor's will struggles, then relaxes and yields. She kisses his knees. "You love me." He begins kissing her.

> "Yes." The word cost him a painful effort. Not because it wasn't
> true. But because it was too newly true, the *saying* seemed to tear
> open again his newly torn heart. And he hardly wanted it to be true,
> even now.
> She lifted her face to him, and he bent forward and kissed her on
> the mouth, gently . . . He never intended to love her. But now it was
> over. He had crossed over the gulf to her, and all that he had left be-
> hind had shriveled and become void.

This is tame stuff, for even an American junior high class. Every teacher can imagine the seventh-grade smart aleck piping up, "But nothing really happens!" It could hardly get you in trouble with the Lutheran Ladies Aid. But "The Horse Dealer's Daughter" is the real thing, alive with true eros. Those Chinese students felt it and it moved them. For them, it became what literature should always be, a necessary volcanic eruption in the soul.

"Where can we find more of these stories, Comrade Bill?" they asked. When was the last time a visibly moved American class demanded more work from a writer?

I came back to America after my year in China and tried teaching again. I sunk as close to clinical depression as I have ever come. In the middle of the silence or the diddling, I tried superimposing the faces of my Chinese students on the clean-cut blond heads. I tried teleporting myself back into the dust and spittle of a Xi'an classroom. I stood gawking in the parking lot at my students' cars. I surveyed the piles of unpurchased text books for my classes. I dutifully graded the almost illiterate hen-scratched essays. What insufferable arrogance, I thought to myself, to throw the chance for a real mental life away on people who don't want it. American life doesn't want them to want it, not, at any rate, to want more than the name, surely not the fact. Nor do the Chinese party hacks want Chinese students to want it, but they do.

And even after the tanks in Tiananmen Square, those students will still want it, and neither Deng Xiaoping, nor the next Deng Xiaoping by another name, has enough bullets or tanks to do anything about it.

MI LAO SHU:
MICKEY MOUSE

米老鼠

At 6:00 on Sunday evening, China stops. Not once and for all, but each week. Not to worship, but to laugh (though a Transcendentalist can't tell the difference). The Middle Kingdom of Confucius and Lao Tze settles down in front of its collective televisions, from one end of the Chinese vastness to the other, all eyes on Minnie Mouse serenading Mickey with "The St. Louis Blues," backed by the whole "toon" orchestra hitting hot licks and cool riffs. Minnie sings in impeccable Beijing Chinese, and, so far as I can tell by the perfectly synchronized lip syncing, did so in 1937. Didn't she?

* * *

On any day down any street in Xi'an, a parade of cartoon mice, ducks, hound dogs and rabbits walks past you. In the thermos shop, you can buy decorated plastic cylinders painted in gaudy colors with Mickey, Minnie, Donald and Goofy. The precious "only" toddlers wear dancing cartoon mice T-shirts. The red-kerchiefed Young Pioneers carry school notebooks decorated not with pictures of Marx but with the perpetually smiling Mickey. In the candy store, small fists that will build the Four Modernizations reach over the counter clutching aluminum *fens* in sweaty fingers to order Shanghai *tang guo*, hard fruit candy that comes in plastic sacks stamped with Minnie Mouse holding hands with the famous Shanghai white rabbit.

"Trixon" and "Mow the Helmsman" didn't open China to the West;

Walt Disney did. The evidence walks the streets, spends money on doo-dads and clusters in front of the telly. Maybe the Chinese secretly know that the real loony tunes live in Washington and Zhongnanhai, the Chinese Kremlin.

* * *

My students, brilliant lively people in their twenties and thirties, with sad histories and quick minds, fancied Mickey, Minnie, Donald and Goofy. Disney buttons flowered on shirt lapels. My favorite was Mickey and Donald painted in red, purple and orange, doing the jitterbug. I offered an ironic compliment or two on their taste, and before class one day they presented me with my very own button. Now I belonged to the club. I've got that button in my hand now, two years later, and I will prize it for a long time.

Once, a bunch of us were hauled in by the police for taking a bus trip through a "closed area," probably a town with a gunpowder factory so pointless that even the Pentagon has saved space by deep sixing its detailed satellite photos. The police took passports, cameras, work unit ID cards. We wrote out "confessions" for the authorities to scrutinize. I risked only a fine, but the Chinese felt the threat of ruin—expulsion from jobs, universities, prospective marriages. We were all depressed and afraid. Someone looked at a watch.

"It's 5:30! Where can we find a TV?"

We found one, and a half hour later, I watched a room full of obviously worried watchers turn off the worry switch, glue their faces to the flickering screen with complete attention, and giggle and guffaw at the high pitched quarrels of Mickey and Donald. Later, we ate dumplings with hot pepper and laughed more. It's cheaper than therapy or prescriptions for Valium.

* * *

Why Disney mania in the Middle Kingdom? I have two ideas about this, one the dark view and the other the praise view.

Disney doesn't survive childhood in America. The middle-aged remember fondly cartoons of their youth—eating *real* buttery popcorn in art deco theaters with names like ROXY or JOY, their still short legs dangling off red plush seats as they cheered Pluto's pursuit of bones. They bore and irritate their own children with this nostalgia. For this generation, Disney is a theme park, a duty children extort from parents with guilt and nasal cajoling, where popcorn is flavored with a "butter-flavored" product and costs too much. Last year's hit movie in America was a soul-less technical tour de force with "toons" and humans acting together. As critics noted, the "toons" were more human than the paid actors. The movie paddled briskly into that swamp of fantasy and nostalgia where most American political life takes place.

The Chinese blame themselves for living in a state of perpetual artificial childhood, passively obedient to a brute authority playing stern father, but quarrelsome, jealous and conniving in their day-to-day dealings with each other. Partly, this seems true to me. The Chinese adore pointless secrecy of a grade-school kind: "I know something Teacher said, that you don't know! Na nana na na!" This secretiveness gives a Byzantine undercurrent to friendships, business deals, even courtships and marriages. Chinese warned me continually not to lay all my cards on the table. "Adults speak plain," I said, frequently disappointing them. On August 28, 1989, a boy from Hangzhou was sentenced to nine years' hard labor for telling the truth about the Tiananmen massacre. "Spreading counter-revolutionary rumors to the 'Voice of America,'" was the official name of his crime.

Children are constitutional stool pigeons. They either grow out of it and into a sense of honor, sometimes with great effort, or never become human, much less adult. The Party uses the unfortunate Chinese propensity to turn others in to save their own skin by ratting—even on parents, brothers, sisters—for political views, class secrets, dealings with counter-revolutionaries. They are then rewarded and patted on the head like good children and praised for doing their duty to the Party, putting Caesar above your father. This disgusts grown humans almost beyond endurance. It is reptilian and vile here as well as there. Minnesota is now full of "hot lines" where you can turn in your neighbors anonymously: for welfare cheating, for game poaching, or for other things. Civility leaks out of this once decent place like air out of a balloon. Ratting shrivels any possibility of human honor or of true community. Deal with injustice yourself; don't trust authority to do it for you. Authorities are not trustworthy, here or there.

After my cousin Chuck from Tucson had been in China for a few days, bicycling past gray concrete blocks of flats almost bare of furniture, with bad or nonexistent plumbing, erratic electricity, deliberate discomfort planned into the architectural scheme, he said, "It's a Lutheran Bible camp or Boy Scout camp, only the grown-ups live here all the time." He was right. As if they were suffering to "Live with Jesus" for a week, or to imitate Lord Baden-Powell and the artificial strenuous life, the world's oldest civilization seems camped in temporary quarters. One first imagines they will soon go home to their real houses with cozy stoves, old carved Chinese beds, overflowing book shelves, brilliantly colored paintings and old chipped porcelain rice bowls from great Grandmother. They won't.

This is not only poverty—the Chinese are geniuses at surviving that with grace and elegance; rather, it is Orwellian state planning to keep home as dismal and bare as possible, to purgate the body in order to force the mind to "higher things." Maybe it explains the absence of dry martinis, hot showers and private cabins at Lutheran Bible Camp.

The taste for Disney fantasy characters is children's taste. The Maoist state, playing father, guards the family morals by keeping out Western imports tainted with adult sexual life, political ideas about standing up for yourself against authority, and dangerously "free talk." Thus, Disney. A world of "loony toons," silliness and baby English rendered into baby Chinese. This is the dark view.

* * *

When you watch Chinese Disney fans viewing, also watch for the raised eyebrow. The Chinese are experienced ironists and have suffered enough to understand the double meaning of almost everything. When Minnie plays the shrew, the audience probably sees Jiang Qing. When Donald Duck gets flattened by a runaway steam roller, there is a big Party potato's head flattened under it, too. Disney offers great relief from the genuine misery and dreary tedium of so much daily life in the kingdom of *mei you*. I found myself laughing at the cartoons almost as hard as the Chinese. But I had an exit visa in my pocket. An hour's escape meant more to them than to me. I really could, when necessary, escape. American movie audiences in the thirties adored watching the idle rich playing pointless games because they saw no other escape from their own dreary lives.

Whatever else is true of Disney's work, it is brilliantly well made. The Chinese, who have watched so much high quality in their own civilization consciously destroyed, admire quality when they see it in others. In a land of kitsch, Disney is the best made kitsch possible. That is not small praise.

Finally, the love of "toons" connects to the Chinese tenderness toward children, a kind of touchstone in the Chinese soul. Though a harsh place for adults, China is a lovely place to be a child, cooed over, fondled and tended by everyone—relatives or otherwise—with great warmth and feeling. The middle class of Europe and North America regards children these days as a burden, a spur to guilt, an impediment to travel, and tries to buy itself a little free time with expensive toys. The Chinese love children in the old way. Watching the silliness of Disney "toons" as intelligent adults, they must feel some yearning back toward that warmth and safety. Part of them becomes a child again, becomes Mickey, becomes Donald. Disney "toons," from this angle, tell an unexpected truth about the Chinese soul.

* * *

I was in China in January 1987 for the drive against bourgeois liberalism that resulted in the firing of Hu Yaobang as party secretary, a dress rehearsal for the Tiananmen massacre. Hu was thought to be an enlightened man, a voice of reason. All my students admired him and feared for the future of China. We sat around looking glum in February, a glum time in chilly, gray Xi'an. The students talked about Hu's career, his belief in real progress.

One voice spoke up: "Hu was as naïve as Mickey Mouse to believe he could win against the old Long March types." Many voices chimed in to agree. After a while, we set up a whimsical and hypothetical club for foolishly hopeful idealists, "The International Association of Naïve Persons," chaired by Comrades Hu Yaobang and Mi Lao Shu. Everyone agreed to join.

"Can a Barbarian join, too?" I asked.

"Certainly," they all said, "you are the most naïve of all! We shall put you on the Central Committee of Naïve Persons!"

I signed gladly. It was almost time to fry peanuts, open Xi'an beer and turn on the television, 6:00 Sunday. Communion for the naïve.

I was not in China when Hu Yaobang died, when the mourning for him began the events that lead to that bloody morning, to the gates swinging shut on a sane China. Over Tiananmen Square, I thought I saw on television the shadow of a cartoon mouse weeping and howling in grief and rage.

MOSQUE

清真寺

China rejuvenated my passion for collecting stamps. Whenever mail arrived for me while I was in the classroom teaching, with envelopes from America, Iceland, Singapore, Sweden, or wherever, Darwin's theory of natural selection swung into action, the desk was circled by students: wolves tearing at the corpse of a moose, buzzards swarming over road kill. "My turn for the airmail! Unhand that commemorative!" At age ten or eleven, I was a little that way myself, so it amused me to watch this ferocity for new philatelic delights. When puberty arrived I retired my stamps for other interests but kept them intact and hidden in a corner of the house, intending always to resume the pleasures of the perforation gauge in old age, should I have one. FDR was my role model. I loved the pictures of Roosevelt in his wheelchair, squinting through his pince-nez at his mint Columbia Exposition set, relaxed, calm and absorbed while World War II raged about him.

Surrounded as I was by this universal Chinese passion for stamps, old age came early in Xi'an and I began going regularly to the philatelic counter of the main post office. It was a lively place, next to the old Ming bell tower, always crowded with stationery and post card peddlers, the black market currency traders and window-shopping stamp collectors. On facing walls of the fifties-era concrete building were painted huge revolutionary murals. One picture showed a handsome young Mao walking alone on a hilltop in a romantic gray light. He wears a kind of monastic gray gown and looks like a sensitive Chinese priest. On the other wall, a broadly smiling avuncular Mao sits surrounded by adoring Shaanxi peasants and their quaintly darling children. Everyone, in fact, smiles beatifically. If I had seen that picture in a Lutheran church, I might have called it "Suffer the little children . . . " I hoped the Chinese at least exercised the courtesy and good taste not to put those paintings on postage stamps.

To get through the front door, I ran the gauntlet of English practicers. If they spotted a Barbarian (fairly easy), they swooped and tried out their eighteen or nineteen-word vocabulary, usually to the great amusement of their friends and a sometimes considerable crowd of gawkers. Once or twice, this small drama amuses Barbarians, but after fifty replays most do their best to avoid it. I usually played deaf, and sometimes that worked.

One day, I leaned over the stamp counter admiring a new bird commemorative, wondering how to get the clerk's attention, when I heard a small, precise voice behind me.

"Hello. You are a foreign guest in our city? Welcome. Do you speak English? Hello? You are . . . " The voice went on, repeating its opening lines. I kept strict focus on the two *yuan* flying cranes engraved on a blue background.

"Hello. Perhaps you do not, in fact, speak English as a native language. Are you from elsewhere in Europe?" I think it was "elsewhere," "in fact," and the precise syntax that turned me around. These were not usual post office language skills.

There stood a tiny ancient man with a wispy, beard, under the quizzical face of an old temple sage. He wore a shabby black padded coat and a black skull cap perched on the crown of his almost bald head.

"I am American," I said. "A foreign teacher at a university here. Your English is quite remarkable."

"Oh, not remarkable at all." He shook his head modestly, a standard Chinese gesture of courteous self-abasement. "I learned the language fifty or sixty years ago and always enjoyed reading and conversing in it. But for the past years now, you know, it has not been so easy. I do enjoy greeting guests and welcoming them to our city. Are you American, did you say?"

"Yes."

"Have you been to London?"

"Yes."

"My teacher was an Englishman from London. He showed me many pictures of his beautiful city. Has it changed?"

"When did you see the pictures?"

"In 1930."

"It is still a beautiful city. It was bombed, you know. Some things are different now. So many cars, people from the empire."

"He left me his postcards of London. I don't suppose I will ever go there now. I am so old. . . ."

"Was he a missionary?"

"No. I am not a Christian. Are you?"

"Well, not exactly . . ." I never quite knew how to answer this question. The Chinese, particularly old ones, expected you, like the missionaries in the thirties, to be an enthusiastic Christian. It was your excuse to be in China.

"I respect Jesus very much. And his followers," he said.

"If you are not . . . "

"I am Muslim, from the Great Mosque by the Drum Tower. Have you visited our Mosque?"

"It is the loveliest place in Xi'an. I go there often."

"Yes. We are lucky it was not so damaged by . . . the troubles."

Until you knew a Chinese well, they would not utter the name, Great Proletarian Cultural Revolution, in your presence. Muslims were victims too. I heard a story that the Red Guard cut off a pig's head and took it, still bleeding, into the mosque, where they forced the old Muslim Imams to drink pig blood. Then they smeared the *Koran* with it. The story is probably true.

"So you speak and read Arabic?"

"Oh, no," he chuckled, "only the old language of the prophet. I teach the *Koran*, but only pronounce the old words. Do you mind if I ask you a question?"

He went through the classic Chinese sequence, questioning my age, marital status and number of children, looking steadily more downcast as the answers, in his view, got progressively sadder. With his papery old hand, he patted mine, assured me there was still time to find a Chinese wife and have plenty of children.

He told me he was eighty on his next birthday. Whenever I met old and intact Chinese, I thought to myself: what history and what grief they had seen and experienced since 1911. Every life was a novel, more fantastic than any by Tolkien.

"Come and visit again to our mosque. It has been a great pleasure talking to you."

The black padded coat disappeared into the milling post office crowd. I saw him often afterwards in the streets around the old mosque, but we never again had such a long talk.

Through wars, famines, pogroms, invasions, cultural revolutions, his old mosque had survived, almost intact. To get there, you walk out of modernized socialist cement into the unimproved China, low mud

122   *COMING HOME CRAZY*

houses with uneven tile roofs, courtyards, cobbled, winding, narrow streets, walk past lamb and goat butchers, calligraphy shops selling ink-stones, brushes, silk and rice paper, an old opera theater, spicy bar-becued mutton peddlers, continue under the arch of the Ming dynasty drum tower. Turn down a curving, narrow lane lined with souvenir ped-dlers, until you come to a red wood door. Open it, and you are in another world, back a thousand years or so.

In its gravy days as Chang'an, Xi'an was a world trade center, a capi-tal, the key town on the old Silk Road through central Asia. It was cos-mopolitan as no Chinese town has been since then—except possibly Hong Kong or Shanghai. A little of everything lived there—Africans, Arabs, Maronite Christians, Mongols, Buddhists, Turks, Jews. Who knows—maybe the Irish too? Anything new or strange arrived there and mixed up in a fine stew. Xi'an suffered more from the closed Chinese door than any other city. The result was a big poor farm town, a back-water, full of the ghosts of a noble history walled in by political and cul-tural xenophobia.

The surface of a modern Chinese city is a confused frenzy of the senses. Mobs, clots, swarms of people everywhere, haggling, arguing, de-bating, shouting in loud clangorous tones, walking continually, sweating, breathing garlic pickles, farting, spitting, gesticulating, the smell of sew-ers, vegetable markets, boiling oil and chilies, diesel fumes, coal fires, in-cense, burnt sugar and a cacophony of traffic, clanking machine parts, car and bicycle horns, bells, broken truck mufflers, top volume ghetto blasters, loudspeakers blaring brass band tunes. For most Barbarians, as indeed, for most Chinese, it is sometimes too much. Where is the still point in the turning chaos of this world?

The Great Mosque, for some reason unknown to me, was the only place in Xi'an with uncaged birds perching in trees, flitting from bush to bush, singing. The interior was a series of courtyards and gardens, en-closed by prayer halls, temples and Imam's quarters. A large sign in several languages told people not to spit or smoke, and this was the only place in town, maybe in China, where people seemed to obey. In other places, the signs function as ashtrays or spittoons. The gardens and rooms were scrupulously clean, the flowers and bushes watered and trimmed, the omnipresent coal dust washed off. The architecture seemed hardly Islamic, instead, old Chinese-temple style with gates lead-ing to carved gates capped by upswept tiled roofs. This mosque began in 742 A.D., less than eighty years after the Prophet's death, and the Chi-nese adapted it to local tastes. The flagstones seemed worn down by a thousand years of feet. Have they been here since Chang'an? Under a

Chinese gazebo stood old stones with lines from the *Koran* carved into them, Arabic facing Chinese. What an impenetrable wall of languages to a European! Old men in skull caps sat on their haunches around the courtyards talking quietly, praying, or just watching the birds. Almost complete silence and calm.

Whenever China was too much, I walked down that narrow, serpentine lane. When others wanted to find the Great Mosque, you often had either to take them, or trust that intuition would get them to the right turn. Many got lost and never arrived, probably for good reason. I almost always went alone and sat in the garden silently, sometimes jotting in a notebook, sometimes just breathing. I never saw crowds, winter or summer. If other Barbarians found their way there, they had need of the same silence and sat away in another corner of the garden. Inside the rooms of the mosque stood lovely antiques, carved mahogany furniture, fine calligraphy in both Arabic and Chinese, paintings, and old porcelain. But simply to sit in the garden with nothing but birds and insects for company was the best thing. Aside from bloody intrusions from Chinese history, this mosque must have been an island of silence since the eighth century. I thought of the old Imam in the post office bowing toward Allah five times a day, toward a Mecca so far away. Maybe he imagined it looked like London in 1930.

That mosque is a visible sign of what happens when something un-Chinese comes nose to nose with the steamroller of Chinese civilization. It is Chinafied, of course, and suffers the same sea-change as any foreign idea, but it gives China back the gift of the "other." That means it is always in danger, always frail, but if it lives, develops the sweetness and beauty of tiny strawberries that ripen in harsh places. I loved it better than the famous clay warriors that tourists flock to see. They are images only of megalomaniac brutality. Whatever violence is hatched in mosques in Iran, Mecca, Bradford, there is nothing but calm and loveliness here, so many light years away.

NIGHT SOIL

大粪

A Shaanxi carrot is almost red, the flavor dense and sweet beyond any American carrot I have ever eaten.

"Almost sugary," said one Barbarian, contemplating the dark carrot slice between his chopsticks.

"The night soil, I suppose," another remarked phlegmatically, pushing his bowl away.

The Chinese live more intimately with shit than we do. Conventional genteel English conspires to distance the word, but "defecate" and "fecal matter" remain more vulgar than the old simple "shit." We hide toilets inside houses, as inside language. The comfort station, the water closet, the powder room, the John, the head. It is the shithouse, and it is inside your house. You shit there. You do not see a man about a horse.

The Chinese shithouse is more direct—a hole over an open pit. Someone empties that pit periodically. The shit is carried out in pails balanced over the shoulder, then fed to wheat, to carrots, or to flowers. Noodles come back to you, a gift that returns itself forever in a circle. Nothing is lost, nothing wasted. There is a cosmic neatness in this, even if we do not want to think about it.

I grew up on a farm with pigs. When the wind blew from the southeast, my mother closed windows and cursed farms.

"Candy," my father said. "Money in the bank."

On the rare occasions when I could not escape helping clean that pighouse, I soaked for hours in the clawfoot bathtub, scrubbing my fingernails over and over, then smelling them. As either a Chinese or a Minnesota farmer will tell you, pigs are cleaner, less malodorous than humans. Minnesota wheat, like Chinese wheat, waited with trembling beards for mouthfuls of that shit. The Bread of Life.

In every Chinese town, you will find the night soil man with his mule cart and stinky barrel. His may be the oldest profession of all, and the most useful. When humans gather together in large cities, they shit vast quantities. The vegetables are fine and sweet in Shanghai, not so sugary in lightly-peopled Gansu.

If you apply an intense enough fire to your vegetables, you exterminate the bacteria that they have eaten in the field. The first sentence in every Chinese cookbook begins: "Into a very hot wok . . . " Whatever else you believe, believe that!

There are now well over one billion Chinese. Most of them eat regularly and, therefore, shit. What shall we do with this mountain if we don't give it back to the earth? Because humans breed unwisely, they must at least try to keep down the mess. Until Mao's industrialization campaigns, the Chinese did that.

Currently human messes are of a different order, more ominous. A giant oil tanker shits in Alaska. But oil, too, is refuse and the sea eats it as time goes by, just as cabbages, carrots, wheat, eat what remains of us.

COMING HOME CRAZY

OPERA
戏剧

If you were a composer of bad opera, capable of the plot of *Lucia di Lammermoor*, but not of Donizetti's music, and you were assigned to invent a title for a sort of hysterical political shindig, you would call it the Great Proletarian Cultural Revolution. As if the name were not satire enough, you would then invent operatic details: little children denouncing their parents' political opinions, huge mobs wearing Mao buttons on their lapels, shaking red Testaments under each other's noses and chanting in chorus, a whole population of intelligent people singing to each other entirely in memorized quotations of third-rate prose, full of jargon, clichés and empty abstractions. In grade school, you would begin teaching a complicated written language to children not with "See Dick run," but with "Long live the Commendatore!" You would, in the course of a decade or so, destroy the universities, the intelligentsia, the greatest art, architecture and sculpture in your history, most of your books and musical instruments, the economy, and the finest culinary tradition on the planet. Rehearse not once, but periodically, under various names and for various excuses, in case anything decent or valuable should survive. For one of the directors, hire a Chinese Lady Macbeth married to the senile composer of the score. Let her have a try at re-inventing culture from the ground up. Since you love opera, let her ban the entire thousands of years of old repertoire at once and replace it with her own purer, more correct work. Let these works have catchy titles like *The Red Detachment of Women*. It's time to open the house again. Lights! Overture! Beat the drum! Let the loudspeakers sing! Let the tanks roll!

* * *

There is an operatic quality in Chinese daily life that no book, no description prepared me for. One of my students had a long crisis of the heart with her parents, with her work unit, with her childhood conditioning to Chinese duty and obedience. She was a very pretty girl who whitened her face the color of an eggshell and fancied brilliant colors in her clothes. The whole *deus ex machina* of Chinese family and political life decided on the right husband for her and presented the poor fellow as an accomplished fact. She came to my room for advice and to wail against fate. I listened patiently and always told her what I thought: "You must follow your heart in this. But do it sensibly, bruising as few egos as possible." I sounded like a cross between *Redbook* and a kindly grandfather. Her eggshell face darkened as she walked into a shadowy corner of the room. She struck her forehead with the back of her hand, tilted her head backward and held the blocking.

"There is no way out. It is all too terrible; I am lost." And now with an even grander sweep of the arm, "Life is meaningless!" A pause for breath — maybe applause, "Or don't you think so?" Then, as a little coda, or maybe a bridge to the next scene, "You must tell no one of this. They would laugh and use it against me." There was not a trace of dissembling or insincerity in this performance. It was not an act, but a world view. She rehearsed it again and again. Maria Callas would not have been ashamed to add this aria to her repertoire.

* * *

I often thought, looking at Chinese life, that the country was geographically misplaced in Asia. It ought to have been a peninsula shaped like a boot stepping into the Mediterranean. Only my Euro-centered world view. A Chinese saw the mirror image of this, probably imagined Milan a city just north of Shanghai.

An operatic culture is Manichaean, every choice a matter of life and death, from buying vegetables to having a revolution. Bargaining in the market is a duet with cabeletta, the chorus echoing the lines, offering commentary and solace.

"That is a ridiculous chicken!"

"It is a fine fat hen, my daughter's pet!"

"Three *kwai*, not a *fen* more!"

"Don't be silly. That chicken is worth six!"

The tonal, sung quality of the Chinese language puts exclamation points at the ends of even simple sentences. "Where is the toilet!" A bargaining, as Aristotle demanded of the drama, has a beginning, a middle, and an end. It offers catharsis, sometimes tragic: "Oh woe! I have been cheated!" Nothing happens singly in a well-made bargain; the *da capo* form prevails. Always refuse food at table, or a proffered cigarette, or more hot water for the tea. Do so three times. Have faith, the tune will come round again and you will eat, smoke and have a second infusion of the leaves. Even bribes are offered three times, melodically and formally: "These Marlboros . . . "

There is also a quality of tragic opera in large movements of Chinese history: Medea murdering her children, Tristan and Isolde defying the king and dying for love, Manon going into exile (it would be Qinghai rather than America), Chinese cadre Scarpias rigging Cavaradossi's execution and slavering over Tosca. An operatic culture seems spontaneous on the surface but rehearses all its movements, gestures, speeches, massacres unconsciously through every day of its history. It knows what it is going to do because it is living out a form, a *convenienze*, as Verdi used to say.

* * *

The state television broadcast Peking operas almost daily in 1987. These operas are long, brilliantly costumed, loud, melodramatic, acted in broad stylized gestures and interminably shrieky and tedious to most Western tastes. But so are *La Sonambula*, or *Turandot*, or *Götterdämmerung* to Barbarian fanciers of Mantovani, Johnny Cash, or Barry Manilow. Young Chinese, like young Barbarians, thought opera old fogey music and preferred "Disco."

"I am an old fogey," I said to them. "Where can I go to the opera?"

"You will not understand what is going on," they countered.

"So much the better. *Lucia* should never be translated, and sensible people should not learn Italian for fear they might understand it."

Opera theaters reopened after the Cultural Revolution with their old repertoire and at least some of their old musicians. The greatest Chinese opera diva, almost destroyed in the holocaust, was still alive, her sad autobiography a local best seller. I found a couple of opera theaters in Xi'an. They were in old neighborhoods and were patronized by old Chinese farmers and workers who had waited patiently for Jiang Qing to finish with her cultural tantrums, for *The Red Detachment of Women* and its cousins to sink under the murky waters of the Yellow River, and for the real fun to start again. Chinese opera, whether Peking, Sichuan, Shaanxi, or any other school or style, is after all fun before it is anything else. Of course it is exaggerated, melodramatic and noisy. Do you want a refined and quietly elegant circus? Chinese opera remains, after its political bludgeoning, a live art form. The audience cheers, boos, eats, smokes, spits, sighs, weeps, faints, guffaws and hums along. The Chinese, practical to a fault, do not buy tickets unless they plan to be amused. The orchestra, with its drums, gongs, bells, two-stringed violins, dulcimers, lutes, zithers, pan pipes, blasty horns, reed flutes and a few Western instruments thrown in to swell the cacophony, is a noisy prospect. The singers rise to the occasion both in pitch and volume. If you want to be soothed, stay home. This is China, the Asian Italy, not the home of the almost silent Japanese theater that Yeats fancied.

* * *

There are at least three operatic occasions in your own life: birth, marriage, and death. I don't know anything about the Chinese delivery room, but they have obviously rehearsed. There are, after all, 1,200,000,000 of them. Marriage is a noisy party. The Chinese orchestra plays loud, the bride wears red, you shoot firecrackers, everyone eats "full to death" and there is a parade. A funeral is a noisy party. The Chinese orchestra plays loud, the mourners wear white, carry white wreaths, the guest of honor, when not cremated, rides in a gaily carved and painted coffin, you shoot firecrackers, everyone eats "full to death," wails and sings dramatically, and there is a big parade, ending in a bonfire where you burn paper money.

In America these natural occasions are as operatic, as full of melodrama as in China, but we go at them like constipated Puritans with the brakes on, with pursed lips. William Carlos Williams wanted to teach Americans to perform a funeral, but they didn't listen—"I will teach you my townspeople/how to perform a funeral . . . "

It is no accident we had to wait for *Porgy and Bess* to get a real American opera. Yet most Americans listen to it under the mistaken notion it is something else—a Broadway musical maybe. Scott Joplin tried to make American opera out of black life and music much earlier, but no one was listening. He was on the right track: the misery, irony and occasional grandeur of black life will hatch true operatic gestures on this continent. We will not invent moving arias about fixing the Volvo, or shopping at Saks. Philip Glass is to opera what Velveeta is to cheese.

* * *

I gave piano lessons to a brilliant and charming nine-year-old boy whose father worked as a teacher at the provincial opera high school.

Mr. Hou composed and orchestrated opera music and had begun monkeying around writing twelve-tone pieces. Once I came to give a lesson, and he told me that a new production of a local opera with his orchestrations and some of his tunes was set to go in a few days — famous singers, a gala night. I accepted his invitation gleefully, and also got tickets for my friend, Marcy, my musician cousin, Chuck, from Tucson, Arizona, and a handful of students who thought they could endure a single night of boredom for the pleasure of watching me watch. We arrived early, were escorted backstage where we met the orchestra having their last smoke before the overture. We also met the director and, best of all, saw the stars — already in their costumes and dead-white makeup, doing their last primping. The director gave final instructions on fan holding to the two female leads: how to fold the fan into the giant sweeping sleeves of the costumes, then expose it suddenly. Either their hands were naturally pale, or they too were made up dead-white so the audience could follow the expression in the fingers. Their gorgeous silk and brocade costumes in brilliant colors were embroidered with dragons and exotic birds in gold and silver thread. They wore huge hats twice the size of a head and opera boots with square three or four-inch soles to give them height, majesty and the characteristic shuffling opera walk. I had no idea whether these wonderful creatures were human beings or not. They might have been Jussi Björling and Zinka Milanov in those costumes! The opera was everything an opera should be: grand, stylized, a frontal assault on the emotions — good and evil grappling tunefully (to a Chinese ear). There was a plot but you don't want to know it. Remember *Lucia* . . .

* * *

When I came back to China the next Christmas, Mr. Hou asked me to give a lecture on Western music to his opera school students. I gladly did so. I played Bach and Liszt and Brahms, sang a couple of old German chorales, "*Una Furtiva Lagrima*" (Caruso's old plum), and an aria from *Die Zauberflöte*, and played the Scott Joplin finale from *Treemonisha*. I explained my theory on the universality of the operatic impulse (without taking the metaphor into politics as I do here) and finished by giving my idea about contrary motion in Western music and what it reveals, by contrast, about the differences between the two cultures.

When you are taught to compose in the West, you begin with a bass line, a harmonic foundation that moves and, if it is any good, is a real tune. The melody and all the other voices you invent must move in contrary motion to the bass and to each other. They must be completely independent in themselves but simultaneously good tunes when played one at a time. Music like this is structured, precise, orderly and, if there is any quality to it, the bull-headed independent voices all sing together to make an harmonic whole without sacrificing their linear individuality. Take any single voice from any piece by Bach and play it yourself with one finger. You will see what I mean.

A Chinese orchestra, on the other hand, moves in parallel sliding motion. All the instruments, from bass to treble, double the tune, sometimes in unison, sometimes in chords. A singer or any instrument may embroider a melody, but all players keep the general form of the line. What you hear is one line with a rhythm, either solo or en masse. Debussy liked this effect and introduced it into French music. One manner of conceiving movement inside music is not superior to another, but they are exact opposites.

At the end, I asked these bright-eyed Chinese teenagers if they had any questions. They asked about dating habits, the price of Levis, the status of "Disco" and wanted me to sing their two favorite Christmas songs: "Jingle Bells" and "Rudolph the Red-nosed Reindeer." Then they presented me with a pair of pastel polyester puppy dogs in a plastic box, and sang for me the same two songs in Chinese. As Gertrude Stein might have said, "A teenager is a teenager is a teenager."

But not quite. They invited Marcy and me to a return party at the school where they would have a chance to perform for us. We arrived just at dark to a cold, paint-peeling concrete hall lit by a few bare light bulbs. Chairs and tables were shoved against the wall, orange soda and melon seeds distributed, a piano badly in need of tuning wheeled in. What followed was one of the most amazing nights I spent in China. Those children, from ten to eighteen years old, were not simply talented, they were a Swiss bank full of genius. A beautiful fifteen-year old played a solo on the *pipa*, a Chinese lute, her long black hair falling over the strings as she plucked. One of my students from Inner Mongolia sang a herder's song with the bleating of sheep and ringing of bells in his voice. Two children, no older than eleven or twelve, acted out a whole comic opera scene playing tiger and prey. They were in full costume, singing at the tops of their lungs, and so funny I almost collapsed laughing in a language I couldn't understand. The whole student orchestra played opera tunes and dances. The school's *erhu* teacher played first a heartrending Blind Ai Bing tune and then, for an encore, the old salon favorite for four-stringed violin, Gossec's "Minuet in D," on a two-stringed *banhu* with great style and humor. Xiao Hou, my nine-year-old piano student got up and, feet dangling above the pedals, ripped off one movement of a Mozart sonata and a Bach invention. He imitated his Barbarian teacher by crossing his small legs at the keyboard, smiling wickedly at me as he played. I finished the evening with Scott Joplin and "tears full of my eyes . . . " Chinese opera is safe for one more generation, no matter what the tanks did in Tiananmen!

* * *

China seemed sometimes to me like a stuck recording of the mad scene in *Lucia*, trills and arpeggios and broken lives, over and over and over. As much as I love opera with its grand gestures and fits of feeling, the black-hearted villains and noble heroines that live inside it, countries oughtn't be governed that way. The sober tradition of the Lutheran chorale, with the stubborn independence of the voice leading and its slow placid surface, is probably a better model. But something in me wants to make the texture of daily life in America more operatic in sane ways: more passion, more color, more music, more life. My favorite store in Xi'an was the opera shop where you could buy (for a pittance in dollars), the magnificent embroidered robes, masks, helmets, boots, swords, wigs and mustaches. If I thought dressing up the local Scandinavians in those costumes would do it, I'd open a shop tomorrow and give them away.

PAPERS, PLEASE
请交文件

In China, I always traveled with a full pocket. I carried a white card with my photograph on it that entitled me to spend local money; I carried a brown work-unit card with a photograph that entitled me to the Chinese price for train tickets and admission into the gate of the university where I taught; I carried a green card, ditto photo, that enabled me to travel internally, stay in hotels and amuse police officers. Sometimes I was asked for my American passport, so I frequently carried that, too, and sometimes I had special letters in both Chinese and English from the *Waiban*, the foreign office (or as the Chinese understand it, "Barbarian Handler's Office") with red official seals stamped all over, further attesting to the certainty of my identity as myself and establishing almost, though not entirely beyond question, the legality of doing whatever it was I was doing or being at whatever place I was at. My pocket had nice wear from folding and unfolding these documents for ticket sellers, policemen, office functionaries, bankers, store clerks, keepers of gate keys, and, in general, anyone with a uniform or anyone who claimed to be an official who demanded to see them for whatever purpose.

This seemed more pointless, laborious and irritating to me than to my Chinese comrades, who were used to it. They carry the Chinese version of the same documents stamped with an equal number of official seals, and in addition carry a marriage license in case they want to stay at a hotel with their own spouse. The Chinese are used to folding and unfolding documents and to establishing their personal existence, their identity and their authorization on demand, daily, sometimes hourly if they are active. The discomfiture of foreigners, particularly Americans with their slow adjustment to the fact of this process, amuses the Chi-

COMING HOME CRAZY

nese. Documents are life, as they know from longer experience than we can imagine.

"America is not all peaches and cream," I would tell them when they asked, as they continually did. "It is neither so elegant and rich, nor so rapacious and mean-spirited as you have been told or have imagined.

"For instance, I do not miss cheese, my Chevrolet, clean toilets to sit on, soft toilet paper or the *New York Times*, but I do miss the pleasure of telling bureaucrats who gratuitously demand that I establish my identity with paper into which part of their body they might, with my kindest good wishes, file that demand. In America," I said over and again — with just the smallest trace of self-righteousness in my voice, "you travel wherever you please, stay at whatever hotel you like or can afford, do whatever work you wish that someone is willing to pay you for, and it is none of the police's or the state's damn business.

"I am forty-three years old," I added smugly, "and aside from a trip to East Germany, a couple of traffic tickets that required a driver's license, and the usual presentation of a passport to a customs man, I have never shown papers to a soul.

"Americans," I said, voice rising in patriotic crescendo, "do not carry papers. Indeed, most Americans couldn't even find them at the bottom of the dead-relative-photograph drawer, if a bureaucrat were silly or rude enough to ask for them."

"It must be a wonderful country," my Chinese comrades said with envious voices.

"Yes," I sighed, "that is the way it is."

I came back to Minnesota in August to start my old job, teaching English at a state college in Marshall. I ate my first pizza, fired up the rusty Chevy, bought a bag of lemons and a *People* magazine, paid bills by check, dialed long-distance on a mostly functioning telephone and, in general, had a fast re-acculturation before entering the classroom.

I started school on Monday and found a memo informing me that I needed to change my health insurance from fully "Aware" to partly "Aware" and to sign a few other odds and ends before getting my paycheck. I arrived at the personnel office, enrolled my teeth in Delta Dental, left a deposit slip for the Minneota bank and was about to leave when I heard a voice ask for my driver's license. I dropped it in front of the clerk and resumed smoking.

"And your Social Security card."

"The number is right there in front of you on the health insurance form."

"I have to see the card. The original."

"You have to see my Social Security card? What in God's name for?"

"The immigration form."

"But I'm not immigrating anywhere. I'm already here."

"A birth certificate will do."

"Lost it when I got my last passport."

"A passport is fine, too."

"Do I understand this correctly? You are asking to see my passport inside the United States?"

"Yes, indeed."

"You may not do so, now or at any time in the future."

"Then you won't get paid. It's federal law."

"Are we in the United States now?"

"What a silly question! We're in Marshall, Minnesota."

"Show me the form."

The woman handed me xeroxed page 8795 from the Federal Register, "Employment Eligibility Verification," Form 1–9 (03/06/87) from the U.S. Department of Justice. It indeed demanded that I produce the required identification—in her presence. She was, like every Chinese bureaucrat I met, "only doing my job" in asking for my papers and documents.

"This," I said, "is a piece of shit, and you may see nothing. I refuse either to sign it or have it signed without my consent."

"Then you won't be paid."

"I signed my contract, and it did not require me to produce my papers. I'll continue teaching anyway, thank you."

"You will not be paid."

"So be it."

"Everyone has to sign the form—all new employees. It's federal law. No one else complained."

"Somebody's got to be first. If I signed that form, then in ten years we'll have national identity cards carried by your own children, keyed to a federal computer. Any policeman or bureaucrat will be legally able to demand that you prove you are who, indeed, you say you are."

"You won't get paid."

"I'm too fat anyway. By the way, this is still the United States, isn't it? We haven't been annexed as a new Chinese province?"

"Just remember, you don't get paid."

No pay . . . the great American threat, before which our good sense and courage always crumble. No house payment . . . no tenure . . . no trip . . . no car . . . no salary . . . no honor . . . maybe honor lives someplace else . . .

A Chinese bureaucrat in the same situation would offer us different

136

choices: first, thought examination and self-criticism; then, Xinjiang, Qinghai, the pig yard, the night soil bucket, no marriage, no university, a bullet in the back of the head and a bill to your family for two *yuan* for wasted ammunition from the public arsenal.

No papers, no pay. It's an interesting equation, and I think it has not surfaced before in Minnesota. Neither of my Icelandic grandfathers, for instance, had papers enough to work in Marshall, and if you're an old Minnesotan, it's unlikely that your grandfathers did, either. Viking wet-backs, they were.

Though Section 1324A, Title 8, of the U.S. Immigration Code was passed by Congress during my non-newspaper-reading absence in central China, it doesn't take much thinking to figure out its rationale: it is intended, to use the vulgar cliché, to "stem the flood" of illegal Mexican labor. It also doesn't take much intelligence to figure out that if you're a Mexican laborer in southern California and know you have to sign this silly form, you will promptly dummy up an "original" Social Security card and a driver's license or birth certificate. Meanwhile, imagine Enrique Lopez, whose family has been in California since before Plymouth Rock, being abused by an officious bureaucrat because, like the rest of us, his "original" Social Security card disappeared down his Maytag twenty-five years ago. Visualize this. And then visualize the Senate debate on this legislation. As Mark Twain said, the true native American criminal class must certainly be Congress, and its behavior in this case is a nice mixture of hypocrisy, cowardice and thoughtlessness.

A friend, after hearing me in high dudgeon and confessing that he had himself signed such a form with silent misgivings, suggested that I might be more sensitive to such issues because of my recent return from China. If this is true, it is a harsh and sad comment both about me and about American citizens generally. If we have to spend a year in an authoritarian country producing papers on demand before we become sensitized to the moral and political dangers of Section 1324A, then we are already a nation of slaves, passive and agreeable, ready for Orwell's eternal "boot in the human face."

Walt Whitman, our great poet of human liberty, warned us that if we ever start producing papers and carrying cards, then we are lost. The bill won't be repealed, either in our lifetime or in our grandchildren's. Ask the Chinese about identity cards. See if they enjoy them. Then listen to Whitman:

> To the States or any one of them [even Minnesota],
>   or any city of the States

[even Marshall]: *Resist much, obey little.*
Once unquestioning obedience, once fully enslaved,
Once fully enslaved, no nation, state, city of this earth, ever
    afterward resumes its liberty.

Let it not be said of us in another century that we became our own slave masters.

PASTORALE

田园曲

It is the Ides of March, a Sunday, 1987. I am not in Rome waiting for
Caesar's assassination but in Xi'an waiting for spring. The last two weeks
have been cold and raw, gray snow slushing down through a gray sky.
Inside my gray room in a gray cement building, the gray steam-heat pipe
which at its best is not at its best, is, to use the most popular Chinese
word, *mei you* (not have). The ten Barbarian teachers are chilled, cheese-
less and crabby. They suffer from the Chinese version of cabin fever.

We decide to go to the country. From the university garage we book
the banana-yellow mini-bus with the bucktoothed driver and, at 10:00
a.m., we are off. Xiao Zhang, the guest house English factotum and skid
greaser, is our native guide and interpreter.

Chinese Sunday traffic is movement without system. The police, in
crisp green uniforms with white gloves, conduct the traffic, but the orchestra ignores them, playing in its own key, in its own sweet rhythm.
Like any philharmonic, it is in sections — the bass tractor, the tenor tractor, the soprano tractor, all unmuffled and unmuted, four mule carts in
sequence, a chorus of pedicabs, the contrabass accordion buses and a
full chorus of bicycles, rattling along at a majestic *largo*. The Banana
threads slowly through this maze to the edge of town where we find ourselves following an enormous shiny black limousine with silk curtains,
polished wood interior and a uniformed chauffeur. I think at first it's an
old forties Cadillac miraculously preserved.

"What is it?" I ask Xiao Zhang.

"*Hong Qi*," he says, a "Red Flag," probably on its way to Shaanxi
Guest House with a big potato." We follow it.

"Is that a socialist car?" I ask. No answer.

The Shaanxi Guest House is a walled pavilion, ten or fifteen miles into the countryside. Zhou Enlai had a room there. Reagan and the Queen of England stayed there. The *Hong Qi* glides unquestioned past two green police guards. Inside the gates, we see palms, manicured gardens, curving drives. We are not allowed in—no permission. Irene from Louisiana wants to use the bathroom at the gate house. The guard refuses. We drive on to our first stop.

We stop at a little market town to buy peanuts, fruit, and beer for a picnic. The one village street is packed, old men in black pajamas peddling tobacco and chilies, old ladies with bound feet weighing out cauliflowers, hay wagons pulled by mules moving through the crowd, a brace of pig trotters hanging from a clothesline by a hook, children mobbed around a TV blaring out a Kung Fu movie, two scraggly looking white goats nursing from a bored nanny by the roadside.

Andrew, the British engineer, looks at a pair of sunglasses at a street stall. "Fifty *kwai*," the old man says without smiling. Fifty *kwai* is the equivalent of a month's salary. He can't tell an Englishman from an oil sheik, and, in this town, has probably never seen a Barbarian before. Andrew resists buying. The apples were wormy, the peanuts soggy, the beer warm. We are the main attraction. Off to the temple.

The Grass Palace Temple sits, as its name says, in the middle of a lush meadow. A ten-ton bell covered with ancient Chinese characters stands just inside the gate. When they arrived from across the Himalayas, translators brought the first Buddhist texts to this temple. These texts became the first, and so far, the only foreign idea to fertilize and energize China. I do not forget Marx. The ten of us are probably part of some second idea.

After months in a city, the Barbarians are stir-crazy. A bicycle in China will take you any place in town, but town is, after all, still town, more of what your body longs to escape. Here at the temple, though, grass is not merely grass, and every flowering crab owns a private soul, including the just-blooming one inside the temple gates. Above its pink blossoms, jagged crags surround us. We have stumbled into a Chinese painting. We reached the end of the plains and didn't know it, our city eye still dodging night-soil wagons and crowds of gawkers. *Mei you* that, here in this green meadow.

The temple building is only a few hundred years old, new in Chinese terms, and, after the Cultural Revolution, active again. Gray-robed monks wander here and there lighting incense, banging gongs, tending their wheat, cabbage and rape garden, now and then kowtowing to the red and gold Bodhisattva. A Buddhist temple with its gaiety, color and whimsy is to a Chinese cement building as a Spanish Baroque cathedral is to a Dutch Reformed country church. Six months of China are enough to drive any Puritan asceticism out of you. You want color, light, pageant, excess. No more gray, not ever again on this planet! If you are going to live at all, live beautifully.

We drive up into the mountains, arriving finally at a muddy parking lot on a low slope of Wutai Shan (Five Terrace Mountain). Spring is here, too, and the mountain lives up to its name. Wearing new spring wheat, it looks like a five-layered pistachio cake. We walk through a stone gate; below us is a small gorge of white stones with a waterfall. Though a little dehydrated after a dry winter on the higher slopes, it still tumbles downward in three or four leaps. Like so many Chinese "good view scenes," this one does not overwhelm with its sublimity an American used to Yosemite, Yellowstone or Alaska, but it is sweet and necessary and well arranged.

The white stones in the half-dry river bed gather the heat and warm our bodies as we lie picnicking and lazing in the sun. Irene falls into the river and soaks her socks. Bill splits the crotch on his threadbare corduroys while crawling up a rock. Irene eats mutton sandwiches. Earlene celebrates with the last can of tuna fish for ten thousand miles. Yuki (ever a patriotic Japanese), dines on rice balls with miso and seaweed. The Brits, Andrew, Min and Simon, are into beer, boiled eggs, and Chinese potato chips. We exchange food, pass beer bottles and tea cups, tell stories, laugh, congratulate each other on the weather and our escape from town. A few Chinese locals give us an eye and pass on to the higher slopes.

The next hill is pink with flowering crabs. Up a hundred feet, white crêpe wreaths rot away on gravestones in the village burial ground. The air is full of birds again. Little girls in orange and pink jackets pick herbs on the slope leading to the river. The water gurgles dependably. It is Sunday, and we have all been to church (albeit Buddhist), have gotten into the habit of praise again, and are now having communion — the true Eucharist of human joy.

On the way out, a young girl stands at the gate collecting money. We missed her on the way in — nap time. "Twenty *kwai*," she says to Xiao Zhang, "for the Barbarians."

"Are you crazy?" he asks. "How much for me?"

"Two *jiao*," she says. That is one-tenth of two *kwai*.

"Does a Barbarian breathe ten times as much air as a Chinese?" he asks her.

There is a flurry of acrimonious argument in Chinese, much shouting and gesticulating, always more exciting in a tonal language. He finally throws her two *kwai*, and we troop behind him to the banana bus. We have arrived back in the city early, without ever leaving the waterfall. Church is over.

PIG

猪

In China, if you have not eaten pig, you have not eaten. Many an innocent vegetarian has ordered a wokful of vegetables, eaten them thinking
them uncommonly tasty and never dreamt they were fried in lard, the
favorite Chinese cooking grease.

If you travel in the Chinese countryside, you share the road with
pigs as well as humans; live pigs being driven to market, butchered pigs
carted home, aimless pigs foraging in the ditches. I once saw a farmer
carrying two grown live pigs lashed together over the back of a bicycle.
They balanced each other, presumably.

Chinese pigs are not the graceful long, lean, low-cholesterol modern
hybrid hogs of western Minnesota. They are lard hogs, heavy-bellied
snufflers. When they arrive at a market on the back of a bicycle cart
(pedicab), Chinese housewives swarm to get the fat pieces. When I
bought pork, I asked the farmer to trim. He did so without complaint but
thought I was crazy. "No fat, no good," he would say. Pure lard sold for
almost the same price as pork.

The cooks in Sichuan rival black cooks in the south for using every
part of the pig but the squeal. In the genius cuisines of the world, nothing is wasted. The unlikeliest parts are made magnificent; there is a sense
of neatness and economy in the use of ingredients. Ingenious cooking
is a fruit of poverty, not of munificence. Witness the tasteless and un-
imaginative cooking of most Americans, residents of the richest agricultural land on the planet. Give a Sichuan cook the garbage from an
American suburb, and he will construct an emperor's banquet. In the
mountains of Jiuzhaigou in western China, I ate a first course of cold pig
ears, pig stomachs, pig balls, pig heart and pig kidney all spiced in prickly
ash. It was wonderful. In America, it would have been dog food, or a hot

dog. Among America's poor, only blacks have managed, like the Chinese, to eat brilliantly.

Behind the building where I slept in Xi'an was a farm commune. It was hidden from view by a Chinese wall, but walls do not stop sound. For my first few months, I was awakened at night by what I thought were gun shots followed by a foul burnt smell. I thought it was the local execution grounds. To begin with, I didn't know how to ask, but after a while I did. The commune slaughtered pigs during the day, burnt bristles off hides all night. The noise was hog bristles exploding. In the mornings, the alley behind the dormitory frequently ran with pig blood. I walked through it on my way to teach, leaving footprints under the sycamores all the way to the classroom.

The real execution grounds were on the west side of town, well away from the universities. Later, I heard the noise from them. It sounded like exploding hair bristles.

When my students found that I fancied pigs, too, they began bringing me presents to decorate my little flat. I got a plastic pig pencil sharpener, a couple of fine pottery banks, posters of Pig from *The Monkey King,* a pig mask with movable ears and mouth, a black, quilted pig made by local peasants, a gingerbread pig, and a set of little porcelain pigs playing Chinese musical instruments. It was like having a tiny farm of my own in that concrete room. At night, as I lay listening to the exploding bristles, I looked around at my artificial pigs in the dim light. I did not expect them to move. They didn't.

QIGONG

气功

On rare mornings, usually in fall, tail ends of the south China monsoons gasped over the Qin Ling mountains and dropped their last few hysterical buckets of rain on the courtyard below my apartment window. On all other mornings at eight, whatever the weather or occasion, an old wooden speaker, hung by chicken wire from a second floor balcony, started scratchily playing its familiar 4/4 jingling tune. I never learned the name of the tune, and, for the year I lived there, it never varied. It was an ordinary Chinese tune, in ordinary ambling tempo. It signaled the beginning of neighborhood geriatric exercise in the parking lot.

Between twenty and thirty people arrived, some on foot, some on bicycle, most wearing old-fashioned gray or blue padded jackets, baggy pants, and black cloth shoes. I knew they were very old by their unashamed silver hair. I learned one Chinese state secret in that year. The great Chinese vanity is black hair. Hair dye sold briskly even during the darkest stretches of the Great Proletarian Cultural Revolution. Until the proper time, the Chinese defeat nature with art and keep their hair black. Even Mao did. When my students guessed my age, they first tried sixty-two, because of my gray beard.

"Forty-four," I said.

"You are too young to be so old," they commiserated. "Maybe we can help you buy some hair dye." If these thirty in the courtyard had let their manes go silver, they were at least seventy, many probably eighty or over.

I climbed out the window onto the flat concrete roof over the courtyard, an invisible spy with a zoom lens, and watched. The neighborhood ancients visited a little, swung their arms and, when the tune came around to a cadence, arranged themselves in rows four or five feet apart to begin. They moved in unison, not like dancers, but like normal, though decently agile, people connected to their physical bodies. The movements were neither quick, nor did they defy gravity. They were liquid rather than athletic, without frenzy or violence. One old lady with snowy hair clipped short was particularly beautiful and graceful, her face, calm and serene as a carved Buddha's on a cliff wall, her agile body and easy movements contradicting evidence that she was well over seventy. She might have been the Chinese Martha Graham, but her shabby clothes and residence in this block said she was someone's grandmother from a farm or a factory. Whatever she was, I more than half fell in love with her wonderful face and graceful body and admired her like a rooftop knight errant.

They began with a counting exercise — *yi, er, san, si* (one, two, three, four), and when they felt their bones limbering, commenced with the real business. They "greeted the sun," "clasped the sword," and "turned as slowly as a mill wheel pulled around by a half asleep mule." Their limbs didn't fight the air; they became part of it. They were "flying cranes"; "they bent to get a pearl at the bottom of the sea"; "they stroked the horse's mane." Chinese taste in exercise and dance, as in landscape description, is metaphorical and narrative rather than scientific or historical. In any form of *Qigong* or *Taichi*, you tell a story and make images with your body and your breathing. You don't tone up your pectorals or get the fat off those thighs. You do this not so much because it will make you firm or sexually attractive or able to go on making money in the investment business until the next heart attack, but to come into harmony with the earth, the air, your own body, the universe — not to improve and grow (two favorite American words), but to melt into balance with the big WHAT IS.

When Chinese tourists travel to mountains and caves, they want fanciful resemblances and fantastic stories. That mountain is an old man leaning on a long staff as he meets a wolf. That is the princess's face on the cliff, the waterfall her tears. Chinese tourists do not inquire after geology. Upthrust, overthrust and the foibles of the last Ice Age do not interest them. "But when the great Dragon carved out this river valley with his tail . . . " The Four Modernizations may be a long time coming; part of me wants to head them off at the pass.

Judging by the evidence of that handful of ancient exercisers, the Chinese age more elegantly than Barbarians. Those were not the arthritic, gouty bodies of most American old. They walked and moved with buoyant spring. Their muscles still obeyed. They were impeccably skinny and that helped. Whenever I looked at them, I felt my own stomach bulge. I thought of the popped shirt buttons on middle-aged men, the flabby limbs of elderly ladies eating brownies and lemon bars at bridge clubs and coffee parties. Chinese history and economics have, of course, helped to keep them trim. Those flying cranes in the courtyard lived through the age of warlords, the Japanese invasion and occupation, the civil war (with massive inflation and famine), Mao's Great Leap Forward and Great Proletarian Cultural Revolution (both occasions for mass starvation), endemic poverty, and more public violence than we can imagine. Yet here they are, lucky, tough survivors, lean and limber at the end, with enough memories and close calls to fill novels the size of Tolstoy's. *Yi, er, san, si* . . . embrace the moon rising through the branches.

One morning on my rooftop perch, the same scratchy tune they played began to irritate me. I had been a month or two in China without pianos, libraries, book shops, or public radio, feeling smothered by a language and civilization in which not only was I unsophisticated, I was a retarded baby. I missed the grand ideas and works of art that held up my own mental pilings. I got my Chinese cassette player and one of the dozen of my touchstone tapes that I had smuggled into China — Bach's cantata "*Wachet Auf, Ruft Uns die Stimme!*" ("Wake up! cries to us the voice of the watchman high up in the tower.") I turned it on, trying to defeat psychically — if not physically — the morning *Qigong* music. The piece begins with an immense surging of dotted rhythms in complex counterpoint and a series of grindingly dissonant suspensions. Perhaps no piece of Western music contains more mental and physical energy, precise, mathematical, completely ordered, with a powerful but calm surface. All the energy is inside the music itself. Whatever inside you does not obey external orders, join groups, or make do, stands up to be counted in the presence of this music. The count leaps directly from one to the infinite universe. Two do not care and share together inside Bach. I am aware that this is music composed for a public Lutheran service, but Bach and I know better. So does Robert Bly who said:

> There is someone inside this music
> who is not well described by the names
> of Jesus, or Jehovah, or the Lord of Hosts!

This is not music that ought to be permitted inside dictatorships, of the proletariat or otherwise, because its interior message is this: because I am a human and I have imagined this music, this energy, then you are a human too and need never be bullied by fools or power again. All they can do is kill you, and now you are awake so it doesn't make any difference. Kill them first.

It was not good music for morning exercise, and my little experiment in rooftop counterpoint was disturbing the flies and crickets, so I clicked off the knob. The silver-haired lady was reaching for a pearl at the bottom of the sea, her old body bent as lithely as a teenager's. I was not sure for a minute which was the true civilization: the sweet calm melding with the impervious Qi of the universe, or the coiled energy of, "one at a time," me and the gods, inside Bach. They were two things. They lived on the same planet. Both trailed wars and blood stains behind them.

At the end of the session, everyone relaxed for a few minutes, smoking and visiting, then went off to their morning labors, monitoring phones, guarding gates, tending grandchildren. Walking away, they looked more like gray-haired adolescents than like candidates for the misery of an American nursing home. Should we spend more of our lives as flying cranes, reaching for the sun, stroking the manes of invisible horses?

RED RIVER VALLEY

红河谷

Every morning in China, I woke at 6:30 to "The East Is Red" played soothingly by a loudspeaker stuck up in the courtyard behind my room. After that, exercise music, then silence until Sleepy, the sturdy but lethargic young man who made a pretense at vacuuming my floor, shuffled down the hall an hour or two later, always whistling or humming the same rather pretty, four-square melody. I had heard it often before on Chinese tuneboxes. "What is it?" I asked.

"New Chinese song . . . " said Sleepy. "Very beautiful. Can't translate the words. . . ."

One of my students could. The song came out of China's interminable border war with Vietnam. A husband, leaving to protect China against the Vietnamese threat, says to his wife that she should always think of his bravely shed blood when she sees the red star flag fluttering in the wind. In the next verse, the patriotic wife does just that, expressing her gratitude to her dead husband for saving the Fatherland and the red flag. The song was popularized by a local singer. He'd had a leg blown off in Vietnam and was trotted out everywhere by the army to croon the song in his best Dennis Day tenor, empty pant leg fluttering patriotically as the red flag. The Chinese did what the Chinese always do in the face of propaganda. They liked the tune, so they hummed it, paying scant attention to the bloodthirsty words.

Music followed you everywhere in China: old men singing opera tunes on street corners, teenagers bumping along to disco, riders in an overcrowded bus singing humorous songs to take their minds off the miseries of travel. The state loudspeakers with their gravelly, mechanical voices chimed in, but the Chinese preferred live human music.

At the endless rounds of parties and banquets that the Chinese loved so much, Barbarians were expected to sing the songs of their own country, solo! After the chairs were pushed back against the wall, and watermelon and pumpkin seeds, hard candy and orange soda passed out, the Barbarians were introduced to a great flurry of delighted applause. Now what?

No trouble for me. I sang Bach chorales, Joe Hill labor songs, and operatic arias, but singing frequently struck other Americans with terror. Americans don't often sing to each other sober and don't burst into spontaneous a cappella song on public occasions. The Chinese do, and our embarrassment puzzles them.

My Chinese students knew more American songs, both words and music, than most Americans, but their skewed information systems gave them an odd idea of what was popular: "Auld Lang Syne," "Old Black Joe," "Jingle Bells," "Sounds of Silence," "Rocky Mountain High," "Swing Low, Sweet Chariot," and their favorite of all, "Red River Valley."

"Do not all American youth love the beautiful 'Red River Valley'? " they asked.

"Maybe their grandmothers did," I said sadly.

In addition, they knew all these songs in Chinese translation. I heard nothing more bizarre than a Chinese disco version of "Jingle Bells" blaring out of a loudspeaker on a blistering day in mid-July.

In the spring semester, I went on a small trip with some students. Wang Xiao was a Gansu girl from the next province west, the Chinese equivalent of Wyoming. She wanted to visit a school friend who had just come back from six months as an exchange teacher in America. Six of us decided to make a holiday of it, four Chinese students and two American teachers, Marcy and I. We bought hard seat train tickets for the day trip west into Gansu. This was Old Hundred Names class, sometimes so crowded that passengers hadn't enough room to stand with both feet on the floor. The tracks followed the north ridge of the Qin Ling mountains, the country gradually turning into desert as the train poked its way west toward central Asia.

Just at dark, we arrived in Tianshui—Heavenly Water. Here, the Chinese population begins thinning out drastically; soon there is no water to support even the pretense of agriculture. This harsh, dry, windblown country looks like much of the American west with even something approaching western emptiness and space. It is not tourist country, and we were clearly the only two Barbarians in town. There were no legal hotels for our mixed group of Chinese and Barbarians. In fact, no Barbarian hotel at all. What to do?

Chinese ingenuity! The two women went off to stay with Wang

COMING HOME CRAZY

Xiao's friend in her tiny apartment. The four men would find a cheap hotel and pass me off as a Xinjiang comrade, a non-Chinese speaking Kazakh from the Siberian border. They advised me to grumble in something that sounded like Russian. It worked. We were soon safely installed, cackling about the scheme, in our own four-bed room in an army hotel. I paid the Chinese price—two *kwai*, about fifty cents. My student, the Old Fish, took off his Chinese towel pillow cover (a standard feature of hotel rooms) and discovered two black footprints on the pillow. I turned mine over—more footprints. Water seemed hard to come by, here in Heavenly Water. We wrapped coats around our pillows, sighed, and slept.

The Chinese invented the idea of Mount Rushmore a couple of thousands years before Gutzon Borglum. Instead of politicians, they carved thousands of Buddhas, big and tiny, into their cliff faces. Maiji Shan, a famous Buddhist mountain, was just outside town. The next day we caught a bus and toured. Maiji Shan was a perpendicular red wall of soft crumbly stone carved with giant bas-reliefs and caves. New wood staircases hung from the cliff. You could stroll straight up the mountain and get close to the Buddhas. The mountain was finished about 700 A.D. Though erosion had damaged many of the carvings, the Red Guards missed this remote place with their sledge hammers and picks.

I saw a half dozen of these Buddhist cliffs during my year in China and they always moved me. Buddhism was the only foreign idea that ever made any real difference to the Chinese—an electrical shock (maybe even a volcanic eruption) of spiritual and artistic energy inside a civilization that, even as early as 300 A.D., badly needed it. China was in danger of drying up from feeding on itself before most civilizations even hatched.

In any cliff face, you could watch the faces of the Buddhas transformed over three or four hundred years—from Indian features to a mixture to completely Chinese. When the process of metamorphosis was complete, the last Tang emperors began persecuting the Buddhists. It was a foreign idea, after all. Thus ended the great age of Buddhist cliffs. But most of them survived, partly ramshackle, partly like new, and you could still feel sweetness and energy coming out of them. We spent all day climbing the stairs, feeling the Buddha's nose or foot, shaking his hands until our own were covered with red Gansu dust.

After this hard day's Buddha watching, we gathered at the apartment of Wang Xiao's friend and her husband to make dumplings. It was an eight-human job: two to roll dough, two to cut skins, and two to stuff with pork and vegetables. Since the husband had a guitar, and played it, two traded off singing and telling stories to give the dumpling rollers heart for their work. I asked the hostess, newly returned from America, what she liked best about her experience.

"I took showers twice a day. There was hot water everywhere you went. You could shower whenever you liked."

"There is a joke," I said, "about Americans singing in the shower. Did you?"

"Hot water is happiness enough . . . "

It was a lovely night, sitting around that jolly, tiny apartment in that dry remote town, eating juicy dumplings, drinking local beer, joking, laughing, watching the sun go down over the edge of the desert. We decided to work off our dumplings by strolling down to the Heavenly Water River that gave the town its name. Like most Chinese towns at night, this little one was alive with eaters, strollers, arguers, gamblers, peddlers, even lovers. It was a fine spring night with stars coming out over the desert, the same dipper, the same North Star, here on the opposite side of the planet. The river was a poor excuse for heavenly, mostly a dry stone bed, with scattered rivulets sloshing along toward the Yellow River. We sat down on stones, watched some little boys fishing. They were having a good time but no luck.

Chinese life is so much confined behind walls and barriers, physical, economic, sexual, and political, and is so often made harsh by Chinese duty and necessity, that everyone on that riverbank felt amazing freedom and joy. We were affectionate friends, out of the Chinese box, on a lovely night, in a lovely place! A chorus of raucous frogs almost drowned out conversation, but no one cared. They were friendly frogs.

Finally someone piped up: "Wang Xiao, return the favor to our comrade frogs! Sing for them!"

"Oh no, I could not do that," said a small shy voice.

More coaxing from everyone, an old routine.

"Well—perhaps. Shall I sing an American song?"

Dear reader, you must see this picture: Wang Xiao, the woman who is about to sing, is twenty-five but looks like a little girl. She is disarmingly pretty, and speaks English with a soft British accent. She blushes when she is praised. She is famous among her friends for her lovely voice, not the high sharp voice of a Chinese opera singer, but a soft, clear, delicate voice with a slight fluttering vibrato the quality of water shivered by a small wind. If she were blond and Swedish, she would be the Christmas angel and sing the St. Lucia song. There would not be a single dry eye in church. She is not Swedish, but Chinese, and her long black hair keeps falling over one eye. She is stylishly dressed in Chinese blue jeans and a bright red sweater. The moon has just come up over the stone bridge and lights both her face in profile and the brilliant red of her sweater. One of the men who listens is already in love with her but dares say nothing. He is too poor. Within a year of this night, he will marry her. He doesn't know this now. The night booms with the croaking of frogs — the little boys have stopped fishing and look at Wang Xiao — the shreds of river glide over stones in almost, though not complete, silence. Wang Xiao sings very slowly and with great tenderness, "Red River Valley," as if it were "Dido's Lament," or as if she were Desdemona singing the duet with Othello, but poor Othello was only the Gansu frogs croaking over the heavenly water. Wang Xiao sang a line, the frogs stopped, listening. Another line, a few ribbits, another line —

> Come and sit by my side if you love me
> *ribbit ribbit ribbit*
> Do not hasten to bid me adieu
> *ribbit ribbit ribbit*
> Just remember the Red River Valley
> *ribbit ribbit ribbit*
> And the cowboy who loved you so true
> *a timpani roll of ribbits*

This went on through four or five verses and closed with a chorus in Chinese. It was simultaneously funny and romantic. No one knew whether to weep or giggle. At the end, we were all in love — with each other, with Wang Xiao, with the frogs, with the desert night, with heavenly water, with the cowboy who loved us, with the Red River Valley, with our own lives.

Fie on politics that keeps human beings from living those nights! Fie on lies and loudspeakers! Fie on governments! Fie on "The East is Red" and "The Star Spangled Banner" and "God Save the Queen!" Let us have real music! Let us sing to each other!

SWISS ARMY KNIFE: A HISTORY

瑞士军刀：一个故事

When I found out I was off to teach in China, I felt like a man making a trip into space. The China I imagined was not another country but another planet. I didn't know where or what Xi'an was until I read a brochure describing it as Chang'an in the Tang dynasty. I knew Arthur Waley, so that helped, but I was still over a thousand years out of date. Like Pangloss, who searched all over the kingdom for answers to his query, "Should I get married?" I asked everyone I could find, "What should I take to China? What am I likely to need? What is not there?"

After a frenzy of letters to strangers, phone calls, connections leading to connections, and small trips, I accumulated, like a good research scientist, a body of raw information — of data. This lump of response fell into three main assertions:

1) Everything is not there.
2) You are likely to need most things and not find them.
3) Do not neglect to take as comprehensive a Swiss Army Knife as you can afford. Do not take the hardware store special brand or, should there be such a thing, the Belgian Army Knife. Take only the real thing. It is dependable; it is necessary. Do not lose it!

No Swiss Army Knives in Minneota, so on a hot August morning, I drove to Marshall to a surplus store called Poor Borch's on Highway 68. Poor Borch's logo, a twenty-foot-high wooden revolver advertising specials on Nikes, Levis, and shotgun shells, pointed me in.

"I want a comprehensive Swiss Army Knife," I said.

"Huh?" the man at the counter said.

"A big one."

"Biggest we got." He handed me a five-pound behemoth with a hundred dollar price tag, too comprehensive even for China.

"The Motorist for you, I think." He handed me a forty-dollar knife.

"There are no private cars in China," I replied, "so I won't be driving. I can't fix a car anyway."

"This is what makes it the 'Motorist,' " he said, and pulled out a magnifying glass. "For map reading."

I bought it.

The familiar red handle with the Swiss Army cross housed:

> 1) the magnifying glass with a regular
> screwdriver on the end
> 2) a large blade
> 3) a small blade
> 4) a file
> 5) a tweezers
> 6) an ivory tooth pick
> 7) a scissors
> 8) a Phillips screwdriver
> 9) an awl
> 10) a can opener
> 11) a corkscrew
> 12) a bottle opener

A Swiss Army Knife appeals to those whose musical taste runs to one-man bands or who spent too much time playing with Chinese boxes as children. Until that afternoon, I had never owned one, thinking them an overpriced affectation. Why, after all, unless one were walking along through lonesome stretches of the Continental Divide, would you carry an iron lump of these simple gadgets and tools, more easily and functionally available in any American kitchen or glove box—unless, of course, you were the sort who ate in cafes that did not provide a plastic dispenser of toothpicks next to the cash register and had need of your personal ivory model for tableside hygiene?

The knife flew in my pocket from Minnesota to Beijing, and, unlike the rest of my luggage, arrived. It proved, from the beginning, as useful as my advisors claimed. In moments of high irrationality and American optimism, I even imagined that China, given a few billion Swiss Army

Knives and rolls of duct tape, could be put back together and made to work. Like a good American, I had neglected to factor in the inertia of history that not all the Swiss Army Knives in the universe could repair. Here is an inventory of some uses:

I

China has not invented, or does not prefer to make available, the can opener. The Chinese, great tinners of food, pry off the tops with chop sticks, nails, or any sharp object at hand. More than one can of stewed doggery meat or some similar delicacy was more scientifically opened by my Swiss.

II

The Chinese brew, bottle and peddle splendid beer in every town I visited. Beer, unlike potable water, is cheap, safe and available. But if you prefer to open beer bottles, not by pounding the cap on the edge of a stone, or by pulling it off with your teeth (a great visual stunt, and possible if you know what you are doing), use your Swiss.

III

Chinese red wine, celebrated by Li Bai and Su Dongpo, among others, is to my Barbarian palate heavy, thick, overwhelmingly sweet and aromatic, and generally undrinkable. It comes in a screw-top bottle and presents no challenge. On rare occasions, however, bottles of Great Wall or Dynasty appeared in odd stores. Barbarians snapped them up briskly. But what to do? As "export wines" made probably for Beijing hotels, they are corked. Under the cork is a perfectly drinkable table wine. I have seen Chinese open these bottles with nails. But no need . . . Here, on the Swiss we have . . .

IV

Classroom floors, train cars, ancient temples, are alike carpeted with piles of fruit peels. The Chinese are enthusiastic fruit eaters and, conscious of the night soil that fertilizes orchards, equally enthusiastic peelers. They peel even oranges with knives and are remarkably adept at it. Clumsier Barbarians have recourse to their trusty Swiss.

V

If you own a Chinese bicycle, it will rattle. Major parts will be loosely attached. In the middle of a clot of thousand-bicycle traffic, something important will fall off or cease functioning. You will want your Swiss with its various screwdrivers.

VI

Chicken, in Xi'an at any rate, is the dearest Chinese meat. The Chinese adore chickens, prefer to buy them live, hauling them home squawking over the back of a bicycle, to be garroted next to a hot wok. When you are served a chicken in a Chinese house it still owns its head and feet. Proof that it was indeed a chicken? "Very nourishing meat," says the family daughter, picking up the head with her chopsticks and gnawing on the comb. But there is a hazard for the unwary Barbarian. A Chinese chicken has worked hard to reach adulthood and has grown muscles to prove it. Like his fellow citizens in the Middle Kingdom, he is lean and a good deal older than he looks. The Chinese manner of chicken dissection is more unusual even than Colonel Sanders's. Chicken carvers seem to put on a blindfold, arm themselves with a heavy cleaver and whack until the chicken corpse lies vanquished in a chaotic heap. The most innocent looking part of that chicken is stringy and full of bone chips. Those chips will find their way into your teeth. The normal solution to this involves a good deal of sucking and spitting, but Lutheran Barbarians come armed with personal ivory toothpicks sheathed like Excalibur in their red Swiss.

VII

About twenty Minnesotans arrived in Xi'an when I did. Some were old, some middle-aged, some young, but all Midwesterners united by their fat, by continual complaining about it and by imaginative and expensive plans to do something about it. Unconsciously they had done the only useful thing possible. They arrived in China for a long stretch. Dieting, planned exercising and the twelve-step program are about as effective against fat as slingshots against howitzers, or herbal teas against brain tumors. They pass conversational time and facilitate the exchange of goods but leave the belly pressed snugly against its buttons. But China works. You walk or ride a clunker bicycle slowly for miles a day; you shiver indoors for six months and sweat for six; both activities dispose of your stomach; you eat when you can and what you can and buy whatever you have language enough to ask for, if it is available, though probably not; you have diarrhea occasionally, a gift from the local bacteria, and therefore think intelligently about what you put in your mouth, something no hare-brained spiritual or body-building principle has ever accomplished; you drink less because the world you live in is sufficiently interesting without a buzz, though indeed China presents you with occasions that truly demand a stiff drink as American situations so seldom do. After a few months your belly has ceased to press against your Levis. After a few more months, they fit. After a few more months, they sag on your hips and newly muscled legs. Finally, they are as baggy as Chinese trousers, and, on a hot day, can be rolled halfway up to your butt Chinese style. Your belt no longer has enough holes to function. Time for your Swiss army awl. Every Minnesotan needed that awl after six months. Those I have seen since, including the one I watch in my mirror, have backslid into their old belt holes. There are a few things a Swiss Army Knife can't fix. Living in America is one of them.

VIII

The first night I stayed in my Xi'an apartment, I pulled the chain on my floor lamp. It shivered on its base. One bulb lit up, flickered and went out. I reached in to unscrew the other bulb and got a violent electric jolt. I swore, reached down, unplugged the lamp. When the plug came out, it threw a shower of sparks. I reached for the pull chain again. It had disappeared inside the lamp, as if into a malevolent electrical maw. I complained. The guest house manager, a woman who was a former PLA police sergeant referred to by Barbarians as "Hatchet Face," pointed out to me that the Chinese people had fulfilled their proper contractual responsibility to me by providing a floor lamp. If it didn't work, I must have broken it. It was my duty to see to it that the Chinese People's own floor lamp functioned or pay up. She meant to inspect it and collect a substantial deposit, too, all this delivered in rat-a-tat high-pitched Chinese. I was, for not the only time in China, speechless.

I went back to my room, raging and fulminating. As I stomped around, cursing the floor lamp and the whole *malebolge* of human incompetence and venality, a knock came. I went to the door. There stood two students, a married couple. Yu and Liang. I calmed down and we chatted.

"Why is it so dark?" asked Liang.

"It's dark because of that god-damn . . . " and the whole rage followed.

"Well, it must be fixable . . . " said Liang calmly, squinting at the wiring. His ravishing wife, Yu, giggled. A beautiful woman giggling averts almost any disaster. Liang was prying for the pull chain with his Tiger brand ball point. "If I had a tool . . . ," he mused. I handed him the Swiss Army Knife and a roll of duct tape. He unfolded the full panoply of its blades. "What a wonderful tool," he said. "We have nothing like this in China. It must be American."

"Swiss." I said.

"Ahh!"

He pried the pull chain out with the tweezers, unscrewed the stand with the Phillips and trimmed off a bad section of cord with the scissors. He gently pried apart the interior wiring with the toothpick, examined the positive and negative wires with the magnifying glass. He made a few adjustments, tightened the screws, sutured the wounds with duct tape, and splinted the disappearing pull chain. When he replugged it, the same shower of sparks came out. "Be careful!" I said.

"Only Chinese wiring. No matter . . . "

The lamp lit on both sides. It was still an aesthetic and mechanical disaster, a piece of cheap crap. The Swiss Amy Knife and duct tape couldn't help that, but, disaster though it was, patience and ingenuity brought it to life for a little while. Liang's repair work had to be done monthly. Gradually the screws would loosen and the pull chain would find a way to throw off its duct tape shackles and disappear to freedom back inside the middle of the lamp. The whole wobbling contraption would throw ever-widening showers of sparks. Liang and Yu, frequent visitors and, after a short time, good friends, would invariably notice the decrepit lamp and say, "Ah, your poor Chinese lamp . . . Do you still have your wonderful knife?" And with the delicate patience that the continual disasters of Chinese history have left so well fixed in the soul, Liang brought the lamp back to life one more time, an accident waiting to happen. Only that expenditure of infinite patience staved it off for a little while.

Surely there are better ways for widely read, multi-lingual Chinese to spend their energy than in repairing lamps that ought never to have left the factory in the first place. But if the lamp worked, or if there were enough electricity to light it with some regularity, then there would be time to think of deeper maladies that need fixing. Swiss Army Knives, whatever they had to do with precipitating the disaster in Tiananmen Square, might, from one dark angle, not be any service to the Chinese at all. Repairs might only deepen this blackness, expose the haywire circuitry. Presumably the next foreign expert who lived in Room 207 contended with the same wretched lamp, though without Hatchet Face (she was sent back to her regiment), and presumably the pull chain was at the point of being devoured again when he was shuffled off abruptly to Hong Kong with the other guest Barbarians in June 1989, probably taking his own new Swiss Army Knife with him, back to the world where it isn't necessary for small repairs.

***

Midway through my Chinese year, the unthinkable happened. I lost the Swiss Army Knife, only defense against ancient chickens, tin cans, beer bottles, and floor lamps.

After a semester of China, I was exhausted, claustrophobic, confused by the speed and contradiction with which experience had assaulted me, and cold. Foreign teachers got, by contract, one day off for Christmas. Some local colleges made this up by extra teaching on Saturday or Sunday. Still, the semester soon afterwards ground to a halt, leaving everyone free for about a month during Chinese New Year. The Chinese graduate students, since they had passed enough examinations to go to a "key" university that recruited from all over China rather than just the province, were from homes as far flung as the Siberian border in Xinjiang, southern Hunan, old Manchuria, Suzhou (home of gardens) and Qinghai (home of prison camps). They had been six months without wives, husbands, children, parents, and friends, and were, as they described it, "lonesome to death." One moony Hunanese genius in his early thirties had married a beautiful woman in August and left her immediately for school—Chinese Virgilian "duty." He sat dreamily at the back of the room, writing love poems in Chinese and English, looking like a Hunanese Percy Shelley as he stared longingly south through the cracked dusty windows. The Sichuanese contingent had almost starved to death. Shaanxi, the province we were in, was famous in China for bad cooking. The analogy might be imagining a French county with American truck-stop cooks. Sichuan was, not without reason, famous for its gourmets and chefs. The Sichuan crew looked sadly at me over their chopsticks whenever we ate together. "Poor comrade Bill, having to eat this terrible Shaanxi slop. Do not judge our whole country by this. The pigs of Chengdu would decline to fill their rice bowls at a Shaanxi banquet." As a result, when I received an invitation to stop in Sichuan and visit one of my students on the way south, I accepted. To eat in Sichuan and to cruise slowly on a boat through the Yangtze gorges! When such pleasures come toward you in this world, smile sweetly and say, "Thank you very much."

I wanted also to escape from China for a while. The campaign against "bourgeois liberals" had started. The *China Daily* was full of dark threats. Political education meetings had been beefed up (usually they were excuses for magazine reading and naps). Students were fearful and edgy. Real information was impossible to come by, the phones impossible to use. The loudspeakers sounded more 1984ish than usual, trumpeting out their "think good thought" slogans and Maoist marching songs. It was almost enough to make you lonesome for the good old days of the Great Proletarian Cultural Revolution or, at the least, a good pogrom. Life without information, without ease of movement, without connection, was making Barbarians edgy, too. I longed to get into a car, drive somewhere on pure whim, make a direct phone call with no one or no machine listening, give someone a credit card and have them write up a slip briskly without questions, go into a book store or newspaper kiosk and buy whatever I pleased. I longed to drink tap water, eat lemons and oysters, hear the tinkling of ice cubes in a gin and tonic, see and smell an ocean — any would do. I wanted to not need my Swiss Army Knife for a little while.

Some Barbarians went to Tibet for adventure, then to Nepal for relief. Some went to Hong Kong for shopping and total collapse. A few went home to Canada or America or Britain. No one could afford Japan. I had old friends in Singapore (my old next-door neighbors in Iceland, in fact, had moved to another somewhat warmer island). I called a travel agent in Hong Kong, found a cheap flight and arranged my month: half in Sichuan, a quick plunge over the border, and then the luxurious Confucian tropics, gin, lemons, ice, orchids, the sea!

Travel in China is not a sport for the punctilious. It is impossible to book a return ticket or connection. All travel is one way. From one town you buy a ticket to the next. To get a ticket on an airplane, you must have to buy a ticket to get a ticket. To get that ticket, you have to buy a ticket ticket. You must give CAAC, the airlines, a day or two to examine your papers and determine whether you ought to be flying or not. They may have other itineraries in mind for you. For flying CAAC (they have no competition of course; they are the people's airline) you will, should you survive, be given some candy and a little plastic-wrapped present. As booty on various flights, I got a make-up kit, a rabbit key ring, a plastic bird pin, and a billfold with a mirror and a secret pocket. For these treats, your big foreign nose is charged three or four times the "Chinese" price.

Train tickets operate mostly on the elaborate Chinese system of *guanxi* (connection). Without cigarettes or relatives, they are *mei you*. A Chinese train ticket office is the visible embodiment of Milton's description of Chaos and Hell. Foreigners usually pay considerable money for someone Chinese to buy their tickets. Not even J.P. Morgan or God can buy a connecting ticket.

Given those facts of Chinese travel and the absence of functional travel agents, I found Sun Travel in Hong Kong and gave my credit card number to a brisk-voiced British women named Jane. When I called back, she had a cheap night flight to Singapore and return. "I suggest you pick it up here in Hong Kong," she said. "The mails, you know, are not entirely dependable . . . " This is an understatement on the magnitude of predicting snow in Minnesota.

"I'll be there on February 3," I replied cheerfully.

"Leave plenty of time," she continued. "The unexpected, you know . . . " Indeed.

***

With two British teachers, Simon and Andrew, I took the night train to Chengdu, found the only Barbarian hotel in town and collapsed. We ate, we slept, we ate again. We strolled through the famous duck market, a whole street where a couple of thousand ducks sit quietly in orderly rows. A huge heap of feathers, webs, and bills uttering hardly a quack, while sharp-tongued Chengdu housewives haggle and cajole farmers for a bargain. They stroke the duck's neck, point out with jabs his skinniness and shortcomings, pinch his belly, trying to shave off a *kwai* or two. The duck farmers, a jaunty-looking crew in high, brilliantly polished black leather boots and Russian hats pulled rakishly over one black eye, stand firm. A bargain at five *kwai*! A choice fat duck! The traveling Barbarians stand amazed. What language do these ducks speak? Why no bedlam of ducks? Are Chinese ducks as obedient as the Party prefers the citizens to be? Are the old opium dens open for ducks? As with all supernatural phenomena, the calm silence of these soon-wokked ducks gave rise to wonder, not scientific inquiry.

Mao in gigantic white marble still watched over the main street of Chengdu in 1987. By then, helmsmen statues were almost collector's items in China — so many empty pedestals waiting for the next emperor. But in Chengdu of all places! A city of teahouses, monuments to great poets (Du Fu lived and wrote here), bamboo groves, succulent sweet rice balls, genius cooks, lively and pretty women, cranky truthful journalists (Liu Binyan's home base), markets full of blood oranges and succulent pomelos, strolling Tibetans gay and colorful as carnival gypsies — and a bit fragrant with a few years' dirt. Chengdu, aside from its utterly destroyed main street strewn with typically ugly Party-style public buildings, is one of the liveliest, least doctrinaire places in China. But there stands the old boy, wart and all, right hand raised. Simon, Andrew and I took each other's pictures wickedly satirizing the great helmsman's heroic posture. No thunder rumbled under Chengdu . . . Then . . .

***

After a few days of pig ears in numb spice (prickly ash), smoked duck hearts and sticky rice balls, it was time to move downriver. Simon and Andrew left for Kunming in the tropics, then to Hong Kong. On the advice of my waiting student, the sage Old Fish of Sichuan, I booked a night train to Chongqing, intending to buy a boat ticket with my nose in person on the following morning. Only luxury class was available: a wood-paneled sleeper with four bunks, covered with lace doilies and quilts, a plastic thermos of hot water, and four only-a-bit-chipped covered tea cups. The train was perhaps 1930 vintage, pulled by a steam locomotive. I settled in for the night and was soon joined by a pair of young Japanese students. They were squeaky clean, well-dressed, and had hardly a word of English. They giggled and blushed a good deal.

I got up and stepped out to smoke in the hallway. A dignified Chinese gentleman of about sixty, wearing a tweed coat, was already puffing. He inquired, in English, if I was American. I found it always safe, in China, to confess my nationality. Whatever the stupidity of our government, most Chinese are inclined to be affectionately curious about us as humans and to forgive our private foibles. Two years later, Westerners should keep in mind the same distinction. Whatever the Chinese government does, or however much it argues otherwise, it has almost nothing to do with Chinese humans. I no more wanted to be held accountable for "Lonald Leagan" than that Chinese gentleman did for Mao or Deng.

My smoking partner turned out to be an agronomist who had studied in Michigan and Iowa, pursuing the science of soybeans. We farm-talked for a good while. He told me a wonderful story. A group of Chinese farmers toured the Midwest and wound up strolling in a section-sized cornfield in Illinois. They were amazed at the eight-foot height and vitality of the corn.

"But where," they asked the farmer, "are your ditches and conduits? How do you water this heroic corn?"

The puzzled American farmer finally pointed up and said, "It rains."

"Only rain?"

"Only rain."

Inconceivable to these Chinese farmers that nature could be so benevolent. To any Chinese farmer, my own grandfather's free 160 acres of western Minnesota would seem the equivalent of winning a cosmic lottery, wealth and ease beyond imagining. And yet, out of that hard and uncooperative Chinese ground, the farmers — not the emperors, not the Party hacks and bosses — kept a civilization going for 6,000 years. The agronomist and I smoked till late in the night as the train clacked and rolled over the steep fertile Sichuan farmland, me praising the succulent local pomelo, he dazzled by Iowa soybean yields. When I came back to the compartment, the Japanese students were still awake. The loud-speaker, omnipresent on Chinese trains, was playing martial music and warning passengers to be wary of bourgeois liberals and not to spit. This at 2:00 in the morning! The poor Japanese fellow was trying to figure out how to disconnect the speaker but the button was broken off. It wanted a screwdriver. I handed him my Swiss Army Knife.

"Ah, very good," he said in English and quickly shorted out "The East is Red."

"Good night," I said, re-pocketing the knife, ever so pleased to be of service to Japanese technical ingenuity. And sleep.

***

Chongqing is the only big Chinese town without bicycles. It rises too steeply from the Yangtze. A ski lift might be more useful. It is the most ramshackle, unimproved big town I saw in China. I liked it.

I arrived early in the morning and began pulling my heavy book-laden suitcase through the mob on the train platform. All Chinese train stations are crowded, but this was beyond anything I had seen. It was a clot of flesh armed with red, white and blue plastic bags tied up with twine. Old ladies carried pigs; children had upside-down poultry attached to them. I stopped as the mob surged past. On the opposite platform were closed freight cars, painted green. There were a few foot-square air holes in the side. Out of those holes stuck human heads. My God, I thought, that can't be a carload of people. I moved on. A few box cars down, a door was open. A policeman stood at the edge with what looked like a cattle prod. Behind him was an amorphous mass of arms, legs, heads, torsos, looking out at me. Westerners shudder at sights like this. It reminds them of the awful old photographs of boxcars full of Jews arriving at Auschwitz or Buchenwald. "Only extra transportation for Chinese New Year, when everyone in this enormous country goes visiting at once," I was told later. So many Chinese, so few seats. This did not cheer me as to boat tickets, but I carried on.

I found the boat ticket office on the river at the bottom of a perpendicular hill. "One way to Wanxian," I looked questioningly. The girl answered me in French. I shrugged and was about to begin *"Eine Piao nach Wanxian . . . "* when a tall thin woman with a camera around her neck came up. She saved me in an obviously effortless mixture of French and Chinese. She handed me a Barbarian-class ticket.

"They have only soft class left. The girl speaks good French, little English, but she was confused that you wanted a ticket only to Wanxian. Foreigners never go there, except for a boat stop." Her accent was French.

"I'm going to visit a student, stay a few days. Your Chinese seems very good. Did you learn it in France?"

"No. In Shanghai and Tianjin, the same place I learned English."

I looked puzzled, obviously.

"I am French. I don't like English or the English, refused to learn it. But I went to China years ago to study Chinese. Everyone came up to me on the street wanting to practice English with the *waiguoren*. I shouted at them in Chinese, 'I am French, not English, and you should speak Chinese to me.' But they all wanted to practice their damn English, so I learned it in self-defense. It was the only way I could practice my Chinese."

Francine was working as a stringer for a French paper, traveling through China with her man friend, John, a photographer, gathering material on the student demonstrations that led to Hu Yaobang's firing. The "Voice of America" had been jammed, mail was arriving more erratically than usual, and the old Long March guard on the politburo was calling for a campaign against bourgeois liberals whom they identified as "bad westernized elements and hooligans." To borrow a word from Francine's own language—it's so terribly *déjà vu*.

I was in Chongqing until early the next morning. I decided to telegram my arrival, find a hotel and spend the day touring in Chiang's old wartime capital. Francine and John took me off to a restaurant. Chongqing, like Chengdu, is a city of gourmets, and Francine, with her splendid Chinese, found us a good one. She studied the menu carefully. We had eels, pork, Yangtze carp, and local noodles. The Chinese men at the next table were astonished at the sound of this tall, thin, pale French woman ordering like a native. They invited us to join their noisy drinking game played with fists and fingers and great boisterous shouts and *ganbeis*. It was all a bit childish, I suppose, but there was some pleasure in hearing Francine tell them demotically the local equivalent of "Fuck off!" They returned imperturbably to their noisy game as plates of chili eels and pork in prickly ash appeared. I couldn't feel my lips for the rest of the afternoon.

I tried to find the telegraph office alone, with only a Chinese map on which the hotel clerk had drawn a red X. I found the old clock tower and stood squinting in the middle of the charging throng, trying to figure out just which Chinese character said telegraph office. An old man came up and took my elbow. "You are American perhaps, and in need of help?" I confessed. He guided me across the street, got my telegram safely sent to the Old Fish in Wanxian. He inquired whether I might like to see the Temple of Five Hundred Buddhas and take tea. I did. He learned English in World War II, was a clerk, had a bad time of it in the Cultural Revolution, wanted to buy foreign exchange currency from me at the standard Chongqing black market rate. I had none, so he went on to tell me about his family and to take out of his jacket pocket a bundle of old postcards from America, England, Australia, Holland.

"From my foreign friends . . . " he said. They dated from the thirties and forties, then skipped a generation to the eighties. I was oddly touched by the man. After we had sat in the almost empty tea house next to the temple for a couple of hours, he asked how I enjoyed the tea.

"Very much."

"Chongqing Tuocha — winner of many awards both here and in Europe. But you must always wait for the second or third infusion. Then the flavor comes." All Chinese have tea theories. "You cannot leave without tea." He grabbed my elbow again and marched me to a tea shop where he bought me a box of tea for a few cents. "It has been a great honor . . . " he said. I took his name and address in Chinese, later sent him a postcard from Singapore to add to his collection. I wonder if he ever got it or if the neighborhood committee inquired about his "foreign friend," Mr. Bill.

* * *

The next morning, the boat pushed off through a smoggy acrid mist into strong Yangtze currents. Humid Chongqing is a coal-burning industrial town at the bottom of a sinkhole surrounded by steep mountains. Photographs of it are always bathed in a fuzzy haze, giving it a romantic, ancient look. There is little romance, however, in chemical analysis of the haze.

Around the bend, more mountains, less haze. It was a brisk, sunny, late-January day. Where's the crowd, I thought, looking around? I was sitting in a glassed-in lounge at the front of the boat. There were overstuffed chairs with lace doilies, train-car style tea cups and thermos. I counted five adults and two children. A middle-aged Chinese gentlemen in a well-cut Mao suit sat reading with his back to the river the entire trip. By his chair was a zippered black notebook, sure sign of a big Party potato off in high style on official business. The rest of the passengers were getting acquainted in German. They turned out to be a young Austrian couple with two children, teaching German in Xi'an for the year, and off on the same holiday as me. The elegantly dressed middle-aged couple proved to be a Spanish travel agent and his wife. Most of his business was with groups from Germany, so his German was impeccable. His wife had a Goya face. She smelled strongly of very expensive perfume. She later explained that she found the smell of China difficult. They all chatted away merrily, *"Ya-ing"* and *"Nein-ing"* and *"Und-so-weiter-ing,"* while I gazed absently around wondering where in hell the real Chinese were.

As it turned out, great masses of them were at the back of the boat in third, fourth, fifth and God knows how many lower classes. Once you start, there is no bottom to a class structure. To get aft, I had to find my way out of the Barbarian lounge. This involved several doors, gates and latches, but I finally made it. In marked contrast to the joyless emptiness and boredom of the tourist quarters, the back decks were full of life — eating, gambling, singing, arguing, pointing at the red gorilla and giggling as it ambled through the mobs. This was, after all, the biggest Chinese holiday, older even than Marx, Lenin, and the Long March. Everyone had a few days off from socialist modernization and was going home to eat dumplings and shoot firecrackers.

The boat steamed slowly all day toward Wanxian, past crags, villages, steeply terraced fields, women out pounding their clothes clean on the Yangtze stones, fishing boats with thatched awnings, tributaries flowing into the grand river from both north and south like foreign plenipotentiaries bringing their tribute to swell the glory of the Emperor of Heaven. I found the toilet in the Chinese class—a hole in the boat, straight into the Yangtze. Majestic or not, I decided against drinking the water.

All boats moor overnight in Wanxian, just at the beginning of the gorges, and we arrived a few hours after dark. I was the only departing Barbarian. The Spanish travel agent's wife looked at the mass of poor Chinese with their grain sacks, chicken crates, and plastic bags of New Year food, then, wistfully, at me.

"You leave now? Here? Alone?" By the expression in her face and voice, it looked as if she thought I was going to face a firing squad at dawn. "Here, take this," she said, pressing two traveling packets of expensive men's cologne into my hand. "You will need it in this place."

Old Fish and a couple of his students waited dependably at the end of the gangplank. They picked me out, even in this crowd surge. I was stumbling along with two almost-hundred-pound bags, loaded with books.

"We have no car," Old Fish said. "It is only a mile or two." He looked up at the town, maybe two hundred feet above the river, up a steep stone stairs, then the street winding still further up at twice a San Francisco grade. "It is a nice view from my school . . . ," he sighed apologetically. A sturdy boy not much over five feet tall, carrying a shoulder pole, came up. A little flurry of Sichuan Chinese blew through the air. "He will carry your bags for two *kwai*," Fish said. That's fifty cents or less.

"Give him twenty," I said.

"Two is enough. This is his living."

The boy hooked my two cumbersome bags on his pole, balanced them on his shoulder, and began striding uphill, not fast, not slow, one step at a time, even and dependable as a pendulum on a Swiss clock. The bags easily outweighed him by fifty or sixty pounds. I huffed and puffed to keep up behind him on the stairs, carrying only my heavy body.

"The farmers here have good strong legs from climbing hills all the time," Fish said.

"That boy will collapse from those books," I puffed.

"He makes his living with his shoulders, as you and I do with our mouths."

At the top of the hill, I paid him and thanked him. He nodded, turned on his heel and strode back down the hill, his short powerful legs moving like pistons. Time after time in China, I saw the theory of surplus labor made visible before me. But that young boy, whose shoulders would in ten years have deep ridges worn into them, steep as the local mountains, represented something more. A civilization does not last for five or six thousand years with opinions and theories, but with powerful legs and shoulders and an even stride. It needs neither Chevys, Macintoshes nor a Swiss Army Knife. They are only gadgetry, something that will wind up being carried uphill by a human who doesn't own them and doesn't, considered from the right angle, need them at all.

* * *

The campaign against bourgeois liberalism was in full swing in January of 1987, and the Sichuan loudspeakers endlessly repeated the regulations for New Year's celebrations: no parades, no excessive public crowds, avoid superstitious rituals, study Mao Zedong thought, beware of foreign spies with big noses and Taiwan traitors in your midst. The Chinese walked passed the loudspeakers hearing with half an ear, while

       COMING HOME CRAZY

they bargained for firecrackers, toys, decorations, sweet rice and fat pork. Chinese New Year is the central ritual of an old highly ritualized civilization, and after the decade-long hiatus of the GPCR, it was time for dinner and noise. I got included, nose and all, in the round of wonderful dinners and toasts, and as midnight approached, the firecrackers started.

I think no American Fourth of July was ever quite like it in the ferocity of noise, the stink of gunpowder, the "damn the torpedoes" intensity and mad joy of that bombardment. Wanxian is built at the top of a steep cliff facing still more steep mountains on the other side of the river. The gorge and the huge river itself turned into an echo chamber. There must have been a half million people blowing up firecrackers in earshot, and the noise amplified from rock and water below. Howitzers caromed off the cliff faces, Gatling shots riffled the water, cannonade to left, cannonade to right. The gorge filled up with smoke and powder, an odorous artificial fog. Rat-a-tat-tatting ambuscades fell from tenth story balconies. The air flashed as if with exploding snow. Over it all sounded laughter and screams of delight from the children — and probably from the ancients too! This was the Battle of Borodino refought in the Yangtze gorges at midnight on New Year's Eve.

One of Fish's colleagues took a couple of packages of firecrackers and ran around to the back of his own apartment where he held them up to his window, lit them and dashed quickly away. The firecrackers blasted at the open window like a berserk machine gun.

"To frighten the ghosts away for another year," said Old Fish, the most brilliant, witty, and utterly rational man I met in China, maybe on earth.

And who is to say he is not right? Did any American ever shoot firecrackers under the White House windows when Lyndon Johnson was hatching his war? Did Gordon Liddy consider shooting off firecrackers in the lobby of the Watergate hotel? It's the real guns that anger the ghosts that haunt the houses of government in Beijing, in Washington, in your own town. The inventors of gunpowder have still got the right idea: Eat the best dinner of the year, then go outside and fight an artificial war of heroic size and majesty. The noise of it will cover your belches and farts. Then go home, have a snort of five-grain liquor and a cup of tea, and go to bed surrounded by your relatives. Happy New Year!

* * *

Wanxian is a wonderful town. Aside from boat stops, tourists had not discovered it. I toured the town, saw the old Guomingdang clock tower, met the town gardener who tended magnificent flowers and bushes in the park, met the ancient Catholic bishop who read ten or eleven languages, had survived everything with his irony intact and was considered the most dangerous man in town. I saw a New Year's musical talent show put on by local musicians and introduced them to the pleasure of ragtime afterwards. I found a coffee shop with sweet thick brew popular with teenagers and those with a fancy for the exotic, ate succulent Chengdu noodles in street stands, went paddle-boating at a little mountain reservoir with a parcel of giggling Chinese students who had studied English with Old Fish, and walked up Li Bai's mountain with the same crew to have a picnic. As the legend goes, Li Bai, one of China's greatest poets, lived in Wanxian in the Tang dynasty (eighth century A.D.), and wrote many of his famous poems while living in a hut on the top of the mountain. Li Bai pictured himself in his poems as a heavy drinker, an enthusiastic eater, and a lover of idleness, even sloth. He must have lied—or exercised literary license. The mountain is a thousand-foot climb up perpendicular stone stairs. After the crew of students finished shaming me up the mountain, we sat eating hundred-year-old eggs, duck jerky, and peanuts, washing it all down with local beer and reciting all the Li Bai we knew, in any language we knew it. We opened beer bottles and canned dog with the Swiss Army Knife. Someone had brought thermoses of hot water and cups, so we had tea and sweet rice balls for dessert. The gorge far below us was filled up with gray wintry fog; the river was invisible. It was enough to know it was there, the river that Chinese poets feared and adored so much, sloshing along through the three famous gorges, then toward the new dam, Shanghai, the open Pacific, California. Li Bai may have been looking off the same mountain twelve hundred years ago when he wrote this:

ON THE MOUNTAIN: QUESTION AND ANSWER

You ask me:
     Why do I live
on this green mountain?
   I smile
   No answer
         My heart serene
On flowing water
        peachblow
        quietly going
        far away

                  COMING HOME CRAZY

> This is another earth
>> another sky
> No likeness
>> to that human world below

But the human world beckoned me, as it beckoned Li Bai too. Old Fish decided to go through part of the big three gorges with me, stop in the little town of Wushan where the two of us would go through the small three gorges of the Daning river, a tributary stream coming in between the second and third gorge. We booked tickets, and I said my farewells and received my presents. Fish's eighty-year-old father, the finest calligrapher in the neighborhood, had written Du Fu's "Autumn Meditation" on a rice paper scroll for me. Du Fu, China's other "greatest" poet, was also a Sichuan man and wrote this magnificent poem looking into the very gorge where we now stood:

AUTUMN MEDITATION

Gems of dew wilt and wound the maple trees in the wood:
From Wu mountains, from Wu gorges, the air blows desolate.
The waves between the river-banks merge in the seething sky,
Clouds in the wind above the passes meet their shadows on the
    ground.
Clustered chrysanthemums have opened twice, in tears of other
    days;
The forlorn boat, once and for all, tethers my homeward
    thoughts.
In the houses winter clothes speed scissors and ruler;
The washing-blocks pound, faster each evening, in Pai Ti high
    on the hill.

Those spidery, elegant characters hang on my bedroom wall now. I look at them with the first light of Minnesota day. I know what they mean, though I can't read them. They mean that human beings have made noble, beautiful and intelligent things for a long time, but the powerful river of their stupidity, their ignorance of each other, still carries them daily away in its dark currents toward the sea. And what can be done about it? Can we fix it with a Swiss Army Knife? Or with tanks and bullets?

Old Fish and his wife presented me with a white stone with a fierce portrait of me painted on it by a first-rate local artist. I look like myself, disguised as an amiable Chinese demon, something to frighten children, but not too badly. How unlike America, I thought to myself. I visit people with an income of less than thirty dollars a month, living in a one-room apartment with a dirt floor, no car, no heat, no flush toilet, no running water, no kitchen, not much electricity, two or three changes of clothes, and a wall full of books. I eat them out of house and home for four or five days, am entertained grandly, not allowed to spend a *fen*, and for the pleasure of bankrupting them, they give me elegant gifts for having been their house guest. Where is civilization, Minneota or Wanxian? What has an income accomplished for America?

* * *

Old Fish and I, traveling Chinese class at last, arrived in Wushan early in the morning. The whole town still operated on holiday hours, sound asleep. We went to the telephone office, got the operator out of bed and asked about hiring boats down the Daning: "*Mei you.*" A holiday. But this is a foreigner, a genuine Barbarian tourist. We called the mayor of the little town. In fifteen minutes, he arrived, full of "*huanying* to Wu-shan," and told us the news that, in fifteen minutes, a boat full of journalists from Chengdu was leaving to go down the river. We would travel with them, tour for the day and banquet at the little hotel in town that night.

Hen Hao! Xiexie! Very good! Thanks! Thanks!

The sun shone brilliantly, and the day was beginning to warm up when we arrived at the pier. The journalists from Chengdu turned out to be women, all pretty and all full of jokes.

"There is nothing so sexy as Chengdu dialect spoken by women," said Old Fish. "A little lisping, a little bounce of laughter off the roof of the mouth . . . "

A sage observer, Old Fish; the journalists were wonderful company, adventurous, curious and funny. With them were a couple from Shanghai, and a young fellow from Hong Kong, traveling alone and looking well dressed and confused in this decidedly un-urban wilderness. The two boatman were local farmers, their thin bony faces covered not with skin, but tautly stretched mahogany leather. Sizable ventilating spaces separated their seven or eight teeth. They had the look about them of fellows who had been up and down the river once or twice before. They were powerfully amused by the presence of the heavy pink Barbarian, sure that he was illegal, but delighted by the prospect of tweaking the regulations.

The Daning, in mid-winter, was a puddle compared to the Yang-tze—a shallow clear little stream rippling over colored pebbles in its wide places—but full of vigorous rapids when the canyon narrowed, musical but not life-threatening. The current carried us up to the rapids, and only once or twice did we have to get out of the boat and wade through cold water while the boatmen poled the empty boat upstream. One of the Chengdu women brought out a bag of local pomolos (a grapefruit relative), and with the help of my Swiss Army Knife, we sucked on the acidy fruit, trailing a hand in the river while we floated through the canyons.

The walls of the gorge were—what? Extraordinary, gorgeous, unexpected? The small three gorges were sheerer, higher, more brilliantly colored in red and gold, narrower (in places only fifteen or twenty feet wide), and in almost every way grander than the Yangtze gorges themselves. Only the river was smaller. What it was like in full flood between those narrow canyon walls, I can only imagine, but on this February day, it was like floating down the Little Colorado except with fertile patches between the gorges instead of bony desert. The Chengdu women lispingly warbled folk songs. The Shanghai banker told jokes. The Hong Kong fellow looked dazzled. The boatman told legends of the rock formations in the cliffs: the weeping princess, the shackled demon. He pointed out old Buddhist caves and carvings high on the rock faces. Old Fish translated, though the Chengdu women and the Shanghai banker all had some English. I sighed, basked in the sun, licked pomolo juice out of my beard and thought to myself that I was as happy as I had ever been in my life, here in this boat, with these people, in this place, on this day. *Hoka-hey!*, the original inhabitants of my Grandfather's farm might have said. *Hoka-hey!*

As we came back downstream, the setting sun turned the cliff faces wedding red and dragon gold; the light lit the pebbles by the side of the boat like tiny lanterns. I thought I had fallen into a Chinese painting. We returned to the hotel tired and ecstatic. For almost the only time in Sichuan, the food was terrible, but the beer was lovely, and everyone drank too much of it, toasting the day, the beauties of Chengdu, and the river gods. Old Fish arranged to pass me off into the custody of the Shanghai banker and his wife for the trip downriver to Wuhan and the flight to Hong Kong and Singapore. The hotel had grimy mattresses, broken toilets, a courtyard full of musical roosters who serenaded me all night under a full winter moon. I stumbled up at three in the morning to walk to the boat pier.

Farewell, Daning, you lovely river! May no Barbarian ever find you again. May the Four Modernizations fly past you on their way to Japan and New Jersey. May all your dams crumble, and may the old boatman's teeth find good meat to chew. May the newspapers of Chengdu flower and may all its single children be daughters.

* * *

Gezouba had not crumbled, however. The big dam, with its hundred-and-thirty-foot locks and power towers snaking out to electrify the Chinese countryside, functioned brilliantly and brought all the Chinese tourists out on deck to ogle at the clanking machinery and the rushing water. They liked it better than the scenery in the gorges, I think. China is full of beauty and grandeur, even, maybe mostly, in its poorest, most miserable backwaters, but a piece of engineering that works and does a real job is an unimaginable wonder. The dam marks the end of the gorges and the flattening out of the river for its march over the fertile eastern plains to Shanghai and the sea. Its completion also marked the end of the navigational terrors in the upper gorges that so inspired Bai Juyi and others. Whatever wonders disappeared under Gezouba's silt, I suspect that boat pilots all worship it. It was no use reading selected passages of Edward Abbey to the Chinese tourists. The Shanghai banker and his wife looked like they were watching a gigantic and intricate toy.

"Look, see how the gears turn! See how the water rises!"

After Gezouba, the flat. The boat landed for a while in Yichang, an industrial town. I needed to make fast time to Wuhan and suggested we take a train if there was one.

"*Hen hao!*" said the Shanghai banker, and found the train station. There were six of us, the Shanghai couple, a Chengdu couple, the Hong Kong fellow and me. The line was endless. The locals told us trains were sold out for days because of the New Year's rush.

"No problem," said Shanghai. "Give me your passport, university card and two packs of Marlboros." He disappeared past the front of the line to the office door. After a minute or two, he came back and beckoned me. I followed him. We got to the door and he shoved me in, nose first. Clearly, I was exhibit A. The station master, already smoking a Marlboro, looked up, said, "Hmmm," and began rifling through his desk.

"*Keyi*," said Shanghai, gesturing me back toward the other supplicants. In five minutes, he came back with six tickets, five hard sleepers for the Chinese, and a big nose soft class for me.

"There are six bunks in our car, but I told him you were a famous professor, so he insisted you have a comfortable bed."

"*Keyi*," I said. "You Shanghai types are amazing."

"We are big city people. We know how things work. You are wise to travel with Marlboros, Comrade."

We had a good ride to Wuhan, found the Hankou Hotel almost immediately, got in for the Chinese price, again cleverly negotiated by Comrade Shanghai. The hotel was almost empty, only the top two floors, twelve and fourteen, (superstitious customers . . .) were occupied. We rode up in a creaking elevator, unpacked a bit, then left quickly for the CAAC office to buy a ticket to Canton or Hong Kong. Again, everything was booked for days because of the New Year. More negotiations, more Marlboros (three packs this time, I think), and after an hour of Shanghai fast talk, a ticket for 9:00 a.m.

"Now we celebrate!" said Comrade Shanghai. And so we did.

We ate and drank as grandly as the Hankou Hotel permitted. Wuhan is not the gourmet's capital of China. Comrade Shanghai and his wife went off to see friends in town, and we parted. I thanked him effusively for his urbane negotiating skills. "If you ever come to Minneota . . . ," I said. I expect to see them sometime in this century, whatever happens in China. Everything is possible if you know how to do it, as any New Yorker will tell you.

After they left, I adjourned to the bar for a nightcap or two. The joint venture crew was six or eight drinks ahead of me. One muttered darkly about the "goddamn crooked, incompetent, thieving, commie bastards . . . ". Another tried to calm him down.

"Anybody going to the airport early?" I asked. A young AT&T engineer was flying out to Canton at 9:00 a.m., on his way to Hong Kong, Taipei, and Chicago. He was already fantasizing steaks and Budweiser in Hong Kong. His van left at quarter to eight in the morning and I had an invitation to be on it. I accepted, bought a round, and headed up to the fourteenth (thirteenth) floor.

The elevator had sounded suspicious to me in the afternoon so, having just climbed Li Bai's mountain, I decided to get my exercise on the stairs. All padlocked. I checked the other end of the hall. Same kind of padlock and heavy chain. Padlocks and chains all the way up. A Chinese firetrap, perhaps even incineration chamber. I had been in China long enough to observe the Chinese obsession with locked gates and doors. Not for nothing did they build the Great Wall, invent the Chinese puzzle box, and manufacture the world's most intricate bicycle locks. The world was full of thieves and trespassers, and it was more sensible to lose a bit of surplus population in a fire than risk unauthorized intruders. I took the elevator. It groaned all the way up, like a bloated cow about to explode. I repacked my heavy bags, sealed them with duct tape, set the alarm and slept.

The next morning I stumbled down the hall with the suitcases and ten minutes to spare. The elevator took endless time to arrive from thirteen floors down. Two fellows with Hong Kong-permed hair joined me. I pressed "Lobby." The elevator creaked down. After what seemed an eternity, the elevator stopped dead and the lights went out. What the hell? I flicked my lighter and pressed the "Open" button. Nothing. I pressed the "Alarm" button. A feeble ring. I kept my finger on it. The ring weakened. I banged all the buttons at once, and the lights suddenly flickered on. The elevator's motor growled and the car moved three or four feet. Up. Then stopped. I banged the "Call" button again. I looked at the Hong Kong perms. They seemed as terrified of me as of the elevator. I pressed "Open." The door opened a few inches. I pried it a bit further. We were between floors, about a four-foot climb up to terra firma. I looked at the perms and pointed. They shrugged. The door oozed shut. I pounded it. With a quick shot of adrenalin and a good deal of language learned from my father in the cow barn, I pried it open again.

"Help! God damn it, help!" I shouted at the top of my lungs. Silence. The perms stood impervious. The echos of my cussing reverberated up and down the elevator shaft. Good-bye Singapore, I thought. I am about to perish in a Chinese elevator. What to do?

I stood my large heavy suitcase on end, climbed on top of it, and scrambled up to the floor above. I am not, at two hundred and fifty pounds, a mountain goat, but I was not about to stay in that elevator shaft for even thirty further seconds. I pointed to the suitcase. The perms grunted and passed it up to me. I extended a hand and pulled the two of them up out of the car. There we were! Free at last! Thank God almighty, free at last! I looked around—second floor. Easy! I found the stairs and yanked on the glass paneled double doors. Padlocked shut with a chain wound around and through the door knobs. I could see the lobby through the crack between the doors. I gave the doors a *fortissimo* shake, rattled the chain and yelled:

"Get your goddamn ass up these goddamn stairs and open this goddamn door so I can get in the goddamn van and go to the goddamn airport and go to goddamn Singapore where the goddamn elevators work!"

I had somebody's attention now, and there was a scurrying of feet up the marble stairs.

"Open the goddamn door," I said slowly in "special" English. There was a little rush of Chinese between the two employees as they examined the padlock.

"*Mei you yaoshi* . . . ," they shrugged. I did not need a translation. Not have key. I held my hundred pound suitcase over my head and banged it firmly against the glass door panel.

"Either you open the goddamn door, NOW, or I will smash my goddamn suitcase through your goddamn glass right now. *Dong, bu dong?*" He understood. He pointed to the hinges on the door frame.

"Maybe there, but no tool," he eyed me imploringly.

"Find a goddamn screwdriver and do it. Now! Fast!"

He shrugged. I felt like a character in Stephen Crane's story of "The Open Boat." I could see the AT&T engineer down the stairs ready to leave, wondering where I was. A light came on in my head. I rummaged in my pocket for my Swiss Army Knife. I unsheathed the screwdriver and handed it through the opening between the doors.

"*Ah! Hen hao!*" He set to work and a minute or two later had one door off its hinges so I could squeeze through with suitcases. I swept down the stairs just as the AT&T gang was leaving through the front door. The van honked.

"I'm here! Wait!" I hollered. A Lutheran thought bolted into my head in the middle of the lobby. I hadn't paid my eight *kwai* (two dollar) hotel bill. I extended the proper finger toward the checkout desk and hissed through clenched teeth: "Fuck you and your hotel and your elevator and your goddamn padlocks." I hopped into the van, seven minutes late.

"Where were you?" asked AT&T. "We almost left."

For the first time in Chinese history, a CAAC plane left on time. After we were airborne, I told the now comic story of my elevator and padlock adventure to AT&T. He thought it was funny. The comedy was only gradually making itself plain to me. We sat back to watch the Chinese countryside a few thousand feet below as the stewardess came around with plastic rabbit pins, our present for flying. I noticed that I had broken a fingernail in the course of my adventure. I reached in my pocket for the scissors on my Swiss Army Knife. My Swiss Army Knife? It lived in Wuhan now, presumably in the pocket of the desk clerk whom I had threatened. I had just committed the unforgivable sin in China, and lost "Nothung," the needful sword. I hoped there were no more dragons to slay on the way to Singapore.

* * *

We arrived in Canton to a complete mess, all planes, hydrofoils and trains booked and stuffed till the second coming. Half of Hong Kong had moved north for New Year's and now were headed south. AT&T and I went to a hotel. Full. We looked glumly at each other. Now what? We were Americans! We had currency! Nothing stops an American with a wad! Hong Kong was seventy miles south. We flagged a taxi. Two hundred *kwai*, foreign exchange currency only, about fifty dollars. We divvied up, loaded our bags and ordered the driver to hurry. In an hour and a half, we arrived in Shenzhen, to a crowd of about fifteen thousand already lined up for border inspection. My plane left at eleven o'clock that night and AT&T's the next morning. Not even *guanxi* and a truckload of Marlboros gets you into Hong Kong out of turn. The first lesson the British Empire taught was proper queuing. We queued.

Three hours later, at five minutes to five, we waited to have passports inspected on the Hong Kong side of the creek. My plane ticket waited in downtown Hong Kong in an office that closed in five minutes. I walked up to a border guard in a crisp British uniform and looked pathetic.

"A local call?" he asked. "There's a phone right in the office."

I got Jane at Sun Travel instantly. How strange to dial a phone that connects!

"Oh, don't worry," she said. "I assumed you'd be late and made two bookings. You have the same flight tomorrow for the same price. Stop by the office and pick it up. I've already turned in your credit card number, and it's all ready to go."

If there is a heaven for travel agents, Jane will be queen of it. The vile travel agents will become eternal elevator operators at the Hankou Hotel in Wuhan.

AT&T and I rented a fine room at the Kowloon Hotel, bought a bottle of Jim Beam and went to the San Francisco Steak House for New York cuts. I was violently sick all night.

* * *

Singapore, whatever its physical distance from China, is solar systems removed from it in every other conceivable way. The irony is that it *is* a Chinese city, settled mostly by the poorest, most oppressed Chinese peasants who created lotus land on the equator—a squeaky clean, meticulously efficient and functional place. Singapore is as rich, elegant and well-organized as China is dirty, backward and chaotic. And the same human beings made both of them.

I stayed with my old friends from Iceland, Jón Baldur Sigurdsson and his wife Lee Teng Gee. I slept in a white room with a computer, under a ceiling fan, listening to frangipani leaves clatter against the window blinds, smelling orchids all night. I sailed around the island on a racing yacht under a full moon and the Southern Cross and watched the lights of Malaysia and Indonesia across the straits. I drank icy gin and tonics in gardens full of tropical flowers I had never imagined. I dialed Minnesota directly and found out that the American government had award-ed me twenty thousand dollars for an essay savagely attacking Ronald Reagan and everything he stood for. I listened to Icelandic stories about Reykjavik, and high spirited Scandinavian gossip and arguments. I dined on caviar, oysters and gravlax, and the best Chinese food imaginable on this planet. And I shopped.

I went into a sporting goods store with palmettos and frangipanis growing in front.

"I would like to see a comprehensive Swiss Army Knife, please."

"We carry the complete line, sir," said the Chinese clerk in a crisp British accent.

"The Motorist, I think."

"Very good, sir, and will that be cash or card, sir?"

"Card. Do you take American Express?"

"Of course, sir. That will be one hundred and ten dollars Singapore, plus tax. Shall I wrap it?"

"No. I'll carry it. One never knows, does one, when one might chance upon a dragon?"

"No sir, one never knows."

TICKETS, PLEASE
请交票

When CAAC lost all my luggage on the way into China, a girl at the Beijing airport consoled me with a ticket. I could present it to retrieve my bags if the airline ever found them, though, as I discovered later, they had no intention of looking. At least I had a ticket.

The next day, though I was exhausted with jet lag and anger over lost bags, the *Waiban* (Barbarian Handling Office) man taxied me out to the Great Wall. He bought me a foreigner's ticket—ten times the Chinese price—and we ascended the steep old pile. "Does this mean I have to walk ten times as far as you?" I asked him quizzically. He did not get the joke.

At lunch he bought two tickets, one for me, one for himself. I ate alone, behind a screen; he disappeared into a noisy Chinese dining room. What fun China seemed likely to be! I left lunch early, afflicted with my first case of Chinese rumble guts, and looked for a toilet. I had heard about squatters, but was in no position to be particular. I got to the door of what looked like the right place, was about to bolt in, when a man shouted at me in Chinese and gestured that I should halt. I shrugged my shoulders and started forward.

He stood, held up his hand and said, "Ticket?"

"Ticket?" I asked.

"Ticket." He wiggled his fingers. Before I could resolve the situation, *Waiban*-man came running up behind me, and quickly paid him off—as I later discovered—ten *fen*, one tenth of a quarter, the price for foreigners to shit. Chinese were charged two *fen*. They shit less, presumably. He handed me a ticket, five or six lengths of Chinese toilet paper, pointed me toward the now legal door. I had fed dimes into a bus station door handle, but the ticket to shit was a first.

The next day on the way to the zoo, I rode my first Chinese bus. *Waiban*-man looked apologetic.

"It will be very crowded," he said.

"It's all right," I consoled him.

We both told the truth. The bus stopped, a rusty double-length pile, farting diesel fumes and sputtering, the two halves connected by something that looked like an accordion bellows that presumably allowed the bus to snake around tight corners. I could see no daylight through that bus, all windows and doors stuffed with arms, chins, hair, torsos. The door opened. No one left. Here we go, I thought, and disappeared into the mass. Once safely squeezed on, a hand wriggled through the pile, fingers extended.

Waiban-man said, "*Liange piao*," and fed a small note into the hand. Change came back with two tickets. He handed me one. "Very crowded . . . " he said.

"It's all right," I repeated. "I probably wouldn't want to ride it across the continent."

A Chinese bus at its greatest height is about six feet. I am 6'5". My head whacked the roof whenever the bus hit a pothole. I clutched my ticket. I later discovered the Chinese do indeed ride such buses across the continent. I rode one standing up for an entire day and lived. Shanghai, always more up to date than Beijing, hires bus pushers to cram passengers onto the bus from behind. The pushers make certain the pneumatic door doesn't close on a stray limb. Prostheses are more expensive than bus-pusher salaries.

We bought tickets at the zoo. Inside, we bought tickets at the Panda House. We bought more bus tickets, went to the Forbidden City and Tiananmen Square — more tickets. We went to lunch. First, buy tickets, then order, then eat. Want another dish? Buy another ticket. I shat again. Another ticket. I declined the invitation to see Mao's waxed corpse, no tickets there. I wanted some postcards. We went into a shop, bought a ticket, then found the postcards. We exchanged ticket for receipt. After this long day's touring, *Waiban*-man looked at me and announced, "Now you must fly to Xi'an, to the university."

"Sorry. I have no intention of leaving Beijing until those bastards at CAAC have found my luggage. Remember, I have nothing — no clothes, no books." It was not quite true. After two days in China, I had a half pound of ticket stubs.

"But the ticket has already been reserved."

"To hell with the ticket. Change the reservation till I can find the bags."

"That is not possible."

"Not possible to take a later plane?"

"Once you have bought a ticket, you must use it. No change is possible. I will be in great trouble if you do not . . . "

To quote an old cliché under new circumstances: Use it or lose it. Once money changes hands, the window slams shut. A ticket is not convenience but inexorable fate. Once you have ordered the dish, you are doomed to eat it, as my friend Old Fish often said.

I flew to Xi'an, where the next round of tickets started. At the Barbarians' guest house, you bought, as Joe the Louisiana Baptist called them—*yang guizi fan piao*, foreign devil rice tickets—or you didn't eat. Mere cash was of no use.

The old doorman at the Barbarians' guest house distributed daily pints of milk, a rare commodity in China, if you remembered to buy your milk tickets. To buy bread at the only bakery in the local market required tickets, not cash.

The Party organized the Chinese into *danwei*, work units, and through these units come all tickets necessary for life: grain tickets, rice tickets, meat tickets, egg tickets, bread tickets, tea tickets! Movie or theater tickets are hard to come by on the open market. For most performances, the *danwei* gets blocks of tickets and distributes them to members. Thus, the *danwei* decides what movies you see. Whoever passes out the tickets controls the daily life of the country. A *danwei* might be a factory, a whole university faculty (that was my *danwei*; I even had a work card!), or a farm commune. Presumably, only the safest apparatchik was ever put in charge of ticket distribution. If you wanted to strike off on your own in China, do your own work, travel, live your own life, marry whom you pleased, you left behind the safety net of tickets and walked across the tightrope alone. No tickets: no food, no train, no hospital. Cash is the great equalizer. It spends alike among the obedient as among the rebellious, and leaves no trace in your files.

Students were a *danwei*, too, thus carriers of tickets. They bought tickets to buy shower tickets. They were issued only five a month, at ten or twenty *fen* each. Hot water belongs to the people, after all. This created an active black market in shower tickets since some always hanker to be cleaner than others. They traded books and food for showers; petty larceny blossomed. Don't leave your shower tickets exposed or you suffer centuries of grime. A university of maybe ten thousand students had one public shower. It sported straight iron pipes with no shower heads from which poured unmixed boiling water onto cement floors covered with damp slime. Chinese public showers reminded me of old photos of concentration camp showers, waiting for unsuspecting Jews. Most Barbarians would have gladly peddled their tickets to buy shower tickets for poker change and cheerfully worn their dirt. The Chinese, more devoted to cleanliness than we, gladly jockeyed for what hot water they could get.

The more deeply I entered into Chinese life, the more tickets I accumulated in my billfold. An endless supply of various tickets was visible sign of the prosperity and influence of the bearer. The more tickets required to get something, the more highly it was valued.

I later came to understand what *Waiban*-man meant about the necessity of using my plane ticket to Xi'an. I went to the CAAC terminal myself to get a plane ticket to Hong Kong. I carried my American passport with Chinese exit visa, my Chinese green internal passport entitling me to travel inside China (or even buy a plane ticket), my brown *danwei* card from the university which entitled me to a thirty percent foreign expert's discount (neither the Chinese price, the Party price nor the regular foreigner price but rather, a new price for a new class), my white card entitling me to pay for the ticket with *renminbi* (the people's money) rather than special Barbarians' hard money, and a red-stamped official letter from my *danwei* Barbarian Handling Office, giving me their permission to travel. But this parcel of documents only began the process. I first bought a ticket to buy an application ticket, filled it out in Chinese and English. I then repeated all the information on various cards and, when done, presented it to the proper clerk. He mulled it over, looked suspicious, finally stamped it with his red official chop, kept the documents, and sold me a ticket which I could present to get the airplane ticket . . . three days later, after my travel itinerary and probably my political files had been properly investigated and approved. For an American accustomed to calling a travel agency answering service, leaving dates, a credit card number and instructions to have the completed ticket left at the airport desk, maybe a one-minute procedure, flying began for the first time to seem a heroic and dangerous activity, undertaken only for deepest necessity. Any Barbarians in China for a long time periodically lost their tempers at the hierarchical ticket-pricing system which rose by length of nose. The airplane and the toilet were only two among the thousands of reminders, visible signs of class structure sealed in cement. Anger or conniving sometimes got you the Chinese price, but it didn't seem worth the energy. Only money, after all . . . only tickets. More important to shit or go to Hong Kong.

My favorite Chinese ticket experience involved the premiere performance (in Xi'an) of Beethoven's *Ninth Symphony*, one hundred sixty-five years late, but just in time. I had started giving piano lessons to a brilliant nine-year-old boy, partly as an excuse to practice on his family piano. His father taught at a special high school which trained Chinese opera musicians. One day after a lesson he gleefully told me he had gotten an extra pair of tickets to the Beethoven premiere. Did I want them? The tickets came from his *danwei*. They were not only difficult but impossible to come by otherwise. I did, thank you very much.

I never mustered my courage to face Chinese bicycle traffic with my inadequate technique. Images, after the hypothetical crash, of several thin Chinese crushed under a heavy pink Icelandic body haunted me. Generally, I took buses or walked. After a leisurely stroll, I arrived at the music conservatory gate at seven o'clock, an hour early, to wait for my hosts. A brisk black market in Beethoven tickets had already started. I refused several good offers with a smug "got one already." By the time the Hous arrived, a mob had gathered around the still-padlocked door of the People's Revolutionary concert hall.

At five to eight the door was still padlocked. At eight o'clock, still padlocked. The surly crowd milled around. Someone climbed the steps and pounded on the glass door. The guard scowled. The crowd started brandishing tickets in their fists. Somebody rattled the door chain. The guard walked away. He started to open the door, but had lost the key to the padlock holding the chain. The door opened only twelve inches. The guard tried to shoo back the crowd, but the music lovers were not stoppable. He had opened Pandora's box, if only a foot. The crowd of about a thousand began surging into the lobby, a narrow snake of flesh squeezing through that scant opening. The speed and force of that surge defied the laws of physics and, probably, of physiology as well! How Beethoven would have loved the enthusiasm of that attack, "*Seid umschlungen millionen!*" All this to hear a one-hundred-sixty-five-year-old warhorse!

Mr. Hou, smaller and quicker than I, got through fast and beckoned me to follow. Carried along by the mob surge, I finally got to the door. I realized to my horror that, while it was wide enough for a skinny Chinese, it was not wide enough for me. I was about to become a cork in an exploding bottle! Mr. Hou grabbed one arm and began pulling, the crowd behind pushed. I was the human plug. Suddenly I started laughing, thinking to myself that I was to be the guest of honor at history's most comical dismemberment. "Oversized foreigner arrives home in chunks from Beethoven premiere. . . . " But malleability triumphed; I squeezed inside, intact. The crowd seemed pleased. Forces of nature bear their victims no malice.

Inside, it became clear this was no Lincoln Center crowd but, rather, Old Hundred Names fresh from the factory. Seeds crunching all around, flash bulbs exploding, candy wrappers crinkling, laughing, spitting, loud Chinese gossiping, cigarettes burning, babies cooing. The whole tradition of symphony customers knotting necks, de-mothballing furs, and sitting uncomfortably in sleepy Lutheran solemnity through Bruckner symphonies never developed here. This audience is used to Chinese opera, which is fun for the audience too, not expensive nap time for tired businessmen and their hair-dyed matrons.

The conductor appeared—a woman in her sixties, trained under Moscow's best in the Soviet Union years ago. She was evidently one of the grand names of Chinese music. An imposing woman with spectacles, she wore gray pants and a white shirt. She shook her baton at the audience to quiet them down. After a warmup "*huanying*" (welcome), she started lecturing. A student next to me translated. She explained to the audience that Beethoven was a true proletarian who composed to express the soul and struggle of the masses. He was a Marxist before his time, seeking to give voice in his last symphony to the eternal revolutionary striving of the oppressed workers. And so on and so forth . . . She reminded the audience that this was not Chinese music but serious stuff intended to improve them. Therefore they must sit quietly. No seed eating, storytelling, flash-picture taking and, most important of all, no spitting during the movements. She said she would pause between movements to explain the story of the thematic material—D minor was the key of struggle, the hammerstroke triple rhythm of the scherzo represented the rising anger of the oppressed, the placid tune of the adagio was the repose after victorious political struggle. Finally, in the last movement, "the workers raise voices to sing together their desire for international peace and justice."

And so she did. Between each movement she delivered a schoolmarm lecture on what to listen for, while the audience had five minutes to be Chinese. One peculiarity—Chinese orchestras seem not to tune up before the first chord. Each movement began with four or five bars of terrible cacophony after which the players clicked into tune. Ideologically correct orchestral technique?

Before the last movement, about three hundred white-robed choristers filed on stage. When their time came they bellowed out, "*An Die Freude*," Schiller's "Ode to Joy," in Chinese! It was fine! It was grand! It was a proper premiere for Ludwig's great piece! I think he would have been pleased . . . if he had been able to get a ticket.

An Alphabet of China Essays

They had found the padlock key in time for our exit. I toured the conservatory with Mr. Hou, met his composer buddies, and thumped on the conservatory pianos. Then I walked home three or four miles in the middle of the Chinese autumn night, fingering the still uncollected prize of a ticket in my pocket and smiling.

UNDERWEAR

短裤

In China, south of the Yellow River, it is illegal to heat a house in winter. I knew this abstractly. Still, it is one thing to read a fact in a book, and quite another to sit in a concrete room with loose windows rattled by a northwest wind howling in from the Gobi desert and Siberia. Winter in Xi'an is not of Minnesota magnitude (for that, you go to Harbin), but it is nasty, raw and long. Concrete holds cold. Even when sun warmed the courtyard, the room in which I sat, stood, or huddled under a quilt remained freezing. I often thought of an Icelandic phrase I heard day after day on arctic weather reports, *"fimm styki frost . . . "* literally five pieces of frost—or in conventional English: minus five degrees Celsius. But in China, I first understood the literal truth. Frost does not come by degree, but in stiff pieces.

The Chinese are as used to this as they are used to all the varieties of misery that poverty brings human beings. Only Barbarians whined. Chinese endured their croup, bronchitis and shivering. They tried to remain alive until spring and the great heat. Yet, a long and necessary acquaintance with misery does not require us to love or heroicize it. The Chinese, sensibly, did not. They detested cold and, unlike the Minnesota Lutheran, did not imagine that it built character or made them virtuous. It made them sick so, in practical Chinese fashion, they did something about it. They piled on underwear: silk, wool, cotton, anything they could afford, under shirts, sweaters, light coats, then heavy coats. Small, skinny people became square and forbidding. Little children almost disappeared under the size and weight of the layers, became walking boxes with shuffling appendages. Delicate women were transformed into Amazons, slight men into sumo wrestlers in medieval armor. The fashion for puffy down jackets added bulk. The winter Chinese resembled not human beings but moving closets. They sometimes wore every piece of clothing they owned, indoors and out, night and day.

Thus fortified, they continued the humdrum business of daily life. They went to class or work, managing to maneuver chopsticks past the layers to feed rice into the engine, bulking together in steamy buses, human clothes racks jostling each other.

The Chinese, so numerous and poor, are forced to live piled next to each other at home, in the street, or traveling. However, the necessity has not made them love the fact. They are deeply private people physically, with the reserve of an old culture and an elaborate system of formal courtesy. The touchy-feeliness of the New Age and twelve-step programs will be a long time reaching them. In dress and demeanor they prefer (or are forced to prefer) the drab, utilitarian, sensible color that doesn't show dirt — brown or gray or dull blue. Also, they are sexual Puritans with an underside of wild abandon, again the mark of a very old, maybe doddering culture. These characteristics are exacerbated by constant anti-sexual Marxist cant and fear of anti-egalitarian peacockery.

I strolled into my classroom one freezing November morning. I discovered no electricity and twenty five down-jacketed puff balls breathing visible air into frosty semi-dark. It seemed good weather to teach Thomas Hardy. After a while, the heat from massed bodies and the labor of reading "The Convergence of the Twain" and "Channel Firing" warmed the room a little. Students began unbuttoning the top few of their long series of buttons. First the coat, then the jacket, then the sweaters, then two or three shirts, all drab so far. Then an amazing Chinese phenomenon — underwear! Not white or gray or sensible, but colored like rainbows, or exotic tropical birds, or the Dowager Empress's robes: bright lime green, hot pink, imperial yellow, gay lavender, peacock blue, day-glo orange — layer after layer of brilliant cotton or silk. Down by the boot-tops, where layers pulled over two or three pairs of pants, the bottom end of the same brilliant underwear — lime green or hot pink calves. All brilliant cotton or silk, in a sane world made into scarves, dresses and lovely shirts, but here, underwear; the real China, closest to the heart as closest to the skin. It was a jumbled kaleidoscope of color, a circus of color, a visible emblem of what lives through winter in China just as it lives through the mad repression and violence of endless Chinese regimes from Qin Shihuang to Deng Xiaoping. This is what is hides under endless drab layers of the public self, waiting to burst its cocoon when any fortunate quirk of history turns on the heat at last, lets warm air blow through.

How lovely to teach Thomas Hardy in that half-dark, cold, dusty room full of underwear! Lawrence Ferlinghetti once called poetry "the underwear of the soul." In China he might have called underwear "the poetry of the soul."

Unlike Chinese teachers, I sat on the desk, wandered around the room, or hung halfway out the window while I taught. The students were used to calmer, more doctrinaire teaching but came, I think, to like or, at least, to tolerate my style. That morning I sat on the desk, parked my feet on a chair and pulled up my now baggy pants.

"Comrade Bill!" they cried almost in unison and considerable shock, "You are naked under your pants! Where are your underwear? You will freeze in this awful Chinese cold!"

"Don't worry about me," I said. "I have an Icelandic thermostat and am not happy above fifty degrees. Warmer than that, I prefer to be entirely naked. Will that be all right with the class monitor in the springtime?" There were many giggles. But privately, I regretted being too well insulated for long underwear. Imagine having long layers of lime green, pink or orange silk next to your body—in secret!

Spring finally came and passed in fifteen minutes (as it does in continental climates like Shaanxi and Minnesota), and the great enervating heat began. Then there was a new and delightful transubstantiation of underwear. Sheer skirts and blouses of filmy see-through nylon were high fashion for Chinese women. It was sweetly comic to watch the exposed underwear on pretty Chinese girls bicycling languidly through the streets. Chinese women are extremely modest. The exposed underwear thumbed its nose at you is if saying:

"I am covered, quite decent and practical. What you see, and what you choose to make of it, is your own business."

That's poetry of the soul, poetry of things that survive everything, no matter the fierce cold of unheated winter, no matter the brutal stupidity of power.

VIOLIN
小提琴

After a month in China, I had still found no piano, and my fingers began practicing unconsciously on the bed sheets at night while I slept. I was an alcoholic without whiskey, a junkie without heroin. Music, like anything else, is a habit, an addiction, a fix, and I was in the middle of withdrawal, delirium tremens brought on by the absence of Mozart, Bach, Liszt, under my hands. My neighbors in the next Barbarian apartment knew an engineer on the faculty who played the violin. Perhaps he would know where to find a piano in the neighborhood.

The engineer turned out to be an amiable and sweet-tempered man of about fifty who missed playing violin sonatas as much as I missed the piano. "Maybe we could practice together. It has been a long time . . ." I agreed.

We started going once a week to the apartment of one of his colleagues, a power engineer who had been lucky enough (or had a back door) to get hold of a new Pearl River piano from Canton. It was a cheaply made upright but serviceable and close to being in tune. Mr. Zhang's wife and daughter both took piano lessons. The whole family loved music. I would come an hour early to violin rehearsal, and play Chinese favorites for them. They brought out glasses of steaming tea and bowls of Shanghai candy while I played Mozart's "Turkish March," Beethoven's *"Für Elise"* (the best-loved piece in China, I think!), the "Moonlight Sonata," *"Liebestraum #3,"* Schubert's "Serenade," "Military March," and a little Scott Joplin ragtime. They liked these pieces and could listen to them over and over. Between numbers, or while they drank tea and chatted, I played Bach fugues which they did not like so much. The Chinese prefer Western music with color, dash, grand rhetoric and sweeps of melancholy. In orchestral music they like Tchaikovsky and the noisy parts of Beethoven. I never met a Chinese who was moved by Bach. Bach's music may be too interior or mathematical for Chinese who, for whatever reason, seem to prefer nineteenth-century grand romantic gestures. Perhaps Russians in the fifties left them this taste. Whatever else Bach is, he is not Slavic.

Lao Wei arrived with his violin. More tea, more candy, more cigarettes. He handed me his music: Mozart's A *Major Concerto* with piano as orchestra, Beethoven's "Spring Sonata," Grieg's "C Minor Sonata," a handful of virtuoso salon favorites by Weiniawski, Sarasate, Drdla, Fritz Kreisler. Lao Wei rosined his bow, tuned, nodded. We began with Mozart.

He was a first-rate amateur violinist, with big romantic tone and gestures, who could not count to four. The playing went awkwardly at first. I tried to follow, found myself double timing bars, then taking sweeping *ritards* where none existed. All the notes were there on the violin, but not in time. The rhythm under the piece disappeared into some mysterious ionosphere. After a half hour of stumbling and false starts, things went more smoothly. After an hour, we finished the movement triumphantly. The Zhangs, now moved to the other room to get their own work done, were pleased too. They said, "beautiful," poured more hot water over the tea leaves, and heaped the candy bowl.

Lao Wei apologized for his rhythm while he rosined his bow again. "It's been more than ten years since I played."

"Ten years!" I said. "Your technique is remarkable if you haven't played . . . "

"Oh, I play alone sometimes, not often. But I have not played with an accompanist."

"Are pianists so hard to come by in China?"

"Yes . . . " His voice trailed off. There was more to be said but not now.

After another slurp of tea, we resumed for the last half hour. Now gypsy music by Sarasate and the others. This went better because the piano provided nothing but chords and afterbeats in simple harmony; the violinist had all the fun.

We rehearsed every week through fall, as the temperature steadily dropped. Finally the concrete room was thirty-five or forty degrees. We came with gloves, used tea glasses to warm our hands between movements. The Zhangs sat listening, bundled in mufflers and padded coats. The room clouded with frozen breathing. Damp cold threw the piano badly out of tune. But music is music and we went on playing. Mozart and Beethoven went like silk; Grieg came along.

I went off to Singapore for Chinese New Year in February. I found a music store where I bought Caesar Franck's "A Major Violin Sonata." For some odd reason, the canon in the last movement ran through my head for months in China. I woke at night dreaming one voice, and singing the other a measure later. It haunted me; I craved it.

Though he had never played it, Lao Wei had heard the piece in America where he studied engineering. By mid-February, the temperature indoors was arctic, the piano terminal. The tea was cold before we finished a movement. China almost defeated music just as the simple square quarter-note rhythm of the canon almost defeated us. Lao Wei's rhythmic uncertainty, gone now in Mozart, came back in Franck.

"Are you not fond of counterpoint?" I asked.

"I like a single melody, one beautiful passionate tune."

In Franck, the tune is everywhere, at different times simultaneously. You hear that canon not as a single event, but as an event taking place continually, everywhere you listen. I suspected some truth about the mind of China in this mistrust of counterpoint. It is music without a center, without a master, without a single destination. A canon, once begun, obeys only internal laws.

We gave up on Franck and on winter. We decided to retire our music till spring. Lao Wei invited me to dinner with his family. He lived on the fifth floor of a building exactly like his colleague Zhang's. I huffed up five flights and found Lao Wei on his balcony looking out at clouds of coal dust and smoke hiding the mountains twenty or thirty miles away. His new project was to translate the film script of *Amadeus* into Chinese. I helped him with some of the odd idioms. Mozart was his great passion.

"It is very strange for an American to meet an engineer who plays the violin so well. In America, engineers shoot ducks and play golf, not Mozart. Did you never want to be a violinist?"

"I was a young man in the early days after the liberation. Poor countries have no use for violinists. They need technology."

He said no more, but I had the feeling, as I did so often in China, that most of her technocrats and scientists would rather have been poets, calligraphers, or musicians if the world had been saner and sweeter. I do not have this feeling in America.

He looked down from his high balcony. "My accompanist, my dear friend, jumped from a balcony like this . . . or was pushed. That was during the bad days of the Cultural Revolution. She was a wonderful pianist. We worked hard on Beethoven and Mozart, and I have not felt like playing those pieces for many years."

After a year in China, I had heard countless horror stories of the Cultural Revolution, each one sad and brutal. These stories did not, and will not, lose their power over me. A dead pianist, pianos set afire, violins smashed, Ming drawings shredded into a toilet pit, Tang statues with heads sledge-hammered off, bonfires of old books, heaps of smashed porcelain, more bodies laying crushed under balconies or sunk at the bottom of ponds. How can this civilization, where engineers play Mozart in the middle of the night and hide their violins for years on end from fright, do it to itself again and again and again?

As in a canon, there is another voice waiting to enter this history. It bides its time . . . for awhile.

WAIGUOREN

外国人

American blacks and whites have been at each other's jugulars for so long they might be cheered to discover at least one corner of the world where *neither* is considered quite human. Walk down any shopping and residential street in Xi'an. A Chinese mother comes along, cradling her one-child-family toddler. It is darling: sparkling black eyes, a little twist of black hair, a gold embroidered jacket. The little fist shoots out with a cocked index finger. It shouts gleefully at the top of its lungs, "WAIGUOREN! WAIGUOREN!" and points straight at you.

That intonation might be used to holler: "Elephant!" or "Two-Headed Cat!" or "Bearded Lady!" Sometimes the mother blushes, and tries to shush the child, giving you a shrug and look as if to say, "Sorry, he can't help it. You know how babies are when they see freaks." Sometimes the mother joins him. The two continue chorally, following you down the block, summoning the neighbors. The first time this happens, it is a little disconcerting.

I complained about this to my wise motorcycle anthropologist fellow Barbarian teacher. "Don't let this upset you," he said. "The next time it happens, just smile sweetly, point back and holler, 'ZHONG GUO-REN' at the same decibel level." I did. The child stopped in astonishment; the mother hurried past; no choral aftersong trailed me.

What had I just done and said? The child called me "out-country-person" and I called him "middle-country-person," or in more idiomatic English: "foreigner" and "Chinese." How did he discover my secret so instantly? I am 6'5", red-bearded and green-eyed. What a shrewdly observant child! He would have used the same word for James Baldwin, Miles Davis or Roosevelt Grier and, indeed, for N. Scott Momaday and Chief Dan George. *Waiguoren* all, we are brothers in China.

The Chinese are famous xenophobes and richly deserve their reputation. You (or your nose) can be blamed for everything that goes wrong in the Middle Kingdom: AIDS? *Waiguoren*. Rambunctious demonstrations for a little democracy? *Waiguoren*. Failure of the five-year plan? *Waiguoren*. In a way, it is a kind of compliment to be responsible for so much in a kingdom as ancient and vast as China. We had not known we were so powerful, we *Waiguoren*.

When a native speaker hears the word "*Waiguoren*," he understands it differently than our rather bland, connotationless English word, "foreigner." It means, in Chinese, to be not truly part of human civilization — to be outside the magic circle of the Middle Kingdom. He hears, and our little toddler shouts, "Barbarian." In these essays, I have chosen to translate the word correctly.

Barbarians should also be suspicious of the word "minority." Officials in Beijing drool sentiment over the happy minorities in the Middle Kingdom: their singing and dancing, their unique primitive cultures, their legal right to more than one child. Who are these minorities? Among them are Tibetans, Mongolians, Kazakhs, Manchu, Uygurs, and the tribe we know in America as Hmong. To the Chinese, they are *Waiguoren*; racially and culturally outside the Middle Kingdom of Han. I pointed out to a Chinese acquaintance the similarities between Beijing's notion of governing Tibet and Andrew Jackson's conception of an Indian reservation.

"Absolutely not!" he fumed. "It is a great hardship for us Han to be there in that god-forsaken place. The Tibetans are dirty, illiterate, superstitious, and . . . "

"Uncivilized?" I finished the sentence.

"Yes," he said. "Uncivilized."

I am not sure the Tibetans (or others) are much cheered by Beijing picking up Kipling's "Burden" to uplift and civilize the lower races.

Every county, factory, or university in China that has any cause to deal with Barbarians has a *Waiban*. This literally means foreign office, but is understood as Barbarian Handling Office and thus so translated. Like a circus animal, you are an object to be handled, fed, exercised, amused, but isolated and watched. You are expected to perform your act, whether teaching or doing business, then go back into your reasonably comfortable cage for the night. You will be groomed and tended for the next performance but not allowed to stroll around the grounds or cause trouble among the customers. You are special. You get more hunks of meat, and your more commodious cage is cleaned and serviced. But, try to behave like a human being and leave your Barbarian cage, and the handlers will grab their whips, will send out dragoons to fetch you back and discipline you. Their whole purpose in life is you. Your whole purpose in China is to escape from them unless, of course, you enjoy being a circus animal. Simply because *you* are called a Barbarian is no reason to act like one. Barbarians obey orders; humans don't.

Some *Waiban* people are decent and honorable and try to do their best by you. Others, maybe a majority, are apparatchiks, boot-lickers, and liars. They can be trusted no more than a timber rattler. Still, whether good or bad, their office is inimical to your learning anything, seeing anything real or having any fun in China. Since they start with the official view that they are not dealing with human beings, they are not likely to do you much intentional good.

Barbarians noticed Chinese xenophobia a long time ago. But who finds it useful? Power needs convenient strangers as scapegoats to avoid responsibility for its own incompetence, cruelty and venality. Hitler knew this well, as did the Dowager Empress, the Japanese and a goodly number of American politicians. Deng Xiaoping and Li Peng practice at it too, improving day by day even as you read this sentence.

Xenophobia doesn't need a passport. A cousin of mine was an active Lutheran his entire life — he tithed, worked on the church council, taught Sunday school, was a lay reader. During the Vietnam War, a bunch of students and local pinkos organized a peace walk from Canby to Marshall, about thirty miles. Minneota was halfway, so the marchers wanted to rest their feet in a church basement and have a glass of water. The Catholic and one Lutheran church turned them down. My cousin went to the council of the other (he was a member) and asked permission. They all agreed that the war was a bad thing; they thought the march a reasonable idea.

Finally one council member spoke up, "But there'll be all those strangers here in our church basement." The council voted no permission. The next Sunday my cousin asked to preach and did so. His text was the parable of the Good Samaritan. He asked the question, "Who is a stranger?" The last line of his sermon was, "So, I am the stranger." He walked away from the pulpit, down the aisle and out the front door of the church, alone. He has not been back for twenty years.

My cousin would not do well under a *Waiban*'s thumb. How different is the face of that Minneota council member from the face of the Chinese child? Don't they both stick out their finger, point and holler, "*Waiguoren!*"? It must be a great relief for American blacks and whites to get home from China where they have been clumped together in that uncomfortable brotherhood, and get back to their real business: baiting each other while hollering, "Barbarian!" "*Waiguoren!*"

196   COMING HOME CRAZY

XMAS IN CHINA

中国的圣诞节

The American cliché goes: "Put Christ back in Xmas." In China, well over a billion human beings have either never heard of Christ or, if the name rings a bell at all, think of Him in the same context as famous soccer players, dead movie stars, and inventors of gadgets they can't afford. It seems a good place to put the X back in Christmas.

The Chinese love parties and are eager to please and humor foreigners and their habits. Students brought wonderfully comic Xmas cards to their Barbarian teachers, resplendent with pictures of Mickey Mouse, a very oriental-looking Santa Claus and photos of the Grand Canyon. It would not have surprised me to find Elvis Presley perched on top of a scraggly Xmas tree. They knew the holiday had something to do with popular culture and in that were not far wrong. The favorite Chinese disco Xmas carol was "Ludolph the Led-nosed Leindeer." It played continually well into July.

For years, I have indulged myself in the awful middle class habit of sending xeroxed Xmas letters. Aside from the small pleasure of writing two consecutive English words beginning with X, I find these letters a reasonably good history of what my life in China was like, so I give you three of them: in 1986, a letter smuggled out of Hong Kong by my printer cousin, Chuck Josephson, describing my first view of Chinese daily life; in 1987, a nostalgic letter of longing for China, written on my way back to visit; in 1988, the vaguely discontented letter of a man back too long in America and not sure he wants to be there. Finally, from 1989, I include an essay defending odd Xmases (Xmas with an old-fashioned X) in China and elsewhere from 1989.

And so, dear reader, think of yourself as one of my defenseless old friends who have been opening these xeroxed histories for twenty-five years. Settle yourself into a soft chair with an afghan handy to keep your feet warm, pour a steaming eggnog (make sure there is plenty of brandy in it), clean your spectacles, and have a Merry Chinese Xmas.

I

December 1986

Dear Friends,

This Xmas letter comes to you in a stranger way from a stranger place than any you have yet received. It is five o'clock in the morning in the Mandarin Hotel lobby in Hong Kong, my first morning out of China in over three months. I have done business, bought something, used a credit card, drunk tap water, dialed a telephone that connected, asked directions, read a newspaper, and eaten a lemon. If I had driven a car and been out on the town with a woman, the experience would be complete. The WEST is still coasting along, doing all right for itself, even in my absence.

And where am I that this humdrum life seems so exotic to me? Should you not have heard, I am in China being a "foreign expert" for a year at Xi'an Jiaotong University in central China. What that means is teaching English, a language the Chinese are passionate to learn, and getting in return, not much money, but an experience beyond price—of daily life in what is, after all, still the big OTHER that shares the planet with "us."

What is my life in China like? Jiaotong is a big polytechnic college, mostly for engineers, but with a foreign language program to train teachers.

Without, I think, particularly wanting one, Jiaotong got its token literary intellectual when it hired me. I teach three classes of British and American literature, two essay-writing classes, and a History of the Language class—fifteen hours a week, more than an American teaching load, but less than the twenty or twenty-five hours that some foreign experts have been bamboozled into working.

I start teaching at eight o'clock and teach until noon. The Chinese school week (like their work week) is six days (Saturday), but I teach only four. The Chinese seem appalled that Westerners take off two days a week!—and cannot imagine what we do with all that leisure. They are worse Puritans than Calvin, in this as in other regards, loving the appearance of something more than the reality. A Minnesotan would finish the content of a Chinese work week by Monday afternoon, and go fishing until the next Monday; but the Chinese worker likes to spread it out, take it slowly, and give the appearance of diligence. In doing this, he is supported by the laws of his country and his "work unit."

I live in the Jiaotong Guest House, a combination tourist hotel and settlement camp for foreign teachers. It's about two blocks from the university and, like the countless (though numbered) blocks of flats that surround it, is made from gray cement. It differs from Chinese apartments in having a rug (what an American would call indoor-outdoor patio carpet — cheap and sloppily laid), plastic wallpaper, hot water (a few hours a day, most days, usually . . .), sporadic heat and a sit toilet rather than a squat. A Chinese apartment is all cement, one faucet (or a shared one for the building), a communal squat, and no heat. So we live swell!

My stove is two bare burners attached to a small propane bottle in a kitchen about one yard square (give or take an inch). A Chinese stove burns coal briquettes instead, which makes for interesting atmospheric analysis inside houses.

There are about a dozen foreigners in the building: two Minnesotans, three Louisianans, a few strays from elsewhere, three Brits and four Canadians (all from Manitoba). There is one phone in the lobby that sometimes is answered, and sometimes not, by employees whose three or four words of remembered English do not include your name. The gates of our little home are locked at eleven o'clock at night (to protect us, they say . . .). Almost all of us (even those over seventy) have wound up jumping the gates a time or two and throwing stones at the screen of a sleeping friend. There is a little restaurant connected to the guest house where we are supposed to eat. Like any institutional food, it is boring and offensive after a day or two, and has the further disadvantages of cold food, excess grease, and a price eight or ten times what a Chinese would pay.

Does this sound like a summer camp run by Lutheran Nazis? Do I dislike it? Of course . . . but the point is that the Chinese are not fools. They all dislike the places where they live — places ugly, cold, crowded and uncomfortable. But China is a very poor country and a very overcrowded one and, like the Chinese, even the foreigners come around to being grateful for some sort of roof over their heads and make do, and get on with the business of daily life.

The Chinese day begins at six-thirty with exercise music blaring out of the endless loudspeakers that hang from trees or adorn roof tops. Those ghastly mechanical bullhorns are the only machines that work dependably in China. Unlike the electricity, the heat, the water, the telephone, etc., they can be counted on to function to get you out of bed.

At morning break, they play the "Internationale"; they like military music and loud wind bands: these punctuate the day. If you know me well enough to get this Christmas letter, you don't need to ask my opinions of these things. Those bullhorns are the evil flowers of an authoritarian culture. I sometimes wish my father had taught me to shoot better . . .

So I'm up, waiting for the hot water to come on, brewing my last dregs of contraband Western coffee (the Chinese do sell coffee, not good, but coffee). I grade a few papers, read a poem or two, and char a piece of Chinese bread over my open propane flame. I slather on some date butter, drop a crumb or two, and am off to the eight o'clock class.

It's about a ten-minute walk, and the great hazard is dodging speeding bicycles. The stories you have heard about Chinese bicycle jams are not exaggerations. Chinese bicyles are old junkers, one speed, thick tires, parts falling off, loaded with wives, children, bales, bags, cabbages, live chickens. The air through which we all move is gray, sooty, and thick. The whole crowd is phlegming, rasping and spitting. Many faces have disappeared behind white surgical masks. Chinese factories belch out unfiltered fumes, black coal smoke saturates the air. Mongolia and the Gobi Desert are just north and full of grit, and when the winter northerlies blow . . . suffice it to say that I thought of giving up smoking in China, but decided against it. It's better for you than breathing. Aside from air, water, earth, fire, and ideology, China is a remarkably pure country.

The classroom building (also gray cement) is the same temperature as the out-of-doors. One hundred degrees in July, twenty-five now. The hallways are, to put it mildly, filthy and smelly. Winter has deadened my sensitivity to old urine and uncleaned, unflushed toilets — but not completely. Piles of garbage, overflowing spittoons, rotted fruit peels, waste paper, chalk dust — here's the classroom. The electricity is still off (as it will be all day), so twenty-five Chinese students sit in semidarkness, bundled in five layers of underwear and sweaters, topped by mittens, caps, and down jackets, breathing visibly out into the frosty air . . . Class begins!

If what I have described so far seems dark and uncomfortable, and you don't want to come to China to share my adventure, here comes the payoff. Those twenty-five (and my other classes — all) are among the most delightful, curious, and intelligent human beings I have ever encountered. They are a teacher's dream; they are what I went to graduate school to find. They are not sophisticated; they have never traveled, have seen nothing; they have read and mastered everything put in front of them — but books are almost unavailable in China: no foreign exchange, old cultural xenophobia, sexual puritanism, Marxist dogmatism — the reasons are numberless. But those students want to read — to think (though no one has encouraged them) — to know.

They sleep eight to an unheated room, live on twelve dollars a month, and have frequently been shoved by the bureaucracy into a field they dislike — but they are curious, and when the chips are counted, that's all that matters. I'd move the whole lot to Minneota if I could manage it.

(End of Part one. Part two is written in the middle of the night after a few days "shopping" in Hong Kong.)

My first real culture shock has come on me. Hong Kong is a lovely city, hills plunging to the water, spectacular and elegant skyscrapers, a spotless underground, every gadget and luxury cheerfully up for bargain, credit cards accepted, thank you very much. In a day or so, I go back to the land of *"Mei you"* — not have, not work, not arriving, not available, not possible . . .

No one staring at me in Hong Kong. Though twice the size of the southern Chinese, I am just another shopper, and — for the first time in three months — anonymous. I hadn't realized how much it affected me to be always an object of not entirely kindly interest. At a "bring your own chopsticks" noodle stand, thirty gather to watch me slurp, pressing in close. *Look,* their eyes say, *it eats almost like a human being.* My God, what isolation and poverty do to human beings! Lock them in and let them come to the conclusion that their own culture is the only one on earth. Equate strangeness and newness with corruption of values. Teach people to keep to themselves. Feed them abstractions.

Confused is the right word for my state. Too much has happened, too fast, both interior and exterior, and I haven't had the silence to process it. (What an awful word — process!) I've been too busy living the strange adventure to organize it mentally for your or my benefit. It is chaos — raw mental lava coming at me. Pressed into an argument, all I know is that I know both less and more than when I left, but I don't know which is which!

Holm confused? Without a final word? What is this? A loose screw? No. I am happy, healthy (thinner), have stronger legs (miles a day!), a few words of a new language, remarkable friends and students, and a few old ideas monkey wrenched.

Love from China,

II

In Hong Kong last year, I sat in a hotel at five in the morning trying to describe the strangest life I have ever lived. I was tired, thin and ten thousand miles from Minneota, Minnesota. Now I'm back, fat, sitting at my old kitchen table early in the morning, looking at an inch of ice sheathing the lilac bushes, the grass, the honeysuckle; the whole world quick-frozen and leaning over from the weight of its glittering coat. The coffee is good here in Minneota, and the stove thumps on dependably whenever the thermostat gives it an order. The paycheck arrives punctually, the car works, the new bakery in the old cowboy boot store fills the street with the smell of hot bread every morning, the bank cashes checks efficiently and the Bell telephone squawks like a chirpy young rooster. Things work; it's comfortable; what, me worry? And so I'm going to China again. In some odd way, part of me has never left and is still there, clutching my chopsticks, plotting against bureaucrats, looking for a piano.

The second half of the year of teaching there was both more wonderful and more terrible than the first. The shock of Chinese dirt, squalor and cold wore itself deeply into my body like a new habit. I made new friends, and old friendships deepened, and I found myself charmed and moved by the decency, generosity, dignity and humor of the everyday Chinese I met and whose homes I visited. I started traveling Chinese-style with gangs of students and friends, riding ramshackle buses or third-class hard seat Chinese train coaches to obscure backwaters that had never seen a foreigner (and sometimes landed me in a police office, explaining my odd presence). I was a guest in houses that, in American terms, had nothing and gave everything. On one hand, I dined on cold expensive grease in the Foreigners' Guest House, and on the other I was a guest for magnificent twenty-course meals with plenty of beer and schnapps in plain, cold, damp, cement rooms. But those dreary rooms were full of lively faces, raucous laughter, sardonic jokes about politicians and bureaucrats, first-rate storytelling, flying noodles, smears of pepper sauce, and deep feeling. The Chinese, with so little, have not lost the power of celebration in their daily lives. In America, owning so much, we love and praise so little, and our comfortable lives shrivel as a consequence.

I wrote an essay last year titled *"Mei You"* (Not Have), the first Chinese words a foreigner learns, and their power to describe metaphorically the absence of almost all the comforts and goods one is used to. However, I wasn't quite accurate; simultaneously with *mei you*, one learns *hen hao* (very good), and its usual form spoken twice, *hao de, hao de* (good, good). Good, good is an equal metaphor for life in China, not necessarily because of its connection to the fat life, good suits, BMWs, and oysters, but because it indicates the possibility of the survival of just praise.

There was a young man working in the guest house who made everything possible for foreigners. The usual Chinese difficulties came up when he was faced with any of our problems: a taxi ride, train tickets, a malfunctioning electric heater, a broken camera, a bureaucratic lie, a rude official. He screwed up his face, mounted his bicycle, knocked on any back doors he could find, used Kents and Marlboros judiciously — the common Chinese bribe — and almost always solved the problem in a creative and unexpected way.

"How did it go?" I'd ask.

"Good, good," he said.

We would celebrate with a steamer of *baozi*, the local pork dumplings, at a neighborhood food stand.

"Are they satisfactory?" I'd ask.

"Good, good," he replied, hot sauce flying off the ends of his chopsticks.

One day he walked into my room while I was playing a scratchy tape of the Mozart *Clarinet Concerto* on my Chinese tunebox. "Good, good," he said. "This is good, good."

I christened him Good-Good and began saying it myself. At the bottom of your life, you find out what there is to affirm, and by, God, you had better affirm it! There are duties in this universe larger than yourself and your own imagined discomforts.

The dark side of China, that which cannot be praised but must be fought, was connected to good-good. When you try to violate the pecking order of Chinese bureaucracy and get a little truth laid on the table, someone must lose face, and the consequences are often terrible. Good-Good himself lost his job for being too direct with foreigners, for translating too accurately the convenient lies by which the functionaries survive, there as here. I escaped from the foreign office's vigilant eyes one weekend and disappeared into the vast Chinese desert with one of my students, a brilliant and very pretty young girl. She wanted me to meet her fiancé and see her home country, vast shifting golden sand dunes with the snowcapped Tibetan plateau rearing up around them. We stayed in an old Silk Road trading town, flat-roofed yellow mud houses, carved doors, ancient temples, sunsets brilliant as those on the high plains, streets full of Muslims, Kazakhs, Tibetans, Chinese. When we returned, the authorities got revenge for lost face by punishing the girl. I was untouchable, a foreigner and part of a lucrative exchange program, so to get me, they got her, with the whole ghastly authoritarian apparatus: endless enforced self-criticisms, thought examinations, interrogations and threats by cowardly Party hacks who seemed to take perverse pleasure in persecuting a harmless, innocent and generous girl. I discovered two things in China about bureaucrats. First, every toady in that system, or in this, is a coward. They attack only those with no smell of fight drifting off them; second, the toady has no moral bottom. Most of us who had mothers preserve the illusion that there are some things we wouldn't do, whatever the circumstances. The bureaucratic toady has so such illusion and is capable of unimaginable things. His job is not to do something but to save himself and his own useless job, and to that end he will bite like a nervous rattler. The toady is not only Chinese, but British, Canadian, Swedish, American, Minnesotan . . .

One of my loveliest friendships in China came from my search for a piano. Pianos disappeared from China during the Cultural Revolution, axed apart, burned, drowned, victims of the same fanatical madness that wrecked the statues and burned scores of Mendelssohn in Germany in the thirties. Now, as China comes out of its political fog, the Chinese remember what they have always known: that they love music, any kind, and are good at it. But they are poor, and pianos are hard to come by. I followed rumors of a piano like a young reporter chasing a first scoop and, in the course of one expedition, met a middle-school teacher and composer who had started twelve-tone composing — Schoenberg having arrived in China in 1981 — and needed a sight reader to make sense of his scores. He had not one word of English, and I had no Chinese, so I took a student along to translate. But not necessary! Mr. Hou and I spoke "music" to each other, writing out fugue themes on a score pad, plunking harmonies on his Beijing piano, humming, singing and conducting in the dusty air. Then I met his son, Little Hou, a beautiful nine-year-old boy with a wickedly intelligent grin and twinkling black eyes. The boy ascended the piano bench, his still-too-short legs dangling a foot away from the pedals, and rattled off a Clementi sonatina with perfect fingering.

"He has no teacher," his father said. "Maybe you could tell him something about the piano."

Little Hou was astonishingly talented, the quickest child I've ever met, and every other week or so I'd troop over to his icy, cement half-room, almost filled by the upright piano, and listen to the music I'd given him to play: Bach inventions, Mozart sonatas, Bartok Bulgarian dances, Joplin rags. Between pieces, he would blow on his tiny hands, rub them together and then mitten them to warm them up for the next piece. Our breath curled visibly together above the piano. His mother fortified me during the cold with endless cups of hot jasmine tea, melon seeds and peeled fruit. I was fortified best, though, by the brains and irony in those small black eyes and the amazing life in those undersized fingers. I even rigged up a low stool so he could get to the pedals and start Schumann. The resonant noises pleased him.

In cleaning out my room before leaving China, I took down a big, inflatable Goodyear dirigible (a free gift for buying tires) that had gotten packed by mistake and had spent the year hanging from the light fixture in my cement flat. It had been an object of endless merriment to the Chinese. Now it was to be Little Hou's. I walked over to his apartment through murky July heat and found him playing soccer with his buddies as if he'd never heard of a Bach fugue. He smiled mischievously, cradled the dirigible and thanked me elegantly, in both Chinese and English, a perfect imitation of my own Minnesota accent. Any species that invents excuses to blow up that little boy to fight Communism has no business on the same planet with you and me.

I left in late July, exhausted and ready for the West but not quite ready for Minneota. I sailed in Puget Sound and the San Juan Islands for two or three weeks, trying to put my strange experiences together in my head and/or readjust to gin and tonic, endless cheese, clean toilets, green money and Ronald Reagan.

Sailing was lovely, but I'm afraid the readjustment didn't work very well. I'm still uneasy in America, don't fit so comfortably into my old life. It was fine to see old friends, to be in my wonderful (and perfectly tended) house, to play my Raudenbush and tune my clavichord. I gave poetry readings, went to dinner parties, talked on the telephone, wrote checks, started teaching at my old job, graded papers, complained about reading them, ate too much, drank too much, gained weight, combed through the newspapers for news of China, woke up in the middle of the night listening to machines humming, published short stories and essays, got money from the government for an essay attacking the government, found French roast coffee beans in Marshall, ordered a pig, despaired more about teaching in America, drove my friends crazy with my lovesick mooniness about China, refused to sign my U.S. Government immigration forms, got paid anyway, tried to refuse the paychecks, gave up and collapsed into convention, practiced Brahms' capriccios and intermezzos and transcriptions of Bach organ fugues, got my teeth fixed, a wisdom tooth pulled, raved and ranted to innocent bystanders about not having enough time to write and wrote anyway, but still something isn't right here.

Now, I'm off to China again.

III

December 1988

Dear Friends,

One year ago, I sat at this kitchen table looking out at snow, the sun coming up behind Daren Gislason's red barn, lonesome for China, but with a ticket in my pocket for Xmas. A year later, Dan Quayle is Vice President, my main excuse for going to China is sound asleep upstairs on a Friday morning, and I am still lonesome for China—or Serbo-Croatia, or Singapore, or Burundi—or somewhere the snow doesn't lie so contentedly and regularly white, covering the dry grass for so long, so quietly. While almost all the rest of America seems to me settled into a spiritual earthquake fault, buying furniture, watching TV, making money, and waiting for the end, I keep hearing Walt Whitman's voice:

> Afoot and lighthearted I take to the open road,
> Healthy, free, the world before me.
> The long brown path before me leading wherever I choose.
>
> . . . .
>
> Henceforth I ask not good fortune, I myself am good
>   fortune,
> Henceforth I whimper no more, postpone no more, need
>   nothing . . .
>
> . . . .
>
> (Still I carry my delicious burdens,
> I carry them, men and women, I carry them with me wher-
>   ever I go
> I swear it is impossible for me to be rid of them,
> I am filled with them, and I will fill them in return.)

So the first of my "delicious burdens" is China. I am still lonesome for it. Though my powers as a correspondent have led Chinese friends to think me prematurely dead, I hope this letter, should it reach them, reminds them that a part of my heart is always with them, longing for more mad adventures on the road to Gansu, or Sichuan, or Jiuzhaigou,

206   *COMING HOME CRAZY*

another endless night of stories and local noodles. MJB and I will see you sooner than you think.

Last year, I arrived in Hong Kong in December at midnight, met by Will LaValley, a friend who works for the airlines, but where is Comrade Marcella? I thought: an eight-hour late plane, a crazy bureaucrat at the border, who knows? After waving at Customs, we saw a waiting hall jammed with maybe a thousand anxious Asian faces. But where is the Norwegian? She appeared suddenly from the side, robed in red, and grabbed me in a hammerlock. It was the best hammerlock of the year . . . may it never loosen . . .

We stayed with Will for a few days in his wonderful thirteenth-floor-over-the-harbor apartment, enjoying tropical laziness, and the bizarre menagerie of Hong Kong life, then plunged over the border to Guangzhou, since Marcy had to be back to teach. China again—dust and papers and *mei you*. No flights to Xi'an. Booked for three weeks. *Mei you, mei you, mei you.* At last a seat opened up, then, just before take-off, another.

We landed late in Xi'an to cold gritty mist and a familiar tune: "When you get to Sioux Falls, South Dakota, you know you're getting close ta, the place ya wanna go ta, Minneota, Minnesota . . . " sung by the Chinese "gang," our friends and students. Soon we were eating at an outdoor Sichuan restaurant (they have them in China too!), swaddled in down coats surrounded by eels with chilies, peppered pig ears, flying noodles, fungus soup and raucous laughter.

It was a strange trip. The emotional ups and downs, swinging wildly from depression to delight, from touching thoughtfulness and generosity to unbelievable bureaucratic meanness and ignorance, from the posh comfort of Hong Kong to the stony, bleak poverty of China—a whole year's emotional and physical experience jammed into a few weeks like matter compressed into a black hole. On one day, I saw Little Hou, my wonderful piano student, and suffered "murder by chopsticks" in a twenty-course feast with his parents and neighbors. On the next day, I sat in a dismal, cold police station writing a "confession" for having gone by mistake to a closed town with a military factory. When I left Xi'an, I was exhausted and exalted simultaneously.

I flew to Guangzhou where I had to buy a train ticket over the border. Not so easy as it seems . . . The ticket hall was jammed with a couple of thousand shoving and anxious Chinese, and I was saddled with a ton of luggage and nowhere to go: heat, pressing bodies, shouting—not a word of English or any Chinese I could follow. I waited an hour, then an hour and a half, the last border train now only a half hour from leaving, still ten feet from the window. I was now standing next to a pleasant couple from Hong Kong who warned me about thieves, and wondered why I didn't have someone from the hotel come fetch the ticket for me. "No hotel; just passing through," I mumble.

"The ticket takers have all left for their *xiuxi* (nap)," the Hong Kong lady says. "This is a crazy place. Awful. Nobody works. Not like Hong Kong."

"But soon Hong Kong will be China," I remind her. "Where will you go then?"

"We are working people. We will stay. What happens, happens," she replies.

Fifteen minutes to train time. I'm at the window. I hand the ticket woman Chinese currency. "No! Only Hong Kong dollar!" she snaps.

"*Mei you*," I shrug, "American dollar?"

"Hong Kong dollar!" she repeats, a broken bullhorn. I envision eternity in line in the Guangzhou train station. My face, I assume, collapses. The Hong Kong woman snaps at the ticket taker in Chinese and hands her eight Hong Kong dollars. I have a ticket.

"Hurry to your train," she says.

"But I must pay you!"

"No, no," she says. "Stupid system . . . It is nothing. We are glad to help. Get to your train."

Mumbling gratitude, I rush through the crowd to my train, to the border, to the airplane, to Minneapolis, to the bleak snowy plains to the west. That mixture of kindness and decency, desperation, and stupid, mean inefficiency is the emblem for what happens not only to me but to everyone in China. China may call itself the "Middle Kingdom," but it is the planet of extremes, solar systems removed from the bland evenness of the American Midwest. I love it and will return.

IV

Uncle Scrooge on the Road

I grew up mistrusting holidays—probably mistrusting the whole relentless regularity of public ritual. Always the turkey and dry stuffing, always the Memorial Day guns, always the same Lord's Prayer always coming after the *Nunc Dimittis*. Anything you always did was likely to have the energy and the truth leak out of it like air out of a slow puncture in a tire. After five or six occurrences, it was flat and wouldn't carry you anywhere, either inside or outside. But through some failure of human imagination, or more likely superstitious fear of broken patterns, we went off Christmasing each other into a state of catatonic boredom, throwing money and forced cheerfulness at one another in order to survive until the irregular and unritualized eruption of chaotic daily life could begin again.

Partly this mistrust resulted from being an only child born late in the marriage of unenthusiastic Icelandic Lutherans — or perhaps that is only to say the same thing twice. My mother was a regular at Ladies' Aid because she fancied the gossip and the sociability, but was only an occasional churchgoer. My father squeezed his neck into a buttoned collar once or twice a year, but his expression, a compound of discontent and discomfort, made the experience as trying for those around him as it was for himself. "I went every Sunday until I was fifteen," he'd say, "and I've been improved enough. Every damn crook in Minneota sits in the front row with a long face and a clean suit. It's no place for an honest man." Except on Christmas Eve, when the tug of cultural and social compulsion and the questionable joy of having become a father in his forties pulled him in for "Silent Night," the velvet collection plate, the candle lighting, "a decree went out from Caesar Augustus . . . ," and his plump son soloing away on "O Holy Night" in a boisterous boy soprano.

After church, if he could escape coffee with relatives, we drove out the snowy gravel road eight miles north to the farm, and the three of us disposed of present opening. I quickly shuffled through the underwear, flannel shirts, and knitted mittens to get to the books. I knew them by weight. A gift box of clothes had an undignified feathery lightness about it. They could be worn but not enjoyed. I don't remember a single present my mother received, nor, with one exception, my father. Every year he got a fifth of very old Stitzel-Weller bourbon from one of his cousins and hunting comrades, and a few belts of the rich, brown, twenty-year-old whiskey were consolation for doing his conventional duty at holidays.

I am forty-six now, in the middle of the middle of life, and while I don't think memory has started to fail me, I can remember clearly only a few of those forty-six Christmases — those remarkable in ways not easily described by the conventions and language laid down for us by Dickens and Dayton's, the famous Minneapolis department store.

In 1974 I lived on the Virginia coast, and worked as a schoolteacher, and as a hired tenor in an elegant Episcopal church. I was just divorced, and my mother in Minnesota was two years into a bout with melanoma. I was sitting alone in a town house half empty of its furniture, getting ready to go sing Byrd and Gibbons on Christmas Eve for the Episcopalians. The town house was a few blocks from the sea and next to an old national cemetery full of magnificent magnolias and live oaks. It was about seventy degrees, a balmy winter evening; a good-tempered wind off Chesapeake Bay clattered the heavy magnolia leaves. The rows of old white military gravestones glowed as dusk came on. I opened the door to watch, poured a glass of wine, and decided to open my mother's Christmas box before going off to sing.

It was toys I had owned in the forties and forgotten: a wooden pig, within a wooden pig with another wooden pig inside, pigs all the way down; a couple of other old toys; and a photograph of me giving a poetry reading decoupaged onto a varnished board—a cancer hospital crafts project. All these gifts were labeled with witty notes (where you got this, what it was, etc.) in a squiggly, spidery hand—a dying hand. This fact had not, until that moment, struck me. Like every other human who finds the idea too savage to bear, I had avoided reading the signs of imminent death. There was no mistaking this Christmas box. She was sorting and labeling the house, making her last affectionate pronouncements. I wept like a child on that semi-tropical Virginia Christmas Eve, me and the clattering magnolias, no snow flurries, no "Jingle Bells," no smarmy candle ceremony. It was a fine Christmas for the soul, with that gift of truth.

Five years later I got a Fulbright lectureship at the University of Iceland beginning in January, so I decided to sail rather than fly. Christmas at sea—a first sea trip. Friends argued that I was mad to do it; the North Atlantic in winter is not the Caribbean. "The sea is the sea," I replied smugly, and boarded the freighter *Bakkafoss* on December 22 from Portsmouth, Virginia.

The first two days, going north in the Gulf Stream, were idyllic, windless, warm, and calm, the ocean river as placid and glassy as a stock pond in South Dakota. I was the only passenger, and the only non-Icelandic speaker. Despite my pure genetics, my language skills consisted of swearing at cows, greeting old ladies, and pronouncing names like Hallgrimur and Adalbjorn correctly. A few of the sailors managed some English, but I lived mostly in a splendid solitude of sea and silence.

On Christmas Eve day the ship swung across the Grand Banks on the way toward an American military base in Newfoundland with a load of frozen hamburger patties. Whatever my pleasure at this solitary Christmas, the sailors missed the comforts of Reykjavik, so they spent the day decorating a tree with green glass balls and tinsel and wrapping small gifts for one another. The Chinese cook roasted a turkey and a ham, and there was plentiful brandy, red wine, and Brennivin—the

Icelandic schnapps affectionately known as "the Black Death." During the jolly, boozy Christmas dinner, the wind came up, along with the Grand Banks swells, and the *Bakkafoss* began pitching and rolling in that now confused sea. The brandy snifters, turkey platters, and salt and pepper shakers skated and slid in a confused dance all over the table, clattering into the wall, then banging back into the table guard. People grabbed their forks and snifters, hung on, and continued eating. "Are you all right?" asked one of the sailors.

"Fine," I said bravely and, for the moment, truthfully. The outer rolling hadn't penetrated the inner organs. Yet.

After dinner the crew adjourned to the ship's lounge to gather around the tree for gifts, hymns, and more toasts. The sailors, knowing I was a writer and an Icelander by descent, and honoring my profession more than a ship's crew of Americans might, found me a book of literary essays by a famous Icelandic critic, wrapped it in gay paper, and presented it to me. I was touched — and still own and treasure the book. We sang *Heim Sem Bol* ("Silent Night" in Icelandic) and toasted missing relatives. By this time, the pitching and rolling had turned into a gale, and the Christmas tree was moving back and forth, up and down, at a forty-five degree angle to itself, like a pendulum gone berserk. On each pass, it lost a few of its glass balls, and the Icelandic hymn was accompanied by a descant of clinking broken glass — out-of-tune bells with sharp edges. My eye tried to follow the erratic swaying of the tree, but now the sea decided to confuse my interior plumbing. Two sailors came up beside me and said solicitously: "You are not looking wery vell. Perhaps you should get some air now." They helped me out on deck, where I returned Christmas dinner to the North Atlantic, plus what I imagined was several thousand other dinners I'd eaten during the last decade. I stumbled into my cabin and, as I passed the mirror, noted that my complexion had turned the color of the glass balls on the Christmas tree. I collapsed into my unsteady bed hoping for death but willing to settle for permanent insensibility. Merry Christmas, I thought.

On Christmas morning I woke up hungry and considerably surprised to be still alive. The sea continued pitching and rolling vigorously, but my interior gyroscope had righted itself. I looked at my face in the mirror — pink and healthy. My empty stomach rumbled for bacon and eggs. So this was my Christmas present from the universe — to survive seasickness! I gained ten pounds on the trip to Reykjavik, growing hungrier as the swells grew wilder crashing into the hull of the ship.

I liked these two bleary and solitary Christmases. Neither of them took place in landscapes that much resembled a Norman Rockwell

Christmas card (but then nothing much on this planet ever resembled a Rockwell painting except in his audience's swampy nostalgia for an imaginary golden age when life was less surprising). These Christmases violated the regularity of public ritual, and made their own, and made it new. The gifts were memorable because they were unexpected. Gifts are your teachers, not your obligation or the fulfillment of a bargain. They are supposed to disconnect you from your own life for a few minutes, so you can see it more clearly. A good gift delivers a brisk shock. A good gift cannot be reciprocated without damage to the soul. You must take it and live.

But at least these two holidays took place where Christmas was a normal experience in the culture, even for Jews and agnostics who found themselves Ho-Ho-Ho-ing their way through the season with clenched teeth. My next memorable Christmases were in Xi'an, an old city in central China where I went to teach for a year and where nothing is normal to a Minnesotan.

The Chinese Communists, in their attempts to remold Chinese civilization, tried to do away with the old Chinese holidays, the moon festivals and harvest celebrations, even toning down the usual fireworks of Chinese New Year. Christmas never amounted to much in China, I suspect, but for the handful of Chinese Christians or fanciers of Western habit, it too disappeared. In their place were May Day and Liberation Day. Control the public rituals, and you control the mind of the country.

Christmas was a school day like any other day at Xi'an Jiaotong University. At six-thirty in the morning, the loudspeaker outside the window started singing "The East is Red," vamping into calisthenics music and Party slogans. At ten o'clock the morning exercise show came on, an authoritative voice counting to eight in 3/4 time, until the Chinese began sweating in unison. At noon the "Internationale" and a couple of military marches signaled noodle and nap time.

The foreign teachers' contracts specified their having the day off (along with directions not to steal the silver from the dining room and to be in bed by eleven o'clock). The handful of American, Canadian, and British teachers greeted one another with "Merry Christmas," and someone played a tape of the ceremony of carols from King's College, Cambridge. The sound of little boys singing "Once in Royal David's City" floated up and down the halls of the foreigner dormitory.

In the real China outside the iron fence, coarse grit blew in from the Gobi Desert, the air was gray and acrid with coal smoke from factories and cooking fires, the night soil carts sloshed along in the street, the thickly stuffed and rusty buses snaked in and out between pedestrians

COMING HOME CRAZY

and mule carts delivering the Chinese to work or shop, and bicycles numberless as snowflakes clanked along. It was daily, normal Chinese life, with no Christmas in it. Here was half a planet—replete with an ancient language, noble and coherent philosophies, continuous history older than Plato or Jesus—for whom the major Western ritual meant nothing. Whether Jesus was born was a matter not only of no consequence but of no interest.

My first year in Xi'an, I forgot entirely that it was Christmas Eve until a visiting American teacher from St. Cloud who had arrived that afternoon to give a lecture on American family life and sexual habits stopped by my room and wished me a Merry Christmas. "Well, let's have a Christmas *bailandi* (Chinese brandy) then!" I reciprocated. A couple of my students soon arrived bearing Chinese Christmas cards decorated with Massachusetts clipper ships, paintings of Christmas cactus, or Donald Duck wishing the recipient "the best of Happy Season greeting . . . " Soon the students and the sexologist were deep in a conversation on AIDS, premarital sex, divorce rates, homosexuality, and matchmaking. "Merry Christmas," I thought to myself, and went off to teach school bright and early on Christmas morning, forgetting that I, too, had the day off.

That Christmas, in its bizarre offhandedness, hardly counted as a Christmas at all. I came back to Xi'an for a visit the next year, after having returned for a few months to American comforts in the fall, and the shock of December in central China was more than I expected. Electricity was down to four or five days a week. What small heat they had was turned off to save coal; the grit and pollution were, if anything, nastier, and the winter colder.

Gray snow fell through a thick sky and blew into the cracks between the loose windows in the unheated room where I stayed. Some mornings the snow hardly melted on the bed quilts. It only soiled the quilt cover.

I'd come back to visit students, whom I came to treasure as dear friends, and another American still in Xi'an, who was teaching at a college for mechanical engineers. Three days before Christmas, the whole gang of us, perhaps fifteen people, rented a minibus and went out into the countryside to visit some locally famous limestone caves. When we came out of the caves, green-suited local police waited to arrest us. The caves lay outside a town closed to foreigners because of a military factory. The ticket salesman had cleverly spotted Marcy and me as *waiguoren* (foreigners). None of the Chinese students had ever heard of the factory or the regulation, and my remarking that even the CIA was not stupid enough to send a six-and-a-half-foot, red-bearded, non-Chinese-speaking or -reading Icelander out to spy on a sunny Sunday afternoon did not amuse them. A sense of humor (or, heaven forbid, irony!) probably disqualifies you for police work anywhere on the planet. We all wound up spending December 22 in a police station being interrogated, having passports and cameras confiscated.

The next day, forlorn and without passports, Marcy and I went out to console ourselves with a dish of *yangrou paomo*, a locally famous mutton stew, at a street stand next to her college. Halfway through the stew, a drunk came up to join us and "practice his English"; like drunks the planet over, he was not charming at eleven in the morning. We left abruptly, leaving our half-eaten stew. A half block down the street, I realized I had forgotten my traveling peanut bag on the ground. We ran back. The bag was gone. In it were traveler's checks, cash, a notebook of new poems, an address book, and some half-finished letters and essays.

For fifteen years I carried everywhere a tattered blue cloth Mr. Peanut bag, a gift from an old friend, $2.98 plus five empty Planters peanut bags. It went to poetry readings, carried manuscripts and notebooks, traveled to Ireland, Greece, Iceland, Alaska, China, and a hundred other places. On trips, it usually held my passport and camera. The consolation of having it "nicked" today, I thought, as I rode off to yet another police station to report the loss and sign a complaint, is that, had I not been arrested yesterday, I would have lost them, too. So passed December 23. I sat in a cold cement room in a police station, drinking watery tea, smoking endless Golden Monkey cigarettes (a necessary part of any police experience), and reciting over and over the circumstances of the theft, the contents of the bag.

I spent December 24 going from station to station, eating crow at one and complaining at the other. I came back to the mechanical college exhausted, depressed, and full of Chinese bronchitis. The electricity was out on Christmas Eve — no heat, no hot water, no lights. Marcy and I lit a candle, put on our coats, and opened a Christmas gift box I had carried from America. Shivering, we unpacked it item by item: two three-dimensional foldouts, a paper snowman and a Christmas tree; a box of drugstore chocolate-covered cherries; real mistletoe with plastic berries; a garish orange-haired doll; a miniature John Deere tractor; some tinsel for the paper tree; a Bing Crosby Christmas tape; one red stocking; and a Christmas card that played "O Tannenbaum" when you opened it. "Have a real American Christmas!" the card said. We collapsed, giggling and shivering under the quilt, dusting the snow off onto the cement floor. Merry Christmas again!

COMING HOME CRAZY

On Christmas Day, we took a local bus fifteen miles south of town to visit an art conservatory with some friends. Willow, a talented Chinese painter, fell in love with an American and, after great bureaucratic snags, married him. The two decided to go out for their last nostalgic trip to Willow's school and invited us along. The sun, for the first time in a week, came out brightly the moment we left Xi'an. An old man with a weathered face sat next to us on the bus. He and his grandsons were headed out to the mountains to catch birds. They carried cages, nets, traps, paraphernalia I had never seen before. A Chinese *Papageno* on Christmas Day!

The conservatory was built into the foothills of the Qin Ling Mountains. The main building was a Russian concrete pile from the fifties, but most of the students lived in caves with red doors and half-moon windows cut into the side of the yellow hill. We met Willow's painter friends, all at work in their studios. In honor of the arrival of the foreigners, everyone in the building gathered, armed with their best paintings, ready for an impromptu art show. Not one of them spoke a word of English but, between smiling and pointing at brush strokes, we managed to communicate. There was astonishing talent in that room — a survival of the ancient Chinese passion for beauty of line and detail that even politics and poverty couldn't kill.

Soon it was lunch time. "Join us," the painters said, apologizing that it would be only regular everyday food, since they hadn't known we were coming. "Everyday food" in Xi'an is plain stuff, but the Chinese are geniuses at making celebrations out of nothing by pitching in together. Somebody found a bottle of sweet wine, another went to fetch beer, another had a stash of Sichuan peanuts. Dented enamel bowls and extra chopsticks arrived for the guests. Then the food came: a very old fish, some cauliflower cooked with dried shrimp, a few bowls of elderly cabbage, some pork with vegetables cooked in pork fat. The toasts began, as always — peace, international cooperation, Willow's happiness with Rosario, Leonardo da Vinci, Georgia O'Keeffe, the Tang potters, the Ming painters, and each other. Finally someone, not the Americans, remembered it was Christmas Day. "Melly Clistmas!" one toasted in what undoubtedly were his first spoken English words. Melly Clistmas, indeed! No grand cathedral in the West ever had a celebration like this. It was the unlikeliest church I ever worshipped in.

These Christmases were memorable, both by their physical oddity and by the presence of some new emotion that so captured me that I forgot entirely that I was in the middle of the most conventional of all seasons and rituals.

The Chinese, too, suffer from a heavy-handedly ritualized life, in their case imposed by force. "You will wake every morning to 'The East is Red' at six-thirty, then . . . " But over time, they develop a marvelous power to tune out rituals. They sit blithely reading a book, utterly absorbed, next to a blaring loudspeaker telling them what to do and think at that moment.

"How can you bear this?" I would ask.

"Bear what?" they would answer, smiling quizzically.

God save us from a regular Christmas and deliver us to strange places.

YANGLING
杨陵

China is the smallest huge country on the planet. What you feel inside it is not size and space but claustrophobia, the walls closing in. Too many locked gates, too many crammed-in humans, too many ears listening, too many eyes always fixed on you. I grew up on a farm on the crest of a small hill on the prairie. From the yard, you could see two or three miles in any direction. A car coming at you announced its presence miles away with dust clouds and motor noise. Though I think I am a friendly man, I liked it that way.

Minnesotans grow used to size and privacy. Their inner sense of space expands. Get in a car and drive five hundred miles west from Minneota. There will be few cars, few towns, few people, few trees, only sky and grass. Drive another five hundred miles west, and it thins out more. The privacy of the car and the sparse population gave us this gift of large inner geography. The Chinese never got that gift.

After close to a year in a clot of humans, monitored and locked in by bureaucracy and the facts of politics, my body longed for a cottonwood tree, for an empty sky, for walking all night alone over grass.

One of my students taught English at the farm college in a little town ninety kilometers west of Xi'an. She listened to my complaints for a long time. "Come to Yangling for the weekend," she said. "You will like it there."

Wei Li, a thin elegant woman almost six feet tall, defeated western stereotypes about small Chinese. Her whole family taught at Northwestern Agricultural University. Her father was China's great scholar of watermelons, her mother of grapes. Her husband was the provincial bocce ball coach and wrote poetry. Wei Li taught English to farm students while attending my class in quest of another degree.

Ninety kilometers is sixty miles, a forty-five or fifty-minute drive on country roads in Minnesota when the sheriff is asleep. Even the law abiding drive it in under an hour on state highways. But the Chinese do not own cars; neither you nor they can rent them. It was a three-hour train ride to Yangling after a half-hour bicycle ride to the station. Until I spent a carless year in China, I'd never understood the connection between cars and authority. In a car you cover ground quickly and privately. You don't ask permission or buy tickets, you start and stop when you please, and drive any route that interests you. You become infinitely harder to keep track of, to manage, to police. Chase scenes in movies are metaphors for this. We are all on the outlaw's side at ninety miles an hour. Nothing gives a movie audience greater pleasure than a gumball catapulting off a bridge or over a cliff as the bank robber escapes down a dusty back road. When the Chinese have cars, the authority of the central government is finished.

On a Friday afternoon in spring, six of us hurried from class to train station, where we found a madhouse. The whole province was trying to buy tickets, move livestock, worldly goods, and extended families . . . all today. Our crew was: Wei Li, Small Vinegar (Tango Queen of Taiyuan), Dr. Hoover, Old Fish of Sichuan, David (the romantic Mongolian), Xiao Zhang (the Guest House factotum), and me. One of the native speakers went off to fight for tickets, while the rest of us bulled through the milling mob trying to find the right train. The chaos on the tracks was even worse. We finally found an open car. The hard seat tickets arrived. We all collapsed.

"It'll be good to be out of this mess for a few days," someone commented. Heads nodded. We settled in for our short ride. The steam locomotive belched. We were off. Ten minutes later, when the conductor came by, we discovered we were on the wrong train, going to the wrong town. We were headed for Xingping, the right direction but on the wrong tracks. Xingping was twenty miles away from Yangling, with no connection. What to do?

At moments like this, Chinese genius takes over. Since we couldn't do anything about it, we didn't do anything. Disaster was disaster, so wait and see what happens. One of the other passengers had a guitar, hauled it out, and started singing. Another stranger produced a prized pack of Double Happiness cigarettes and passed them around. David the Mongolian grabbed the guitar and started a slightly out-of-tune Simon and Garfunkel song. Another passenger spoke some English and wanted to know what the hell a Barbarian was doing on a local train out *here*?

Somebody produced a bag of blood oranges from Chengdu. We sat happily smoking, singing and peeling oranges. On the wrong train.

Xingping turned out to be a boondocks farm town with dust streets and no public transport until the next day. What to do? We went to the telephone office in the hotel. The line was down. We drank tea.

Finally a light went on in someone's head: some farmer will have a truck. Off two or three of them went to investigate. Half an hour later, a tiny blue East German truck with a two-stroke engine drove up. The old man offered to take us to Yangling for twenty *kwai* (about five dollars). Old Fish thought it was too much, but I decided to play the rich Barbarian. Six of us piled in the back of the truck. Wei Li sat with the driver to give directions. We trucked off on a sunny afternoon through the Shaanxi wheatfields, the wind in our faces.

The road followed the Weihe River, one of the oldest settled agricultural areas in the world. Yet, despite the presence of a modern agricultural college, the farming I saw was five or six thousand years old. Farmers in rolled-up baggy pants carrying pails of night soil suspended from shoulder poles, children weeding the cabbages with hoes, family graveyards along the edges of fields, pigs and chickens wandering up and down the road, a farmer driving a mule cart loaded with hay, peddlers along the road selling fruit and doodads, fields of wheat blowing lazily in the breeze, hardly a motor, only the same humans moving over the same fields they've moved over since before the pharaohs, before Babylon, before Chicago.

We got to Yangling a few hours late and just on time. It was a small town, perhaps ten thousand people, few cars, little traffic. It seemed without gates, locks and walls, an open, spacious, calm town. The air smelled slightly of manure, strongly of wet wheat. I saw no other Barbarians, no soldiers, no police. A small creek, maybe an irrigation canal, ran along the street. We crossed a little bridge and found Wei Li's parents' apartment. The watermelon king and the grape arbor queen greeted us cordially. They had delayed starting dinner until we came. A special treat tonight! A whole pail of fresh eels from the Weihe River, still alive. We all admired the wriggling water. The women readied the eels for killing; Xiao Zhang heated the wok to begin making the sauce. The rest of us settled in for tea, bowls of fried peanuts and hard candy. We enjoyed front row seats for the demise of the eels.

To kill an eel, first pound a sturdy nail entirely through a thick board. Set the point of the nail towards you on a rock or incline. Grab a fat eel, push the head down over the nail. While the eel still wriggles, make a straight slit down the body with a sharp knife. With a single swipe of your hands, pull out the innards of the eel. Cut off the head and discard. Hack the eel into chopstick-size chunks. Make sure the wok is hot.

Xiao Zhang was peeling garlic, chopping chilies, shaking soy and sesame and *wei xiang* (essence of smell or MSG) into smoking rape-seed oil. In minutes, we smacked our lips over blazing hot eels. The Chinese prefer their food fresh. For dessert? What else? Watermelon at the table of the watermelon king!

It was just sunset when we finished the last of the eels. We decided to stroll through the town. No locked gates or guards demanding papers here. In the courtyard, one of the neighbors sat beheading a crate of chickens with a huge cleaver. He looked up and smiled as we walked through the chicken scraps. A pleasant town for humans but dangerous for chickens and eels. Across from the modern concrete flats where Wei Li's parents lived were old, low Chinese style houses. Through the front room of one of them grew a sizable tree with a foot-and-a-half diameter trunk and branches spreading over the tiled roof. Where the tree escaped through the roof had been well patched and sealed to keep rain out. Yygdrasil in Yangling! Presumably the house of Chinese Vikings.

"Want to go to the movies?" Wei Li said.

"Where?" I asked.

"Here in the courtyard of the school next door."

People had already started to gather with their stools, waiting for full dark. We strolled on along the canal, now full of mallards bedding down for the night. We met a farmer out walking with a fat pig. I admired his pig. Someone translated my bad Chinese into good Chinese for him. He beamed, bowed, thanked me and ambled on. The town was almost silent. A few old farmers on corners squatted smoking long pipes, a dumpling stand still boiling, a little kiosk selling cigarettes and melon seeds, a few idle bicycles, distant radio music. Dark now.

We came to railroad tracks, the same tracks that would have taken us to Yangling if we had found the right train. The smell of wet wheat was intense.

"Those tracks go all the way to Xinjiang, through all Siberia, to Moscow," said Xiao Zhang, looking west.

"Then they go to Europe—to Warsaw, Berlin, Amsterdam, across the water to London," I said.

"Shall we go?" said Xiao Zhang.

We all started walking west, out of town, along the tracks. What a magnificent idea! To walk through China, through Russia, through Europe, take a little boat, and have tea next to Piccadilly Circus. Only the stupidity of politics stopped us. No visas! Do we have diplomatic relations? Won't we pass through closed areas? We would be foreigners, we seven odd friends out for a stroll. I heard a rustling above me that I hadn't heard since I left the Minnesota prairie.

"Are those cottonwood trees?" I asked.

"Look up," said Dr. Hoover. The tracks were lined with huge old cottonwoods, shivering and singing in the night wind beneath a sky full of stars. "Here, we call them sheep trees. The sheep like the leaves and the seeds look like sheep's wool."

"This is a good place," I said. Claustrophobic China dissolved in the wheaty air.

After a while, we turned and walked back toward our beds, happy. When we got to the school courtyard, the movie was in full swing. The whole neighborhood brought wood stools and packed the space. I was about to ask for a translation but, after a minute, I realized I didn't need it. A Hong Kong-style Kung Fu movie with flying fists and feet, fierce battles between noble heroes and slimy villains, pretty girls sighing in the wings. The neighborhood children cheered and clapped wildly. Off to bed.

The next day we walked to the agricultural college to meet Wei Li's husband, who had been at a sports tournament the night before. In the middle of campus stood a statue of Houji, the inventor of agriculture, a fierce-looking old boy with a beard in cast bronze. On the pedestal, a Chinese inscription.

"What does it say?" I ask.

The Old Fish translated, "Houji, the first agricultural big potato, taught humans to grow their first crops on this very site, as it was recorded in the ancient *Book of Songs*."

"So this is the progenitor of Minneota," I mused.

"But did the inventor of farming truly serve the people?" added the cranky Fish. We walked onward to the sports field.

In the middle of a park that looked to me like an arboretum of wonderful old trees and shrubs, we found what was unmistakably a bocce ball court. It can't be! I thought. But it was.

The Governor of Minnesota, a Croatian dentist from Hibbing, once tried to make bocce ball the state game. His home town was full of Italians, Croats and Serbs who played it enthusiastically. It was strange enough to find bocce ball in the middle of Scandinavian Minnesota but to find it in the middle of China? In a tiny, dusty provincial town where agriculture was invented? Zhao came with a box of brightly-colored bocce balls, instructed us on the rules, divided up sides. The game was on!

Small Vinegar, the Tango Queen, giggled whenever she hit an opponent's ball. The Old Fish played like an intellectual—thinking too much. Dr. Hoover couldn't resist banging the ball. David, the big Mongolian, played like a gentleman. Wei Li and Zhao were old pros. I was the wild man. Xiao Zhang was the Napoleon (or the Lin Biao) of the court. Kibitzers gathered. I looked up through the trees and tried to imagine what this scene might look like from fifty feet above, filtered through the eyes of a wise Brobdingnagian strolling through China. He would see happy people together, silly and affectionate, sometimes intelligent, one of them looking a good deal more odd than the rest but probably human anyway. He would not see abstractions like communism, capitalism, Christian, pagan, foreigner. He would see space and light and cottonwood leaves, flowering bushes and trees, eels, ducks and pigs, green and red balls banging into each other, giving birth to the music of human laughter.

Yangling was a good place to come. It is a good place to be . . . wherever you are, whatever you call it.

We caught the right train home on Sunday.

ZOU HOUMEN

走后门

Zou houmen. "Go through the back door." The servants' entrance, where goods arrive, deals are made, cigarettes change hands, where the real economy functions.

If the first Chinese word you learn is *mei you* (not have), the second is *zou houmen.* What you want is usually there if you know whom to get it from, or whose cousin, or whose mother's second brother's best friend who married . . . China much more closely resembles a small town of over a billion than it does a vast and anonymous empire. There really are only a hundred last names and, sometimes, to a Barbarian, it seems they have all intermarried to watch each other. Jealousy is the first fact of Chinese life. Everyone knows who has or can get what. The trick is to pass it off at night, at a private entrance, to say what needs to be said without saying it and thus to build up your own tissue of connections and obligations. This is the spider web in which you trap train tickets, exit visas, fresh chickens, the eight great liquors, taxis, Marlboros, Sonys.

The Chinese invented bureaucracy and its visible stamp, the red chop (a square stone cut with an official seal, used with a pot of red ink). For thousands of years, hands pulled at chins, tea cups tipped; there were nods, sighs, stern looks, explanations, favors offered, before the stone was dipped in ink and moved across the table. To be an official, however petty, must always have meant access to food and favors, so that Chinese history becomes an endless skein of officials clutching their chops, an endless hallway of doors sloping upward that you can open only if you know the secret code, bring a reasonable sacrifice and open your own back door in return.

Is this corruption? The Barbarian's first answer is a loud "yes," as if he were answering a Lutheran confirmation question with Luther's famous, "This is most certainly true." But he has answered, as Luther did, an abstract proposition and done what must always be done if you are to maintain dogma — ignore observed experience.

My first *mei you* in China was in answer to my demands for lost luggage. I threatened lawsuits, imminent departure, international scandal. Nothing worked. Finally, someone remembered a clever woman who worked in a foreign office in Beijing who "knew" people connected with the airline. After a month, my battered luggage finally arrived. "You should thank Miss Wang," a local official told me. "She is very useful and clever." She knows the knock that opens the *houmen*.

In a just world someone will find and return your luggage because it is yours, because they have lost it and because you need it. Those who imagine that this just world exists in America have never been to a draft board, an IRS office, or stood in line at a big-city postal window with a package. We borrowed bureaucracy from the Chinese, and it arrived with a back door. Out of one eye, a self-congratulatory American denies its existence; out of the other, he sees Vice President Quayle motoring off to National Guard meetings during the Tet offensive. Did we fail to elect him because he was a well-connected rich boy who flagrantly marched through the back door? We behave exactly as the Chinese do. We grumble about privilege while wondering if third auntie will bring the hard-sleeper tickets home tonight.

I learned to go through the back door. I made friends and used them just as they used me. We bound ourselves together out of affection and convenience — sometimes out of necessity. I passed Marlboros under the counter and got taxis, butter, and opera tickets in return. I got out of trouble with the police once or twice by knowing someone who knew someone in the department. I failed in a couple of schemes by not knowing the right people, and thought, "if only . . . "

"But this is China," I said to myself, "not America. To live here for a while, I must live intelligently in the Chinese style. But in America . . ."

When I got back to America and looked around, the whole world shifted into reverse, the transmission shuddered. "My brother is in the registrar's office . . . ," "I was going seventy-two miles an hour on that stretch of Highway 40, you know, but Earl, he lives next door to . . . ," "You can't get steaks this good off the truck, but Jack, he drives for . . ." All the way to Ivan Boesky. Beyond that, to the White House. A few days after coming home, I heard that Richard Nixon, in a town somewhere, gave a speech. He was described on the radio as a great statesman. And

Deng Xiaoping is a liberal reformer. And I am the Queen of Romania.

For my first forty-odd years as an American, I never thought much about back doors. In the land of surpluses, you can be a misty idealist and still have plenty of everything . . . if you are a properly articulate white fellow. Every natural gift that came to America without effort or virtue — an empty continent, vast fertile farmlands, easy transport, isolation from history by virtue of lucky geography — came as a blow to the head in China. The first fact is scarcity — and will always be. The second is corruption. They are Siamese twins, whether we like looking at their ugly faces or not. Poverty does not breed nobility, church fathers to the contrary. When the brave Chinese students asked for an end to one and a sharing of the other, the two-headed monster turned and bit them savagely. It then wiped its bloody mouths and said, "Who? Me?" while stamping papers as if nothing had happened. It was only a hydra guarding its own back door. If you imagine it can't happen in America, first imagine scarcity beyond an urban slum, beyond the thirties. Imagine next unarmed idealists demanding some justice, some truth, from the chop stampers with secret door knocks. Imagine all of this on television — in public. Imagine the Colorado coal strike. Imagine Kent State. Ask a high school student if those things ever happened.

No matter how much Americans would prefer that even their small history evaporate like a puddle in the sun, it won't. I learned the weight of history in China and, like Goethe in the famous little poem in which he envies America, was happy for the relative absence of heavy old castles and blood: America, you have things easier than our old continent; you have no ruined castles and no basalt.

But we are connected to the rest of humanity and to their infinitely sadder, longer histories. We gain nothing by playing ostrich except, conceivably, our own extinction. Either we remember, and make conscious connection to the moral and physical lives of others, or we die.

没有结尾的结尾

The Conclusion In Which Nothing Is Concluded

Three small trips
and what I saw,
a homecoming to Minneota,
the story of a fixer and what needs to be fixed.

I

Flies

I spent half a year smashing flies into the ceiling and walls of my Chinese dormitory room. They came in through the screenless windows, along with the yellow loess dust, humidity, and loudspeaker noise. Mosquitos and sparrows were scarce, but the window offered them welcome too. During one of the multitudinous Chinese campaigns—the four antis, the Great Leap Forward, the Great Proletarian Cultural Revolution—the former probably got sprayed to death inside Xi'an and the latter persecuted and then clubbed into local extinction. I heard a story that after the Party issued a directive to kill sparrows who ate grain that could otherwise feed the swelling population, Chinese citizens stayed in the streets for days, banging noise makers, shouting and generally frightening the sparrows off whatever perch they might find. The birds hovered till they dropped in droves from exhaustion, after which the citizens summarily slaughtered them. The Chinese, being practical, and close to starvation at the time, probably ate sparrow stew, stir-fried sparrow, and three-sparrow soup for days afterwards. As an example of what the Party can accomplish when it puts its mind to its task, the campaign succeeded. To this day, Chinese cities are remarkably birdless. Whatever spare grain they saved, the politicos accomplished the murder of music and silenced the fluttering of wings.

But the stubborn flies survived the anti campaigns and gamboled in to keep me company in my Chinese solitude. I was raised Lutheran, and understood the four instruments of spiritual progress: the check book, the dust rag, the coffee pot, and the fly swatter. I rolled up the *China Daily*, stood on a chair, and whacked away until the once-cream-colored ceiling and tan plastic wallpaper were polka-dotted with the splatted remains. This happened daily until the ceiling turned more fly smear than paint. I washed the lower stretches of wallpaper periodically but assumed the God of the Lutherans would forgive me for not scrubbing the ceiling. That was the People's Republic's own work, the fifth modernization. It was their concrete, their flies.

Halfway through the year, my friend Xiao Zhang, who worked the front desk, came in to have morning tea and found me perched on my chair, bloodying the *China Daily*.

"Haven't they invented the goddamn screen in the Middle Kingdom?" I muttered.

"The screens are upstairs, of course; you ought to have some," Xiao Zhang said calmly, sipping his tea. "They keep flies out."

"Upstairs?" I asked.

"Someone else's job to put them on," he said.

"Do you have a key to the screens?"

"Yes."

"As Brecht said: tea later, screens first."

We opened a door and found all the missing screens, heavy iron and badly made, but screens nonetheless. We carried a half dozen downstairs and bolted them to the windows. The flies in the garden growled, then found the opening where the screens came a quarter inch from fitting into the window. I got the duct tape, and closed the border, the Great Wall of flies. The hordes retreated, looking for a screenless room to invade.

"Why weren't the screens already on the window?" I asked, rhetorically. I'd been long enough in China to guess the answer.

"It's Sleepy, your floor man's job. But if you put them on, you have to clean them first, and then take them off in the winter, and clean them again. It's easier just to leave them off. Most of the foreigners don't seem to mind. They think dead flies are part of the Chinese experience."

"Indeed . . . ," I sighed.

For the rest of the year, I waved daily to the bad-tempered flies trying to ooze in past the duct tape, brandishing their little insect visas, demanding free travel to my still polka-dotted ceiling. I played Chinese bureaucrat and remained calmly indifferent to their buzzed complaints.

A year later, I came back to Xi'an, and went to the guest house where, for nostalgia, I asked to see my old room. I missed it. In America, the land of scrubbed ceilings, functioning screens built into triple-paned windows, and zombie democracy, life had lost its edge for me. So much outward comfort had grown, not inward calm and courage, but a kind of interior catatonia, a soul perpetually tuned into a Walkman with a thud bass. Americans made a sort of dull boom-boom noise when you walked by them in a street. If you spoke to them, they told you about running shoes and interest rates, whatever the question. They had considerable feeling about smoking but none about history. Louis Simpson described what I found at home:

THE INNER PART

When they had won the war
And for the first time in history
Americans were the most important people—

When the leading citizens no longer lived in their shirt sleeves,
And their wives did not scratch in public;
Just when they'd stopped saying "Gosh!"—

When their daughters seemed as sensitive
As the tip of a fly rod,
And their sons were as smooth as a V-8 engine—

Priests, examining the entrails of birds,
Found the heart misplaced, and seeds
As black as death, emitting a strange odor.

A new floor girl let me into Room 207. The same tattered red carpet, the same broken deathtrap floor lamp, the same brown plastic couch, the same floral thermos bottle, the same non-functioning heat pipes, the same winter cold, but behold, the screens were gone! I looked up—the same fly smear polka-dotted ceiling, the ghost of my *China Daily* fly swatter still waving through the frosty air. Half of me rejoiced at the dead flies: "Kilroy was here . . . ," "The more things change, the more they remain the same . . . ," "China is always China," "Human nature is everywhere and always constant." Half of me wanted to shout at the floor girl to fetch buckets of hot water, scrub brushes and the keys to the locked-up screens, roll up my sleeves and do the damned job myself to make sure it got done.

Which half was China, which America? I was sure that the propensity to entertain simultaneously two contradictory impulses, both felt and both true, did not belong to either civilization at the moment. Given the election of 1988, and the Beijing Massacre of 1989, the single idea, the old cycle of brainlessness and brutality, the obstinate refusal to learn from experience (or even pay attention to it), seemed safely in the saddle, riding mankind. I stared with affectionate melancholy at the ceiling one more time, thanked the giggling girl in bad Chinese, and left, still crazy.

II

I Know the Police Give You Trouble

On every formal Chinese occasion: a lecture, a party, a banquet, foreigners were expected to sing, and if the Chinese fancied the song, to teach them to sing it in English themselves. The first time this happened to me, my mind turned blank—I failed to remember words to a

single song that was neither obscene nor religious, the only two disqual-
ifiers for these occasions. Finally an old Depression song that I'd heard
Woody Guthrie sing clicked in; I sang them "The Hobo's Lullaby."

> Go to sleep you weary hobo,
> Let the towns drift slowly by,
> Can't you hear the steel rails humming:
> That's the hobo's lullaby.
>
> Do not think about tomorrow,
> Let tomorrow come and go.
> Tonight you're in a nice warm boxcar,
> Safe from all the wind and snow.
> *(Chorus)*
> I know your clothes are torn and tattered,
> And your hair is turning gray.
> But lift your head and smile at trouble,
> You'll find peace and rest some day.
> *(Chorus)*
> I know the police give you trouble;
> Police cause trouble everywhere.
> But when you die and go to heaven,
> There'll be no policemen there.
> *(Chorus)*

Chinese student faces lit up during the police stanza. Here was truth and
beauty united. They all wanted to memorize it instantaneously. They
liked the image of a poor man traveling in a boxcar to unknown places,
of course, but best of all they liked a heaven without police. Police were
a sure means of distinguishing the Middle Kingdom from the Heavenly
Kingdom that the Party assured them already existed locally.

In the course of my year in China and my trip back the next Xmas,
I ran afoul of the police four or five times and saw them work on others
as often. I did not come to enjoy it. China is, of course, a police state,
and was one even during its decade of relative openness from 1979 to
1989. The same apparatus that jailed intellectuals in the fifties and during the Cultural Revolution remained intact, a procedure ready to be
carried out whenever the order might be given. The enthusiastic brutality of police tracking down dissident students and intellectuals in the
summer of 1989 should have come as no surprise. Their bosses simply
opened the doors of the cages and fed them blood.

I took a train far into Gansu in the springtime, to a town in the west-

232   COMING HOME CRAZY

ern desert, Wuwei. Marcy and I traveled with two student friends, a young girl off to visit her boyfriend and an older man back in graduate school after working in a lumber factory for the entire Cultural Revolution. The west of Gansu is wild country, high mountain passes, bleak desert, poor villages that eke out bare livings on the margin of the habitable world. The train parallels the old Silk Road. I loved staring out the train window at the bare brown mountains, crossing and recrossing the murky turbulent Yellow River, watching the huge billows of steam spouting out of the old-fashioned locomotives as they grunted up the steep grades going west. At the top of a high stony pass, the train stopped to blow off steam and refill the boilers. Alongside the tracks, heaps of slag lay scattered. Three poor women, two old ones in tattered dark clothes and a young pretty girl in a dirty pink coat stooped and squatted by the side of the track, sifting through the stony slag for unburnt lumps of coal. A lovely picture, I thought, almost an Edward Curtis scene, as I snapped my camera. Almost simultaneously with the shutter click, I found a policeman shouting at me, waving a blue booklet under my nose and grabbing at my camera. I had no idea what he was saying. I was terrified. I looked helplessly at my student, Old Two Noodle.

He was a calm and courtly man by nature and had honed his skills as a diplomat by having suffered greatly for fifteen years at the mercy of bureaucrats and police. Old Two Noodle wore round owl glasses and had the look about him of a Confucian sage. I needed him now, and he did his best to save me. He asked the policeman what I had done. By this time the policeman had found an English translation in his blue booklet and he waved it at me. "It is illegal for foreigners to take picture from Chinese trains." I had taken maybe two hundred photographs out of train windows in the course of the year, but I was not about to begin quibbling with him. I was unabashedly terrified and afraid that anything other than pure silence would sink me deeper into the quicksand of his blue regulations. Old Two Noodle talked calmly to him, finally asked me to surrender the camera and excused himself as he went off to the next car with the policeman. I stood there stunned in the train aisle, every eye in the hard seat car fixed on me. Marcy and I were the only visible Barbarians here in the middle of nowhere — no, in the middle of central Asia, in a police state.

I studied the Chinese faces and saw not compassion exactly, but something you might call knowledge. They had all been through this before, for years, for centuries, for dynasties, and they wanted nothing to do with it now except to remain anonymous. A few continued munching seeds, some lit cigarettes, some spit, some hid behind newspapers.

After a thousand years, or ten minutes (it seemed the same), Old Two Noodle emerged from the summit meeting with the police.

"You have photographed backwardness and poverty, they say, and they are afraid that you are going to use it to humiliate the Chinese people and Socialist reconstruction. They have agreed not to confiscate your camera but want you to surrender the film."

"The film is done," I said. "Would they be willing to snip off the last three pictures and leave me the rest of the roll?"

A flurry of Chinese, "That is *keyi* (OK)."

With great ceremony, the policeman snipped off the end of the roll, turned on his heel and left.

My shirt was soaked with sweat.

Old Two Noodle explained his negotiations. "They would have arrested you, but I told them you were not a journalist but a professor, a foreign expert and a true friend of China who meant no harm by taking the picture."

"What I saw was courage and beauty, not poverty and despair."

"The police do not think like that."

How differently that policeman and I understand the scene of those three women sifting for coal lumps! It is not that he is Chinese and that I am a Barbarian. For once, culture has nothing to do with this misunderstanding. It is human. It is cellular. He has a "police" mind. I do not. Poe understood this difference in his detective stories. Dupin, his hero, imagines himself in the bodies and spirits of other humans. If you want to find the purloined letter, first imagine the mind that hid it. The police inspector, for all his technical resources, his sense of moral righteousness, his legal search warrants, can only tear up floor boards and empty drawers. Poets solve real crimes, not police inspectors.

By terrifying me and threatening my film, the policeman acted within the letter of Chinese law, such as it is, and managed by doing so to accomplish precisely what he sought to prevent. I tried to capture an image of beauty and courage that I admired. The picture was a failure, and I would have thrown it away. Instead the image of every terrified and embarrassed face in the train car, the Chinese citizens' dread of the police, my own fear—all these things are burned into my consciousness until the end of my life, and I write these words to try to explain them, to tell them to you.

I am not the only Minnesotan to have come nose to nose with Chinese police and not liked it much. The day I returned from Gansu, I had a letter from Jeff and Sue Dean of Minneapolis, teaching that year in the north of China. They were the first burglarized Barbarians in their town, had a window broken and a Walkman, a camera, a clock, and a pair of binoculars nicked. I quote from their letter:

> The police turned out to be much worse than the robbery. We were daily requested to give lists of every Chinese person, including children(!) who'd been in our house. We refused! The police also began a strict check-in of Chinese guests, even went to our eight-year-old son's primary school and called out his classmates one by one and questioned them. Yech!!! The best thing about living in the frozen north has been easy, open access to Chinese friends. The police are now doing their best to put a stop to that. . . .

No sane person cares so much about lost gadgets as about lost friends, lost harmony, lost affection. The police mind is too thick for that truth.

We arrived in Wuwei, a flat-roofed desert town ringed with snow-capped peaks. Wuwei was newly open to Barbarians, and three of us arrived simultaneously: Marcy and I and a Frenchman traveling alone to the caves of Dunhuang. We foiled the police by not staying in the foreigners' hotel where we could be properly registered and watched, and the rumors of police tailing us soon began to resemble a bad spy movie. We did nothing illegal, except behaving like tourists, seeing the sights and meeting the locals, but they had lost us and were panicky. We were, in fact, sleeping in the local judge's apartment, a nice irony!

The town was magnificent: a Chinese Santa Fe—ancient mud courtyard houses, carved wooden doorways, an adobe city wall, almost no socialist concrete—too far away, too poor for improvements. We even spent a night with the town musicians, me playing Chopin etudes and ragtime on an out-of-tune piano, listening to a burly, handsome Gansu baritone do a fine rendition of Emilio the bullfighter's aria from *Carmen*—in good French! We took a hike out onto the shifting dunes of the Gobi desert, where we stood in boiling sand watching the sky blacken with thunderheads, felt the air temperature drop fifty degrees and icy rain that was almost hail evaporate before moistening the desert. We dined grandly on huge platters of roast mutton with chilies at Muslim cafes. After three days of pleasure, during which the police almost slipped my mind, we arrived outside the train station on a sunny Sunday morning. We ordered tea from a little stall and sat outdoors to wait. The Frenchman was already there, waiting for a train going west.

"Ze police," he said, "have been asking for you many times at ze hotel."

At that moment they arrived, curtly demanding papers. We gave them white cards, brown cards, red work-unit cards, green cards, passports. They mulled it all over for fifteen minutes as if it were not enough. Then the train arrived, and with small muttering, they returned our cards. I got on the train and took no more pictures. I didn't have to: they were already fixed inside me, and I knew that I would satisfy the policeman's darkest suspicion and write this account. He left me no choice.

In China, I learned two facts about police: one, the police do whatever they are ordered, here or there. Once it is done, the police will find a justification for it. Trust them. You have hired them for just this work. Two, a policeman who arrests someone who has the power of language has only two choices. He can shoot you or let you go. Almost any half measures are likely to be described and to be used against him (and the state who has hired him) in exactly the way that he worst fears. I doubt that Wei Jingsheng, the "Democracy Wall" leader, will ever leave Qinghai, or wherever he is, or that Fang Lizhi, if he escapes the U.S. Embassy alive, will ever again do scientific work in China. China is not yet heaven, and the police certainly intend to cause more trouble.

III

The Birthplace of Everything

Huangling is a little yellow town, about one hundred miles north of Xi'an in the yellow loess hills. Yellow dust, yellow stones, a little yellow creek winding through yellow fields on its way to the Yellow River, site of the shrine to Huangdi, the Yellow Emperor, first ancestor of the Chinese tribe, thus the progenitor of human consciousness. Maybe myth, but maybe not. Huangdi, five thousand years ago, is said to be the first unifier of China; he brought humans silkworm cultivation, weaving, the cart, the boat, the compass, building bricks, musical instruments, and written language. This page, thus, owes Old Yellow, the ur-father. How could I, worshiper of music and language, not travel these few miles to kowtow to the ancestor who gave me everything, even though I was a genetically debased offshoot from a lost and distant tribe? So I went, of course.

To get there, you take a bus north from the Wei River plains in Xi'an, through some of the oldest farmed area on earth. That is not myth but archaeology. Humans have worked these bare yellow hills with hoes and oxen for what grain they could coax from them for so many thousands of years that it has been deforested, eroded and over-populated since before the gestation of most forests and populations in other younger places like Europe.

Loess is loose yellow dust, and, without tree roots and grass, it blows.

During the rare rains, it runs down in gullies to the little silty creeks that ooze it along into the big Yellow River, a bad-tempered ditch full of more silt than water.

The road soon turns steep and the fields terraced. No tractors or giant combines here—only the same old hoes and shoulder poles and wooden carts and barrels of human shit. Here in this bare, too-peopled, dusty place, poverty is visible out every window, an old yellowed daguerreotype from 1850, or 850, or 850 B.C., or 8050 B.C.

Huangling itself is a ramshackle county town, a little gray cement poured over the yellow silt, but mostly caves in the yellow hillside with mud-walled courtyards, red doors, and ricepaper-covered half-moon windows. Pigs, children and chickens wander freely through the mud lanes that run off along the creek into the countryside. The air is fragrant with garlic shoots, fertilized dust, and coal smoke from cooking fires.

I first visited Huangling in the fall with Minnesota students to tour antiquities. A new dusting of snow had fallen overnight, polka-dotting the yellow countryside. We visited the temple at the bottom of Qiaoshan, bought postcards and then climbed the hill to the mythical tomb. Not much human work is left; a few archeological digs unearthed some suspicious Bronze Age artifacts. On the temple grounds and on the hillside grow thick-trunked, ancient, gnarled cypresses. The trees looked hoary enough to have been full grown when Old Yellow baked his first brick, cut his first reed flutes, and scratched the first Chinese character for human being—a pair of legs, 人 ren—on an ox bone.

There isn't much at the top of the hill besides the grand old cypresses, a plaque or two, a gazebo, a little garden, a place to have your photo taken. The sun was just setting when I heard wild raucous music coming up from the valley floor—bleating, rasping, whinnying horns, punctuated with drum and gong bangs. The music seemed to move from left to right, far below where the lights were just coming on in the town.

"A funeral," said the guide. "The farmers parade with their white wreaths, then burn paper money for the dead one, and sing and play and wail half the night. It is the old way, from before the Liberation."

I suppose that music is as old as Old Yellow but, compared to an electric organ vibrating its way through "Softly and Tenderly, Jesus is Calling," how fine! They need that farmer's funerary orchestra in Minnesota.

We stayed in a drafty old hotel: bare rooms, straw pillows, odorous squatters with uncertain plumbing. The sixteen students and I, and Wolfgang, a wonderfully half-crazed German teacher from Japan, got uproariously drunk that night, circulating from room to room. In the midst of the festivities, there was a knock at the door, and there stood a handsome young Chinese fellow looking a little tight himself. He had heard there was a poet among the Barbarians.

"Me," I said, passing him the Chinese *bailandi*.

He hooked down a swallow, said, "Me, too," rolled his eyes and began reciting: passionately, romantically, histrionically. Even without much language, I knew something was going on here and sobered up suddenly. He hadn't much English, and I had less Chinese, but we were like Henry Miller and the Corfu mayor who, lacking any other tongue, made friends, drunk, in Chinese, on a Greek hilltop. Yellow Poet and I translated, compared poems, recited for each other, told stories and toasted, almost until morning.

"It is good to find poets here in this poor yellow farm town," he said.

"Indeed," I agreed.

We recited the end of Li Bai's famous wine poem together in the dissonant clangor of simultaneous Minnesota English and Shaanxi Chinese:

> While I'm still conscious
> let's rejoice with one another.
> After I'm drunk
> let each one go his way.
> Let us bind ourselves for ever
> for passionless journeyings.
> Let us swear to meet again
> far in the Milky Way.

We did. And we will. With its old cypresses, noisy funerals, and young Lord Byron, Huangling seemed a good place for Old Yellow to have hatched language, consciousness and humanity together.

* * *

I came again to Huangling in the spring, on April 1, this time with Chinese students. We were on our way back from Yan'an, the old Long March terminus, now a revolutionary shrine, almost deserted in 1987 as the Helmsman, his widow, and all his political ideas fell into bad water. We were the only customers in Mao's date-orchard cave. We lounged on his marital *kang* (bed for second wife, another *kang* in another cave for Jiang Qing, the mistress) and took pictures of each other sitting at his little desk holding the writing brush that wielded such power for so long. None of the students had ever paid their respects to Old Yellow, so we decided to stop at Huangling for a few hours, kowtow a bit, and greet the old cypresses as they began their third or fourth millennium of growing.

Huangling is a tiny place, in Chinese or any other terms, and was almost deserted when I came the previous November. But today, it was transformed into Shanghai—teeming thousands, a pedestrian traffic jam of historic proportion.

"What is going on here?" I asked.

The students looked sheepish. "We have all forgotten," said Flower of Chengdu. "It is Qing Ming today. All the farmers have come from the whole county to bring offerings and pay respects to the first emperor."

Qing Ming is a sort of Chinese Memorial Day, the time to decorate graves, pay obeisance to grandfather and make pilgrimages. In a country whose true religion is still reverence for ancestors, that creates considerable holiday mobs. We were in the middle of one.

"How will we get a bus out of here to Xi'an?" I asked.

"Too late to worry about that now," said Hunan Basin. "We may as well join the crowd and have a look at the temple."

And so we did, carried along without volition by the surge—the Chinese masses assembled and moving, servants of a giant unconscious impulse.

At the field in front of the temple, the crowd stopped, though the masses behind continued joining it. We all squeezed tighter as if an invisible visegrip compressed us: jowl to jowl, buttock to buttock, pressing ever denser together.

The red temple door was barricaded and guarded by green soldiers.

"Why isn't it open?" I asked.

A murmur of Chinese went through the crowd. We found out the temple was closed because county officials expected a big potato from Party headquarters in Beijing who was coming to be televised for Qing Ming.

"Has Old Yellow joined the Party?" somebody asked.

One of the soldiers spotted me and hollered in Chinese. I found myself pushed toward the red door.

"They want the foreign guest to come inside and tour the temple," Hunan Basin translated.

"Not on your life," I said. "I will go last, after the farmers."

"You have no choice, nor do we."

The red door inched open and we found ourselves pushed inside into the calm silent garden with the twisted old cypresses. TV cameras stood at the ready, waiting for dignitaries. We strolled around, formed a circle of hands around the biggest old cypress—the belly button of the earth. We kowtowed to the shrine for Old Yellow. It was time to go. How to get out? The county officials whispered nervously to each other, pacing back and forth by the door. A phone rang, an official answered.

"*Wei!*"

"Not coming."

"*Keyi.*"

The eight of us stood by the gift shop next to the doors when they swung open. We were trapped both behind the doors and behind the soldiers who formed a cordon on both sides. The crowd of farmers surged in like a wild river let out of its dam on a hillside—heading for Johnstown. Some soldiers carried truncheons and switches; some took off their leather belts and used them as whips, flailing away at the raging river of humans charging inside, trying to control them, slow them down. An old lady with bound feet was knocked down and almost trampled. A child carried in its father's arms caught the full force of a belt and howled. I looked at Hunan Basin. He was weeping.

"To think they would do this to these poor farmers, the Chinese people, their own comrades."

All the students looked stunned, shocked, embarrassed, perhaps because I was here.

"It happens in America, too," I said, offering weak consolation. "Police and armies always . . . "

And so they do. And so they would, two years later, against these students who now watched.

We walked sadly back down to the town, followed by a crowd of maybe five hundred farmers close on my heels.

"You are the first Barbarian they have seen," said Flower of Chengdu. "Can you say they are very interested?"

I looked over my shoulder at a staring mob. "You can say that," I said nervously.

Old Fish asked for my camera. "When we get to the gate of the hotel, turn quickly around, step backwards and smile as if you are giving a speech. It will make a wonderful photograph."

It did—a pink Barbarian pied piper leading five hundred Shaanxi farmers with their eyes bugged out and their jaws flopped open. We found Yellow Poet, now sober and surprised to see us. He helped us persuade an irate bus driver to load eight more travelers on an already doubly overloaded old rattletrap of a bus. We stood for eight hours on the pothole-filled steep road to Xi'an, banging our heads on the bus roof, singing, telling jokes, praising Old Yellow for discovering language and music, and trying to forget the image of the green-uniformed arm slashing into the surge of backs with his belt.

What a typical Chinese place — Huangling! It stands for everything at once: age, survival, genius, beauty, courage, poverty, the bizarre, the unexpected, the cruel, and brutal. I am a Transcendentalist, of course, so every place, no matter how unlikely, includes everything, if you look with enough penetration, intelligence and love. All the natural facts lay baldly on the surface in China; the spiritual facts are inescapable. You cannot hide from them or deceive or humor yourself with physical comfort, machinery, distraction or sentimentality (the American forms of spiritual Valium). These facts assault you frontally and say: we demand that you see, understand, tell. This is experience; this is humanity; this is you, too. If the acknowledgment drives you crazy, then that is what you are supposed to be. Calm down and enjoy whatever you can. The funeral orchestra is tuning up for you, too. Old Yellow gave you humanity, and this is what it looks like.

IV

Minneota, Minnesota

I came back to Minneota on a sultry August day, driving an old burgundy Chevrolet Caprice at eighty miles an hour over the empty county roads. I turned off the air conditioner and opened the car windows to smell Minnesota — clean, damp, almost odorless. The glassy leaves of the seven-foot corn shivered a little in the afternoon breeze. The fifty-thousand-dollar tractors and air-conditioned combines sat ready and waiting in the farmyards. Not much farm work now, just let it grow, hope for rain, and watch a little afternoon television. Every few miles, I passed a feed lot: too many overheated cows standing hoof deep in fresh shit, swishing flies lazily with their tails, slurping a drink out of a galvanized tank. The cows reminded me more of Chinese life than any of the rest of the human or natural world I drove past: jammed in, over-crowded, bored, hot, and facing an uncertain fate.

I grew up in Minneota, on the Minnesota prairies, and thought it the bleakest, most boring landscape on the world. Today it struck me as indescribably rich and fertile, with its long, straight, well-maintained roads, scattered homestead farms all neat and well tended with their necessary half million dollars of labor-saving machines greased and scrubbed, tiny towns with square white painted houses, cut grass, weeded gardens, sentimental lawn ornaments, signs for high school teams, small stores full of groceries and goods I hadn't been able to get for a year, taverns with cold beer on tap and cheap watery Canadian whiskey, hardware and farm implement stores that sold gadgets and parts that could have fixed half of China, huge elevators crammed with surplus grain that no human being was ever likely to eat, wood and brick churches for sleepy Lutherans and Catholics. I had driven almost two hundred miles without seeing a mountain. I could drive another thousand if I chose. Not a single dangerous river slowed me down. I drove over the Minnesota River on a fine new concrete bridge on a county road. The river was almost dry now in August—full of sand bars and clouds of hungry mosquitos. The river meandered along at the bottom of a fifty-foot green hill thickly grown with spruce and burr oak, western Minnesota's best try at a gorge. At the top of the valley, miles of soybeans waited to become a bumper crop of (as the Department of Agriculture defines them) non-human food products. I thought with pleasure of how much Sichuan bean curd could be fried up out of those acres: cosmic woks-full!

What a lucky landscape my grandfather stumbled into! A quarter mile of free fertile land, no natural impediments to easy transportation for thousands of miles, a population vastly less than the country's carrying capacity, a mostly absent and mostly honest government, all the aboriginals safely dead or moved out, not a single invading army or night bombing raid, decently regular rainfall, plenty of everything to go around. I had been raised listening to the rhetoric of American virtue, the brave, hard-working immigrants who, with God's help (because she liked them best!) and the sweat of their brow, carved out this free and beatific place, stretching from sea to shining . . . blah-blah-blah . . .

My grandfather, and every other settler in the neighborhood, was like a teenage girl at her first poker game: she giggles a lot, asks if three of something is better than two twos, draws one card to a four-five-seven-eight, raises the pot continually, and draws a six. There is nothing wrong with dumb luck in this universe, and, for myself, I certainly thought it all right that things went badly for the old boy in Vopnafjordur; but to assume the superiority of a civilization, a citizenry, a religion, an economic system, a racial stock, a "way of life," or anything else as a result of it was sheer madness and arrogance. It courted the vengeance of the gods. It was the Chinese mistake—to assume that you are the center because you are where and who you are—without even the fragmentary evidence the Chinese had for thinking it. And yet political speeches and newspaper editorials were full of it. It was the fundamental gospel of

Time and *Reader's Digest* and the Hearst newspapers. It was at the bottom of the ten or fifteen first conversations I'd had since getting back:

"Must be good to be home where the machines work, where you can buy stuff, where you've got a car, where it isn't so damned crowded, etc. Sure sounded dirty over there. Bet all those little people sure looked at you funny . . . "

After a few times assuring people I had enjoyed it very much and that the Chinese varied in size as much as Icelanders or Belgians, I gave up, snorted and said, "Yup, sure is." Not meaning it at all.

This went on for months, now for two years. It will go on for the rest of my life. I am crazy.

In the car, Minnesota Public Radio was playing a Schubert quintet when I drove into Minneota, no party slogans, no military bands, but no commercials and no rock and roll either. I passed the trailer houses on the outskirts of town where the welfare mothers, the unemployed hired men, the alcoholics, our own poor, lived. Outside every trailer stood a rusty old car that sputtered but started. Every trailer had a TV, hot water, a toilet that flushed, dependable electricity, a working telephone, and a stove for heat in the winter. Not one of my Chinese students could expect to have any of it — except perhaps a TV and five days of electricity per week.

I stopped in front of my house and looked at it for a minute. Five bedrooms empty for a year, all the pianos, furniture, appliances unused. Twenty Chinese could have lived there, grown all their vegetables in the half acre of ground behind the house. My yard was bigger and more fertile than a great many Chinese farms. They would have raised a pig and a handful of chickens and fished the Yellow Medicine River clean of bullheads. The books would have been dog-eared and the pianos in need of tuning. They would have eaten the burdock that I poison year after year, and beaten the birds' time to get the mulberries for themselves. My hand-carved wooden chess set would be finger-marked from game after game. Yellow Medicine County, that I had just driven through to get here, would be populated not by a few thousand farmers going broke and sinking into despair but by a million thriving inhabitants, all eating better than they ever had before. I blinked my eyes.

I went into the empty house, flipped on the air conditioner, made coffee from fresh beans, and listened to the end of the Schubert quintet. No policeman or bureaucrat had any idea where I was. No one followed me. No one watched me. I sat in silence for a long time, thinking how things would never look the same again.

V

Oscar, the Fixer

On the morning of my first day in China, I went into the flush toilet in my apartment and closed the door. A few minutes later, I discovered I was locked in. The door was stuck — firmly, incorrigibly, hopelessly — stuck. I yanked. I banged. I hollered. Nothing. I hollered again, louder. The floor attendant came in and opened the door with a great heave. A few splinters fell to the floor. I was out.

"The door . . . Fix! . . . Now! . . . ," I mumbled, purple-faced.

"Something in lock," he said. "Don't close."

"Fix!" I repeated. He left.

That afternoon, I told the story to my next door neighbors in the Barbarians' Guest House, Helen and Oscar from Manitoba. They were about seventy, in China for the adventure, just as I was, but better equipped, psychologically and in many other ways.

"They are doing their best," said Helen, trying to calm me down. "It's really a very nice apartment, much better than anything the Chinese might ever have . . . "

"But the damn door . . . " I sputtered.

"I'll just come by and have a look after supper," Oscar said.

Oscar came, bent down despite his new plastic hip, and squinted at the lock in the half-splintered door frame.

"I believe it just needs to be planed a little and tightened up, eh? It's not quite square. If I'm not mistaken, I think I've got something . . . Hmmmm."

He was gone for a few minutes. He came back with a pocket knife, a pliers, a screwdriver, and a small square of sand paper.

"I don't have a plane actually, but this should do it," Oscar said, setting to work and humming a little.

He sanded, shaved, tightened the screws, monkeyed with the latch, swung the door a few times. "Well, that's not much of a job, but it should do for a bit. Don't slam it though." He gently closed the door and it clicked shut. "If a man just had a good sharp plane, eh, and could reset those side screws a bit?"

Oscar gave me a knowing squint over his spectacles, a conspiratorial look that said: if the two of us fellows would put our minds to it instead of our mouths, and if there happened to be a decent hardware store in the neighborhood, we could have things tip-top with no fuss.

Oscar soon became famous for unearthing tools that no one believed possible. He combed the town for hardware.

"There's this little place over by the post office, run by the nicest fellow. Well, I don't know what he was doing with this socket wrench; it's a pretty good one actually, if you don't put pressure on it where the metal is cracked here. Poor job at the foundry, I suppose. But this will come in handy for . . . "

There was no crisis so great that Oscar couldn't make a good try at it with a screwdriver and a pair of pliers. He couldn't truly repair things, because the tools weren't available, and "fixing" was not a concept built into most Chinese gadgets and situations. I could only imagine what Oscar's tool shop looked like in Manitoba. In China, he shined his pliers. They were Seigfried's Nothung, the Needful Sword, and came in handy to boot, if you just took care of them and put them back where they belonged.

He refused to countenance any rages against the Chinese and was a perpetually calm man. "They do pretty well, you know, given how awful it's been, eh? If they could just get a good hardware store . . . "

Oscar was, as you might expect, a meticulously neat man. Dirt and chaos violated something deep inside him, but he didn't complain. He squinted, hummed, and put his mind and hand to the job.

I came back from class one day and found Oscar on his knees scrubbing the marble tile on the hall floor—with a toothbrush.

"What in hell are you doing, Oscar?" I asked, amazed.

"These halls are filthy, you know, and everyone keeps complaining about it. Well, they don't really have good soap, eh, and there's not a brush in the country that will clean anything, but I thought if you just put a bit of baking soda in warm water and scrubbed it . . . "

"With a toothbrush?"

"They've got plenty of toothbrushes. Here, see what it looks like after a little scrub."

A few square feet of floor had changed color and texture. They were bright, cheerful, shiny pale gray marble. The rest of the floor remained caked with dark grainy dirt. This tiny piece of China had been transformed—for a while.

"It only took a half hour," said Oscar.

One day a student asked me to lecture to her high school class, or more accurately, to give them an English lesson. I asked Oscar to come along for fun. We drew pictures on the board, told jokes, and tried to teach a few new English words. At the end of the class, Oscar was mobbed. The Chinese still revere the old and were utterly charmed by Oscar's twinkly, wry humor. They felt his sweetness of soul and wanted to adopt him as Grandfather. The class was mostly girls. After I rescued

Oscar from the mob (he was signing autographs by now), we walked back to the guest house.

"I like this teaching, eh?" he said. "You do some good, and have some fun at it, and all those pretty girls! Felt just like a rock star! Why, Helen would be jealous!"

No, she wouldn't. She had known Oscar for a half century and understood perfectly well why people loved him.

I stayed on after Oscar and Helen left and noticed the dirt gradually cake up on Oscar's scrubbed piece of floor. A guest closed my bathroom door and got stuck. I yanked, and undid Oscar's delicate door salvation.

Two years after China, Oscar died suddenly, in his mid-seventies, of a heart attack. Like Zorba, he was a man who should have lived to be a thousand. There should be a hundred million Oscars on this planet carrying pliers, squinting and getting it calmly working again, with humor, love, and one more set screw right here just to make sure. If I could write like Oscar fixed, I would consider the job honorably done. So long, Camerado! You fixed something in everybody you ever met and will go on doing it for a long time from wherever you are!

VI

What Needs Fixing Now or, Who's Crazy Here?

The tone and content of this book changed after June of 1989, when the outer world barged with such ferocity into all our reveries of peace and sanity. Every American in China then whom I've met since has said to me that they felt all this violence and repression was possible, even probable in retrospect, but still hard to believe. How could humans, even power, sink so far?

Practice, practice, practice, like the piano, or basketball. Because power has done it so many times already, power is good at it, whether we expect them to be or not.

For the thousandth time in Chinese history, life has imitated art. The hottest movie in China in 1986 was *A Small Town Called Hibiscus*, based on a splendidly truthful and brave novel by a young Hunanese writer, Gu Hua. Mr. Gu tells the story of the effects of the politics of the last fifty years on the lives of some citizens in a tiny, out-of-the-way town in the Hunan mountains, a sort of Chinese Minneota, the last boondocks. At the end of the novel, the reforms have come, characters who suffered terribly have been rehabilitated (only after being almost killed by the whims of abstract power), a wastrel Red Guard named Wang Qiushe (Autumn Snake) has lost his power and position and gone bonkers, life for the town is generally cheerful and hopeful again. However, the novel ends eerily with this passage:

> The townsfolk did not know what exactly was meant by the "four modernizations," but already they were having a taste of their advantages.
>
> They also had cause for concern. With memories of the past fresh in their minds, some of them wondered uneasily if the ultra-Left line would make a sudden come-back and stamp out these hopeful new developments. Would their lives be filled with slogans, theories, struggles and political movements instead of oil, salt, fuel and rice for their daily needs . . . ? This seemed a real possibility. Since Wang Qiushe went mad he had slouched through New Street and Old Street every day, bright golden Chairman Mao badges on his ragged tunic, howling like a banshee:
>
> "Never forget class struggle!"
>
> "Every five or six years we'll have a new cultural revolution."
>
> His eerie shrieks could be heard all over Hibiscus. In the daytime when the townsfolk saw him coming, they ran indoors and shut their gates.

Maybe the time has come when none of us, here or there, can shut our gates tight enough to keep out the noise of his crying. We must find another kind of craziness to live inside, or go on in this cycle forever.

THANKS

Many deserve my thanks for this book, but should share no blame for its shortcomings. I start with Bob Carothers, then president of Southwest State University who walked breathless and jet-lagged into my office after his first trip to China and said: "You *must* go! It's the craziest place in the world. You're just the man for the job." So I went on a state university exchange to teach for a year in China. Carothers is a poet, too, and had some sense of what China would do to me.

I have written most of my books sitting on Dr. Mike Doman's deck in Seattle, or at the table of his sailboat in the San Juan Islands. When I can't work in Minneota, I go there. Mike leaves me alone when I pace and mutter, listens with an informed and critical ear to what I've done, and keeps a good supply of coffee beans. I cannot live long enough to thank him for his generosity and his friendship.

And now — Thanks — Alphabetically!

— To John Allen for editing this manuscript tirelessly and brilliantly, and for his long friendship.

— To B.J. Elzinga, computer whiz and editor.

— To Marilyn Helzer and Minnesota Public Radio for asking for and broadcasting my smuggled radio reports from China.

— To the Jiaotong Barbarian Teachers and other China Barbarians; we kept each other alive with humor, dinners, deadly punches, open screens, open doors and late night talks. They are a fine and various crew!

Shirley Bennett, England
Simon Coury, England

Jeff and Sue Dean, Minnesota
Min Dining, England
Andrew Elphinstone, England
Freddie, Japan
Ellen Hewitt, New Hampshire
Janet King, California
Bob and Gini Meittunen, Pennsylvania
Irene Myles, Louisiana
Dale, Toshi and Mina Schwertfeger, Minnesota
Joe and Earlene Strother, Louisiana
Karen Thornton, Manitoba
Oscar and Helen Tonn, Manitoba
Joe Warbansky, Manitoba
Yukki, Japan
Jordanna Zanmiller, Minnesota

—To Wincie Johannsdottir, old friend, for bringing Brennivin, joy and laughter to China. The Iceland essay is hers.

—To cousins Chuck and Lester Josephson for rescuing me in the Mandarin Hotel. To Chuck for coming back to Xi'an to cause creative trouble and for his Inkwell Press.

— To Will LaValley of Hong Kong in whose wonderful apartment many of these ideas hatched.

—To my friend Perry Lueders for his computer, for his running commentary, for his generous support of just about everything, and for his meatballs.

—To the Minneota gang who kept everything together, and whom I treasure: Gary DeCramer, Daren Gislason, Tom Guttormsson, Gail Perrizo.

—To Jón Baldur Sigurdsson and Lee Teng Gee, old friends in Singapore who generously gave a place and time to recover to fight again.

—To Cory Tholen and Wendy Sarazyn, cousins and friends who bravely wrestled my handwriting into a computer.

—To Zheng Weilu and her husband Rosario Aglialoro, for their friendship, their wisdom and their quick Chinese in a moment of trouble.

—To David Wold, editor of the Swedish newspaper *Stora*, who commissioned and published several of these essays.

—Since the phones don't work, and nothing is available, China reduces you to dependence on that noble old institution: the mail. To the correspondents who kept me informed in China: Vladimar Bjornsson (1906-1986) who always answered his mail; Nyla Gislason, Alice Gunlogson, Jim Phillips, David Pichaske, and to those who kept me fed: Donna Anderson, Kathy Bond, John Rezmerski, Pat Ruane, Eileen Thomas.

—Most of all, thanks to my dear Chinese friends and students. You will be named, listed, and honored before this century is over.

Bill Holm of Minneota, Minnesota, is the author of *The Dead Get By with Everything* (Milkweed Editions, 1991), *Boxelder Bug Variations* (Milkweed Editions, 1986), and *The Music of Failure* (Plains Press, 1986), which was issued in hard cover as *Prairie Days* by Saybrook Press. Holm is also an accomplished musician. A successful musical version of *Boxelder Bug Variations*, featuring Holm playing the piano and harpsichord, was staged in the summer of 1988 by the Lyric Theater of Minneapolis. Since his return from China, Holm has been giving readings and lectures in the United States and Canada. He teaches at Southwest State University in Marshall, Minnesota. A letterpress book of Holm's poem, *Brahms: Capriccio in C Major, Op. 76, No. 8*, was published by Ox-Head Press.

Coming Home Crazy

was designed by R.W. Scholes in Elante type.
The book was typeset at Stanton Publication Services and
printed by Princeton University Press.